Galatians

Galatians

Worship for Life by Faith in the Crucified and Risen Lord

JOHN PAUL HEIL

CASCADE Books • Eugene, Oregon

GALATIANS
Worship for Life by Faith in the Crucified and Risen Lord

Copyright © 2019 John Paul Heil. All rights reserved. Except for brief quotations in critical publications or reviews, no part of this book may be reproduced in any manner without prior written permission from the publisher. Write: Permissions, Wipf and Stock Publishers, 199 W. 8th Ave., Suite 3, Eugene, OR 97401.

Cascade Books
An Imprint of Wipf and Stock Publishers
199 W. 8th Ave., Suite 3
Eugene, OR 97401

www.wipfandstock.com

PAPERBACK ISBN: 978-1-5326-5608-8
HARDCOVER ISBN: 978-1-5326-5609-5
EBOOK ISBN: 978-1-5326-5610-1

Cataloging-in-Publication data:

Names: Heil, John Paul, author.

Title: Galatians : worship for life by faith in the crucified and risen Lord / by John Paul Heil.

Description: Eugene, OR : Cascade Books, 2019 | Includes bibliographical references and index.

Identifiers: ISBN 978-1-5326-5608-8 (paperback) | ISBN 978-1-5326-5609-5 (hardcover) | ISBN 978-1-5326-5610-1 (ebook)

Subjects: LCSH: Bible. Galatians—Commentaries. | Bible. Galatians—Criticism, interpretation, etc.

Classification: LCC BS2685.53 H25 2019 (print) | LCC BS2685.53 (ebook)

Manufactured in the U.S.A.   02/19/19

Contents

Abbreviations | vii

1 **Introduction** | 1
2 **Galatians 1:1–10** | 24
3 **Galatians 1:11–24** | 32
4 **Galatians 2:1–14** | 39
5 **Galatians 2:15–21** | 49
6 **Galatians 3:1–5** | 60
7 **Galatians 3:6–16** | 66
8 **Galatians 3:17–29** | 75
9 **Galatians 4:1–7** | 83
10 **Galatians 4:8–20** | 89
11 **Galatians 4:21–31** | 98
12 **Galatians 5:1–13** | 108
13 **Galatians 5:14–26** | 122
14 **Galatians 6:1–18** | 132
15 **Conclusion** | 148

Bibliography | 155
Scripture Index | 159
Author Index | 165

Abbreviations

AB	Anchor Bible
BBR	*Bulletin for Biblical Research*
BDAG	Danker, Frederick W., Walter Bauer, William F. Arndt, and F. Wilbur Gingrich. *Greek- English Lexicon of the New Testament and Other Early Christian Literature*. 3rd ed. Chicago: University of Chicago Press, 2000
BDF	Blass, Fredrich, Albert Debrunner, and Robert W. Funk. *A Greek Grammar of the New Testament and Other Early Christian Literature*. Chicago: University of Chicago Press, 1961
Bib	*Biblica*
BNTC	Black's New Testament Commentaries
CBQMS	Catholic Biblical Quarterly Monograph Series
CurBR	*Currents in Biblical Research*
ECL	Early Christianity and Its Literature
EDNT	*Exegetical Dictionary of the New Testament*. Edited by Horst Balz and Gerhard Schneider. ET. 3 vols. Grand Rapids: Eerdmans, 1990–1993
FRLANT	Forschungen zur Religion und Literatur des Alten und Neuen Testaments
ICC	International Critical Commentary
JBL	*Journal of Biblical Literature*
JSNT	*Journal for the Study of the New Testament*
JSNTSup	Journal for the Study of the New Testament Supplement Series

Abbreviations

LNTS	The Library of New Testament Studies
NBBC	New Beacon Bible Commentary
NICNT	New International Commentary on the New Testament
NIDB	*New Interpreter's Dictionary of the Bible.* Edited by Katharine Doob Sakenfeld. 5 vols. Nashville: Abingdon, 2006–2009
NIGTC	New International Greek Testament Commentary
NovT	*Novum Testamentum*
NovTSup	Supplements to Novum Testamentum
NTL	New Testament Library
NTS	*New Testament Studies*
NTSMS	New Testament Studies Monograph Series
SBLDS	Society of Biblical Literature Dissertation Series
SP	Sacra Pagina
StBibLit	Studies in Biblical Literature (Lang)
WBC	Word Biblical Commentary
WUNT	Wissenschaftliche Untersuchungen zum Neuen Testament
ZECNT	Zondervan Exegetical Commentary on the New Testament

1

Introduction

With this book I aim to present two new proposals regarding Paul's letter to the Galatians (often referred to simply as "Galatians").[1] First, I will demonstrate a new chiastic structure embracing the entire letter, based on strict linguistic and textual criteria, rather than conceptual or theological themes.[2] This chiastic structure accords with the view that Galatians was originally performed orally in a setting of communal worship. Chiastic structures were a common way of organizing or punctuating orally performed NT letters.[3] Secondly, I will offer a new proposal for a key theme of Galatians, as expressed by the subtitle of this book: "Worship for Life by Faith in the Crucified and Risen Lord." I will treat "worship" as a comprehensive concept that includes both liturgical, cultic, or ritual worship, as well as the moral behavior that is to complement it as ethical worship in accord with the biblical tradition. "Life" refers both to the present way of living as well as to future eternal life. "Faith" refers to the acceptance of divine grace available to the believer because of the death and resurrection of the Lord Jesus Christ.

1. I use my own translation for the Scripture cited in this book.

2. For a recent proposal of a chiastic structure for Galatians based on theological themes, see Bedford, *Galatians*, 21–22.

3. I have presented similar chiastic structures for other NT letters. See Heil, "Chiastic Structure and Meaning," 178–206; Heil, *Ephesians*; Heil, *Colossians*; Heil, *Philippians*; Heil, *Hebrews*; Heil, *Letter of James*; Heil, *1 Peter, 2 Peter, and Jude*; Heil, *Book of Revelation*; Heil, *1–3 John*. See also Jeon, *To Exhort and Reprove*; Jeon, *1 Timothy* (3 vols.); Milinovich, *Beyond What Is Written*.

THE THIRTEEN MICROCHIASTIC STRUCTURES OF GALATIANS

Modern day texts employ visual indications of structural organization and punctuation, such as headings, paragraphs, commas, periods, etc. But orally performed texts that are heard rather than seen and read by an audience often rely upon chiasms for their structural organization and punctuation. A chiasm works by leading its audience through introductory elements to a central, pivotal point or points, and then reaching its climactic conclusion by recalling and developing, via the chiastic parallels, aspects of the initial elements. The simplest chiastic units contain three (A-B-A') or four elements (A-B-B'-A'), but chiasms may consist of any number of elements. The original hearers may and need not necessarily have been consciously identifying the chiastic structures as they heard them. They would simply experience the chiastic phenomenon unconsciously as an organizing dynamic that aided their perception and memory of the content. The delineation of these chiastic structures provides the modern reading audience with a visual aid to how the content was originally organized and thus can facilitate the interpretation of it.

In what follows, then, I will first demonstrate how the text of Galatians naturally divides itself into thirteen distinct literary units based upon their microchiastic structures as determined by very precise linguistic parallels found in the text. Where applicable, I will point out how other lexical and grammatical features often confirm the integrity of these chiastic units. I will also point out the various transitional words that closely connect a unit to the immediately preceding unit. These various transitional words, which occur near the conclusion of one unit and close to the beginning of the next, indicate that the chiastic units are heard as a very cohesive and unified sequence. These various transitional words are italicized in my translation of the chiastic units below. Secondly, I will demonstrate how these thirteen microchiastic units form a macrochiastic structure based upon very precise linguistic parallels found in the text of the parallel chiastic units.

INTRODUCTION

1. The Grace and Peace of Our Lord Jesus Christ from All the Brothers (1:1-10)

Glory to God who raised from the dead Jesus Christ who gave himself for our sins[4]

A ¹Paul, an apostle not [οὐκ] from human beings [ἀνθρώπων] nor through a human being [ἀνθρώπου] but through Jesus Christ and God the Father who raised him from the dead, ²and all the brothers with me, to the churches of Galatia,

    B ³grace [χάρις] to you and peace from God our Father and the Lord Jesus Christ, ⁴who gave himself for our sins, that he might free us from the present evil age according to the will of our God and Father,

        C ⁵to whom be the glory for the ages of the ages. Amen!

    B' ⁶I am amazed that you are so quickly turning away from the one who called you in the grace [χάριτι] of Christ for a different gospel,

A' ⁷not [οὐκ] that there is another, but there are some who are troubling you and want to distort the gospel of Christ. ⁸But even if we or an angel from heaven should preach to you a gospel other than the gospel we preached to you, let him be accursed! ⁹As we have said before, and now I say again, if anyone is preaching to you a gospel other than the one you received, let him be accursed! ¹⁰Am I now trying to gain the approval of human beings [ἀνθρώπους] or of God? Or am I seeking to please human beings [ἀνθρώποις]? If I were still pleasing *human beings* [ἀνθρώποις], I would not [οὐκ] be a slave of Christ!⁵

An A-B-C-B'-A' chiastic pattern establishes the integrity and distinctness of this first unit (1:1-10). The only occurrences in this unit of "not" (οὐκ) in 1:1 and 1:7 and of the term for "human being"—ἀνθρώπων and ἀνθρώπου in 1:1, as well as ἀνθρώπους and ἀνθρώποις (twice) in 1:10—constitute the parallelism between the A (1:1-2) and A' (1:7-10) elements

---

4. The main heading of each unit is intended to summarize the unit as it relates to its parallel unit within the macrochiastic structure of Galatians, while the subheading of each unit is intended to summarize or characterize the microchiastic dimension of each unit.

5. This A' element (1:7-10), as well as several of the longer elements in the subsequent chiastic units, forms a chiastic subunit. These various subunits will be delineated and explained in the exegetical chapters to follow. They provide further textual criteria for how I have delineated the elements of the chiastic units.

of this chiasm. The only occurrences in this unit of "grace"—χάρις in 1:3 and χάριτι in 1:6—determine the parallelism between the B (1:3-4) and B' (1:6) elements. Finally, the unparalleled central and pivotal C element (1:5) contains the only occurrence in Galatians of the noun "glory" (δόξα).

2. I Did Not Consult with Flesh and Blood before Preaching the Faith (1:11-24)

They were glorifying in me God

A ¹¹For I want you to know, brothers, that the gospel preached [εὐαγγελισθέν] by me is not according to a *human being*. ¹²For I did not receive it nor was I taught it from a human being, but through a revelation of Jesus Christ [Χριστοῦ]. ¹³For you heard of my former conduct in Judaism, that beyond measure I was persecuting [ἐδίωκον] the church [ἐκκλησίαν] of God and trying to destroy [ἐπόρθουν] it, ¹⁴and I was advancing in Judaism beyond many contemporaries in my race, being far greater a zealot for my ancestral traditions. ¹⁵But when the one who set me apart from my mother's womb and called me through his grace was pleased ¹⁶to reveal his Son in me [ἐν ἐμοί], so that I might preach the gospel [εὐαγγελίζωμαι] about him among the gentiles, I did not immediately consult with flesh and blood,

    B ¹⁷nor did I go up to Jerusalem to those who were apostles before me, rather I went away into Arabia and then returned to Damascus. ¹⁸Then [Ἔπειτα] after three years I did go up to Jerusalem to visit Cephas and I remained with him fifteen days. ¹⁹But I did not see any other of the apostles except James the brother of the Lord.

        C ²⁰What things I am writing to you, behold, before God I am not lying.

    B' ²¹Then [Ἔπειτα] I went into the regions of Syria and Cilicia.

A' ²²But I was unknown personally to the churches [ἐκκλησίαις] of Judea that are in Christ [Χριστῷ]. ²³They were only hearing that "the one who once was persecuting [διώκων] us is now *preaching the gospel* [εὐαγγελίζεται] about the faith he once tried to destroy [ἐπόρθει]." ²⁴So they were glorifying in me [ἐν ἐμοί] God.

"Not according to a human being [ἄνθρωπον]" near the beginning of this unit in 1:11 recalls "If I were still pleasing human beings [ἀνθρώποις]" toward the conclusion of the preceding unit in 1:10. These successive occurrences of the word "human being" thus serve as the transitional terms linking the first (1:1–10) to the second (1:11–24) unit.

An A-B-C-B'-A' chiastic pattern secures the integrity and distinctness of this second unit (1:11–24). Several linguistic occurrences constitute the parallelism between the A (1:11–16a) and the A' (1:22–24) elements: the only occurrences in this unit of forms of the verb "preach the gospel" (εὐαγγελισθέν in 1:11, εὐαγγελίζωμαι in 1:16a, and εὐαγγελίζεται in 1:23), the term "Christ" (Χριστοῦ in 1:12 and Χριστῷ in 1:22), the verb "persecute" (ἐδίωκον in 1:13 and διώκων in 1:23), the noun "church" (ἐκκλησίαν in 1:13 and ἐκκλησίαις in 1:22), the verb "destroy" (ἐπόρθουν in 1:13 and ἐπόρθει in 1:23), and the prepositional phrase "in me" (ἐν ἐμοί in 1:16a and 24). The only occurrences in this unit of the adverb "then" (Ἔπειτα) at the beginnings of 1:18 and 1:21 determine the parallelism between the B (1:16b–19) and the B' (1:21) elements. Finally, the unparalleled central and pivotal C (1:20) element contains the only occurrence in Galatians of the expression "behold, before God I am not lying."

3. Freedom from Circumcision for Worship in Accord with the Truth (2:1–14)

God shows no partiality

A ¹Then after fourteen years I again went up to Jerusalem with Barnabas [Βαρναβᾶ], taking Titus along also. ²I went up according to a revelation, and I presented to them the *gospel* [εὐαγγέλιον] that I proclaim among the gentiles, but privately to those of repute, lest somehow for no purpose I might be running or had run. ³Yet not even Titus, who was with me, although being a Greek, was forced to be circumcised. ⁴But because of the false brothers secretly brought in, who slipped in to spy on our freedom that we have in Christ Jesus, that they might enslave us, ⁵to them not even for a moment did we yield to the subjection, so that the truth [ἀλήθεια] of the gospel [εὐαγγελίου] might remain with you.

    B ⁶ᵃBut to those who were reputed to be something—what they once were means nothing [οὐδέν] to me;

        C ⁶ᵇGod does not show partiality to a human being—

    B' ⁶ᶜthose of repute made me add nothing [οὐδέν].

A' ⁷On the contrary, seeing that I had been entrusted with the gospel [εὐαγγέλιον] of the uncircumcision, just as Peter of the circumcision, ⁸for the one who worked in Peter for an apostolate of the circumcision worked also in me for the gentiles, ⁹and recognizing the grace given to me, James and Cephas and John, who were reputed to be pillars, gave me and Barnabas [Βαρναβᾷ] their right hands in fellowship, that we would go to the gentiles, and they to the circumcision. ¹⁰Only that we might remember the poor, the very thing I also was eager to do.

¹¹But when Cephas came to Antioch, I opposed him to his face, because he was clearly wrong.

¹²For until certain people came from James, he had been eating with the gentiles; but when they came, he drew back and separated himself, fearing those of the circumcision. ¹³And the rest of the Jews also joined with him in this hypocrisy, so that even Barnabas [Βαρναβᾶς] was led astray with them in the hypocrisy. ¹⁴But when I saw that they were not acting rightly with the truth [ἀλήθειαν] of the gospel [εὐαγγελίου], I said to Cephas in front of all, "If you, although being a *Jew*, are living like a gentile and not like a Jew, how can you force the gentiles to live like Jews?"

"I presented to them the gospel [εὐαγγέλιον]" near the beginning of this unit in 2:2 recalls "is now preaching the gospel [εὐαγγελίζεται]" toward the conclusion of the preceding unit in 1:23. These successive references to the gospel serve as the transitional terms linking the second (1:11–24) to the third (2:1–14) unit.

An A-B-C-B'-A' chiastic pattern secures the integrity and distinctness of this third unit (2:1–14). Several linguistic occurrences constitute the parallelism between the A (2:1–5) and the A' (2:7–14) elements: the only occurrences in this unit of forms of the name "Barnabas"—Βαρναβᾷ in 2:1, Βαρναβᾷ in 2:9, and Βαρναβᾶς in 2:13; the noun "gospel"—εὐαγγέλιον in 2:2 and 7, as well as εὐαγγελίου in 2:5 and 14; and the noun "truth"—ἀλήθεια in 2:5 and ἀλήθειαν in 2:14. The only occurrences in this unit of the pronoun "nothing" (οὐδέν) in 2:6a, 6c determine the parallelism between the B (2:6a) and the B' (2:6c) elements. Finally, the unparalleled central and pivotal C element (2:6b) contains the only occurrence in Galatians of the expression "God does not show partiality to a human being."

Introduction

4. I Live by Faith in the Son of God (2:15–21)

Christ lives in me

A ¹⁵We are *Jews* by nature and not sinners from the gentiles. ¹⁶Yet knowing that no one is justified from works of the law [νόμου] but through faith [πίστεως] in Jesus Christ [Χριστοῦ], even we have believed in Christ [Χριστόν] Jesus, that we may be justified from faith [πίστεως] in Christ [Χριστοῦ] and not from works of the law [νόμου], because from works of the law [νόμου] will not be justified any flesh. ¹⁷But if seeking to be justified in Christ [Χριστῷ] we ourselves have also been found to be sinners, is Christ [Χριστός] then an agent of sin? Of course not!

B ¹⁸ᵃFor if those things I tore down I am again building up [οἰκοδομῶ],

B' ¹⁸ᵇthen that I myself am a transgressor I am confirming [συνιστάνω].

A' ¹⁹For I myself through the law [νόμου] to the law [νόμῳ] died, so that I might live for God. I have been crucified with Christ [Χριστῷ]. ²⁰Yet I live, no longer I, but Christ [Χριστός] lives in me; insofar as now I live in flesh, in faith [πίστει] I live, that [faith] in the Son of God who loved me and gave himself up for me. ²¹I do not reject the grace of God; for if through the law [νόμου] is justification, then to no purpose *Christ* [Χριστός] died!

"We are Jews [Ἰουδαῖοι]" at the beginning of this unit in 2:15 recalls "although being a Jew [Ἰουδαῖος]" toward the conclusion of the preceding unit in 2:14. These successive occurrences of forms of the noun "Jew" serve as the transitional terms linking the third (2:1–14) to the fourth (2:15–21) unit.

An A-B-B'-A' chiastic pattern secures the integrity and distinctness of this fourth unit (2:15–21). Several linguistic occurrences constitute the parallelism between the A (2:15–17) and the A' (2:19–21) elements of this chiasm: the only occurrences in this unit of forms of the noun "law" (νόμου in 2:16 [thrice], 19 as well as νόμῳ in 2:19), the noun "faith" (πίστεως in 2:16 [twice] and πίστει in 2:20), and the term "Christ" (Χριστοῦ in 2:16 [twice], Χριστόν in 2:16, Χριστῷ in 2:17, 19, and Χριστός in 2:17, 20, 21). The only occurrences in Galatians of the conceptually and lexically similar forms of the verbs "I am building up" (οἰκοδομῶ) in 2:18a and "I am confirming" (συνιστάνω) in 2:18b establish an alliterative parallelism between the B (2:18a) and the B' (2:18b) elements at the pivotal center of this chiastic unit.

5. Have You Experienced So Many Things in Vain? (3:1–5)

You received the Spirit from the hearing of faith

A   ¹O foolish Galatians! Who has bewitched you, before whose eyes Jesus Christ was publicly proclaimed as crucified? ²This only I want to learn from you: from works of the law [ἐξ ἔργων νόμου] did you receive the Spirit [πνεῦμα] or from the hearing of faith [ἐξ ἀκοῆς πίστεως]? ³Are you so foolish? Having begun with the Spirit [πνεύματι], now with the flesh are you ending?

B   ⁴ᵃHave you experienced so many things in vain [εἰκῇ]?

B'   ⁴ᵇIf indeed it has been in vain [εἰκῇ].

A'   ⁵Does then the one supplying you the Spirit [πνεῦμα] and working mighty deeds among you do so from works of the law [ἐξ ἔργων νόμου] or from the hearing of *faith* [ἐξ ἀκοῆς πίστεως]?

The term "Christ" (Χριστός) at the beginning of this unit in 3:1 repeats the same term toward the conclusion of the preceding unit in 2:21. These successive occurrences of this same term serve as the transitional terms linking the fourth (2:15–21) to the fifth (3:1–5) unit.

An A-B-B'-A' chiastic pattern secures the integrity and distinctness of this fifth unit (3:1–5). Several linguistic occurrences constitute the parallelism between the A (3:1–3) and the A' (3:5) elements: the only occurrences in this unit of the phrase "from works of the law"—ἐξ ἔργων νόμου in 3:2, 5; the term "Spirit"—πνεῦμα in 3:2, 5 as well as πνεύματι in 3:3; and the phrase "from the hearing of faith"—ἐξ ἀκοῆς πίστεως in 3:2 and 5. The only occurrences in this unit of the adverb "in vain" (εἰκῇ) in 3:4a and 4b determine the parallelism between the B (3:4a) and the B' (3:4b) elements at the pivotal center of this chiastic unit.

Christ Redeemed Us from the Curse of the Law (3:6–16)

The just one from faith will live

A   ⁶Just as Abraham [Ἀβραάμ] "*believed* God and it was credited to him as justification" (Gen 15:6), ⁷recognize then that those from faith, these are sons of Abraham [Ἀβραάμ]. ⁸And the scripture, foreseeing that from faith God would justify the gentiles [τὰ ἔθνη], foretold the gospel to Abraham

Introduction

[Ἀβραάμ], saying, "In you will be blessed all the gentiles [τὰ ἔθνη]" [Gen 12:3; 18:18]. ⁹So those from faith are blessed with the believing Abraham [Ἀβραάμ].

B ¹⁰For as many as are from works of the law are under a curse [κατάραν], for it is written, "Cursed is everyone [ἐπικατάρατος πᾶς] who does not remain in all the things written in the book of the law, to do them" [Deut 27:26].

C ¹¹And that by the law no one is justified before God is clear, for "the just one from faith will live [ζήσεται]" [Hab 2:4].

C' ¹²But the law is not from faith, rather, "the one who does these things will live [ζήσεται] by them" [Lev 18:5].

B' ¹³Christ redeemed us from the curse [κατάρας] of the law having become for us a curse [κατάρα], for it is written, "Cursed is everyone [ἐπικατάρατος πᾶς] who hangs on a tree" [Deut 21:23],

A' ¹⁴that to the gentiles [τὰ ἔθνη] the blessing of Abraham [Ἀβραάμ] might come in Christ Jesus, that the promise of the Spirit we might receive through faith. ¹⁵Brothers, as a human being I speak, that even a covenant ratified by a human being no one rejects or amends. ¹⁶Now to Abraham [Ἀβραάμ] were spoken the *promises* and to his descendant; it does not say, "And to descendants," as referring to many but as referring to one, "And to your descendant" [Gen 12:7; 13:15; 17:8; 22:17; 24:7], who is Christ.

The verb "believed" (ἐπίστευσεν) at the beginning of this unit in 3:6 recalls the noun "faith" (πίστεως) at the end of the preceding unit in 3:5. These successive references to faith/believing serve as the transitional terms linking the fifth (3:1–5) to the sixth (3:6–16) unit.

An A-B-C-C'-B'-A' chiastic pattern secures the integrity and distinctness of this sixth unit (3:6–16). Several linguistic occurrences constitute the parallelism between the A (3:6–9) and the A' (3:14–16) elements: the only occurrences in this unit of the name "Abraham" (Ἀβραάμ) in 3:6, 7, 8, 9, 14, 16, and of the term "the gentiles" (τὰ ἔθνη) in 3:8 (twice) and 14. The only occurrences in this unit of the term "curse"—κατάραν in 3:10 and κατάρας in 3:13—as well as the expression "cursed is everyone"—ἐπικατάρατος πᾶς in 3:10, 13—determine the parallelism between the B (3:8) and the B' (3:13) elements. And the only occurrences of the verb "will live" (ζήσεται) in 3:11 and 12 establish the parallelism between the C (3:11) and the C' (3:12) elements at the pivotal center of this chiastic unit.

Galatians

7. Baptized into Christ, with Christ You Have Clothed Yourselves (3:17–29)

All of you are one in Christ Jesus

A ¹⁷This then I am saying: The law that came after four hundred and thirty years does not annul a covenant previously ratified by God so as to remove the *promise* [ἐπαγγελίαν]. ¹⁸For if from the law is the inheritance [κληρονομία], it is no longer from a promise [ἐπαγγελίας], but to Abraham [Ἀβραάμ] through a promise [ἐπαγγελίας] God graciously gave it. ¹⁹Why then the law? It was added for the sake of transgressions, until would come the descendant to whom the promise was made [ἐπήγγελται], ordered through angels at the hand of an intermediary. ²⁰But an intermediary is not of one, yet God is one. ²¹Is the law then against the promises [ἐπαγγελιῶν] of God? Of course not! For if a law had been given that was able to give life, then justification would indeed be from the law. ²²But the scripture confined all things under sin, that the promise [ἐπαγγελία] from faith in Jesus Christ might be given to those who believe.

> B ²³Before faith came we were held in custody under the law, confined for the faith that was about to be revealed, ²⁴so that the law became our guardian [παιδαγωγός] until Christ, that from faith we might be justified.

> B' ²⁵But now that faith has come, we are no longer under a guardian [παιδαγωγόν].

A' ²⁶For all of you through faith are sons of God in Christ Jesus. ²⁷For as many of you as into Christ were baptized, with Christ you have clothed yourselves. ²⁸There is neither Jew nor Greek, there is neither slave nor free, there is not male and female, for all of you are one in Christ Jesus. ²⁹And if you are of Christ, then you are a descendant of Abraham [Ἀβραάμ], *heirs* [κληρονόμοι] according to the promise [ἐπαγγελίαν].

The term "promise" (ἐπαγγελίαν) near the beginning of this unit in 3:17 recalls the term "promises" (ἐπαγγελίαι) toward the conclusion of the preceding unit in 3:16. These successive occurrences of forms of the word for "promise" serve as the transitional terms linking the sixth (3:6–16) to the seventh (3:17–29) unit.

An A-B-B'-A' chiastic pattern secures the integrity and distinctness of this seventh unit (3:17–29). Several linguistic occurrences constitute

Introduction

the parallelism between the A (3:17–22) and the A' (3:26–29) elements: the only occurrences in this unit of expressions for "promise" (ἐπαγγελίαν in 3:17, 29, ἐπαγγελίας in 3:18 [twice], ἐπήγγελται in 3:19, ἐπαγγελιῶν in 3:21, and ἐπαγγελία in 3:22); of the name "Abraham" ([Ἀβραάμ] in 3:18, 29); and of expressions of inheriting ("inheritance" [κληρονομία] in 3:18 and "heirs" [κληρονόμοι] in 3:29). The only occurrences in Galatians of forms of the term "guardian"—παιδαγωγός in 3:24 and παιδαγωγόν in 3:25—determine the parallelism between the B (3:23–24) and the B' (3:25) elements at the pivotal center of this chiastic unit.

8. That the Son of God Might Redeem Those under the Law (4:1–7)

You are sons gifted with the Spirt and thus heirs through God

A ¹I say then, for as long a time as the *heir* [κληρονόμος] is a minor, he does not differ from a slave [δούλου], though being the owner of all, ²but he is under managers and stewards until the date set by the father [πατρός]. ³So also we, when we were minors, we were enslaved [δεδουλωμένοι] under the elemental powers of the world. ⁴ᵃBut when the fullness of time had come, God sent [ἐξαπέστειλεν ὁ θεός] his Son,

B ⁴ᵇborn from a woman, born under the law [ὑπὸ νόμον],

B' ⁵ᵃthat he might redeem those under the law [ὑπὸ νόμον],

A' ⁵ᵇthat we might receive sonship. ⁶And because you are sons, God sent [ἐξαπέστειλεν ὁ θεός] the Spirit of his Son into our hearts, crying out, "Abba, Father [πατήρ]!" ⁷So you are no longer a slave [δοῦλος] but a son, and if a son, also an heir [κληρονόμος] through *God* [θεοῦ].

The term "heir" (κληρονόμος) at the beginning of this unit in 4:1 recalls the term "heirs" (κληρονόμοι) at the end of the preceding unit in 3:29. These successive occurrences of words for "heir" serve as the transitional terms linking the seventh (3:17–29) to the eighth (4:1–7) unit.

An A-B-B'-A' chiastic pattern secures the integrity and distinctness of this eighth unit (4:1–7). Several linguistic occurrences constitute the parallelism between the A (4:1–4a) and the A' (4:5b–7) elements: the only occurrences in this unit of "heir" (κληρονόμος in 4:1, 7); of references to slavery ("slave" [δούλου] in 4:1, "enslaved" [δεδουλωμένοι] in 4:3, and "slave" [δοῦλος] in 4:7); of "father" (πατρός in 4:2 and πατήρ in 4:6); and of expressions involving God ("God sent" [ἐξαπέστειλεν ὁ θεός] in 4:4a, 6 and "God" [θεοῦ] in 4:7). The only occurrences in this unit of the phrase "under the law" (ὑπὸ νόμον) in 4:4b, 5a determine the parallelism between the B (4:4b) and B' (4:5a) elements at the pivotal center of this chiastic unit.

9. I Fear Lest Somehow in Vain I Labored for You (4:8–20)

Become as I am because I also have become as you are

A ⁸Yet when not knowing [εἰδότες] *God*, you were slaves of things that by nature are not gods.
⁹But now recognizing God, or rather being recognized by God, how can you turn back again [πάλιν] to the weak and destitute elemental powers? Do you want [θέλετε] to be slaves of them all over again [πάλιν]? ¹⁰You are observing days and months and seasons and years. ¹¹I fear for you lest somehow in vain I have labored for you.

B ¹²ᵃBecome as I [ἐγώ] am,

B' ¹²ᵇbecause I also [κἀγώ] have become as you are, brothers, I implore you.

A' ¹²ᶜYou did me no wrong. ¹³You know [οἴδατε] that it was because of a weakness of the flesh that I preached the gospel to you previously, ¹⁴and your trial in my flesh you did not despise or reject, but rather as the angel of God you received me, as Christ Jesus. ¹⁵Where then is your blessedness? For I testify to you that if possible, you would have torn out your eyes and given them to me! ¹⁶So have I become your enemy by telling you the truth? ¹⁷They are zealous for you but not commendably,⁶ rather they want [θέλουσιν] to exclude you, that you may be zealous for them. ¹⁸It is always commendable to be zealous in a commendable way and not only when I am present with you. ¹⁹My children, for whom I again [πάλιν] have birth pangs until Christ be formed in you! ²⁰I want [ἤθελον] to be present with you now and change *my* tone, for I am perplexed in you.

The reference to "God" (θεόν) at the beginning of this unit recalls the reference to "God" (θεοῦ) at the end of the preceding unit. These successive occurrences of "God" serve as the transitional terms linking the eighth (4:1–7) to the ninth (4:8–20) unit.

---

6. For the translation "commendably" for καλῶς in Gal 4:17, see BDAG, 505.

Introduction

An A-B-B'-A' chiastic pattern secures the integrity and distinctness of this ninth unit (4:8–20). Several linguistic occurrences constitute the parallelism between the A (4:8–11) and the A' (4:12c–20) elements: the only occurrences in this unit of forms of the verb "know" ("knowing" [εἰδότες] in 4:8 and "you know" [οἴδατε] in 4:18); of the adverb "again" ([πάλιν] in 4:9 [twice], 19); and of forms of the verb "want" ("you want" [θέλετε] in 4:9, "they want" [θέλουσιν] in 4:17, and "I want" [ἤθελον] in 4:20). The only occurrences in this unit of the first person singular pronoun "I" ("I" [ἐγώ] in 4:12a and "I also" [κἀγώ] in 4:12b) determine the parallelism between the B (4:12a) and the B' (4:12b) elements at the pivotal center of this chiastic unit.

10. We Are Children with the Son of the Free Woman (4:21–31)

Drive out the slave woman and her son

A ²¹Tell [Λέγετέ] *me*, you who want to be [εἶναι] under the law, do you not listen to the law? ²²For it is written that Abraham had [ἔσχεν] two sons [υἱούς], one from the slave woman [παιδίσκης] and one from the free woman [ἐλευθέρας]. ²³But the one from the slave woman [παιδίσκης] was born [γεγέννηται] according to the flesh [κατὰ σάρκα], while the one from the free woman [ἐλευθέρας] through the promise [ἐπαγγελίας]. ²⁴Which things are spoken about allegorically. For these are [ἐστιν] two covenants, one from Mount Sinai, giving birth [γεννῶσα] for slavery; this is [ἐστίν] Hagar. ²⁵The Hagar Sinai Mount is [ἐστίν] in Arabia, but corresponds to the present Jerusalem,⁷ for she is in slavery with her children [τέκνων]. ²⁶But the Jerusalem above is [ἐστίν] free [ἐλευθέρα], and she is [ἐστίν] our mother. ²⁷ᵃFor it is written, "Rejoice,

B ²⁷ᵇyou barren one who does not give birth [ἡ οὐ τίκτουσα];

C ²⁷ᶜbreak forth and shout,

B' ²⁷ᵈyou who have no birth pangs [ἡ οὐκ ὠδίνουσα],

A' ²⁷ᵉbecause more are the children [τέκνα] of the barren one than of the one having [ἐχούσης] a husband" (Isa 54:1). ²⁸But you, brothers, like Isaac, are [ἐστέ] children [τέκνα] of the promise [ἐπαγγελίας]. ²⁹But just as then the one born [γεννηθείς] according to the flesh [κατὰ σάρκα] persecuted the one according to the Spirit, so also now. ³⁰But what does the scripture say

---

7. For this reading and translation of 4:25, see Moo, *Galatians*, 302–3.

[λέγει]? "Drive out the slave woman [παιδίσκην] and her son [υἱόν]! For the son [υἱός] of the slave woman [παιδίσκης] will not inherit with the son [υἱοῦ]" (Gen 21:10) of the free woman [ἐλευθέρας]. ³¹Therefore, brothers, we are [ἐσμέν] not children [τέκνα] of the slave woman [παιδίσκης] but of the *free woman* [ἐλευθέρας].

The first person singular pronoun "me" (μοι) at the beginning of this unit in 4:21 recalls the first person singular pronoun "my" (μου) at the end of the preceding unit in 4:20. These successive occurrences of different forms of the same pronoun serve as the transitional terms linking the ninth (4:8–20) to the tenth (4:21–31) unit.

An A-B-C-B'-A' chiastic pattern secures the integrity and distinctness of this tenth unit (4:21–31). Several linguistic occurrences constitute the parallelism between the A (4:21–27a) and the A' (4:27e–31) elements: the only occurrences in this unit of the verb "tell/say" ("tell" [Λέγετέ] in 4:21 and "say" [λέγει] in 4:30); of forms of the verb "to be" (εἶναι in 4:21, ἐστιν in 4:24 [twice], 25, 26 [twice], ἐστέ in 4:28, and ἐσμέν in 4:31); of forms of the verb "to have" ("had" [ἔσχεν] in 4:22 and "having" [ἐχούσης] in 4:27e); of "sons/son" (υἱούς in 4:22, υἱόν, υἱός, and υἱοῦ in 4:30); of "slave woman" (παιδίσκης in 4:22, 23, 30, 31 and παιδίσκην in 4:30); of "free woman/ free" ("free woman" [ἐλευθέρας] in 4:22, 23, 30, 31 and "free" [ἐλευθέρα] in 4:26); of forms of the verb "to give birth" ("was born" [γεγέννηται] in 4:23, "giving birth" [γεννῶσα] in 4:24, and "born" [γεννηθείς] in 4:29); of the phrase "according to the flesh" (κατὰ σάρκα) in 4:23, 29; of "promise" (ἐπαγγελίας) in 4:23, 28; and of "children" (τέκνων in 4:25 and τέκνα in 4:27e, 28, 31).

The only occurrences in this unit of nominative feminine alliterative participles referring to birth—"does not give birth" (ἡ οὐ τίκτουσα) in 4:27b and "have no birth pangs" (ἡ οὐκ ὠδίνουσα) in 4:27d—determine the parallelism between the B (4:27b) and the B' (4:27d) elements. Finally, the unparalleled central and pivotal C element (4:27c) contains the only occurrence in Galatians of the expression "break forth and shout."

Introduction

11. The Truth of Freedom from Circumcision to Serve One Another (5:1–13)

Through love be slaves to one another

A ¹For *freedom* [ἐλευθερίᾳ] Christ set us free [ἠλευθέρωσεν]; stand firm then and do not again to the yoke of slavery [δουλείας] be subjected. ²Look! I, Paul, am saying to you that if you have yourselves circumcised, Christ will benefit you nothing [οὐδέν]. ³And I testify again to every human being who has himself circumcised that he is obligated to do the whole [ὅλον] law. ⁴You have been removed [κατηργήθητε] from Christ, you who [οἵτινες] are trying to be justified by the law; you have fallen away from grace!

    B ⁵For we by the Spirit, from faith [πίστεως], the hope of justification we await.

        C ⁶ᵃFor in Christ Jesus neither [οὔτε] circumcision

            D ⁶ᵇcounts for anything

        C' ⁶ᶜnor [οὔτε] uncircumcision,

    B' ⁶ᵈbut faith [πίστις] working through love.

A' ⁷You were running commendably; who hindered you from being persuaded by the truth?

⁸This persuasion is not from the one who calls you! ⁹A little leaven leavens the whole [ὅλον] batch of dough! ¹⁰I have been persuaded regarding you in the Lord that you will think nothing [οὐδέν] otherwise, but the one troubling you will bear the condemnation, whoever [ὅστις] he may be. ¹¹But as for me, brothers, if I am still proclaiming circumcision, why am I still being persecuted? In that case the stumbling block of the cross has been removed [κατήργηται].

¹²Would that those disturbing you might also castrate themselves! ¹³For you were called to freedom [ἐλευθερίᾳ], brothers; only do not use the freedom [ἐλευθερίαν] as an opportunity for the flesh, but through *love* be slaves [δουλεύετε] to one another.

The word "freedom" (ἐλευθερίᾳ) at the beginning of this unit in 5:1 recalls "free woman" (ἐλευθέρας) at the end of the preceding unit in 4:31.

These successive occurrences of references to freedom serve as the transitional terms linking the tenth (4:21–31) to the eleventh (5:1–13) unit.

An A-B-C-D-C'-B'-A' chiastic pattern secures the integrity and distinctness of this eleventh unit (5:1–13). Several linguistic occurrences constitute the parallelism between the A (5:1–4) and the A' (5:7–13) elements: the only occurrences in this unit of expressions for "freedom" (the noun ἐλευθερία in 5:1, 13 and ἐλευθερίαν in 5:13, as well as the verb "set free" [ἠλευθέρωσεν] in 5:1); of references to "slavery" (the noun "slavery" [δουλείας] in 5:1 and the verb "be slaves" [δουλεύετε] in 5:13); of "nothing" (οὐδέν) in 5:2, 10; of "whole" (ὅλον) in 5:3, 9; of the verb "be removed" ("have been removed" [κατηργήθητε] in 5:4 and "has been removed" [κατήργηται] in 5:11); and of the relative pronoun "who/whoever" ("who" [οἵτινες] in 5:4 and "whoever" [ὅστις] in 5:10).

The only occurrences in this unit of "faith"—πίστεως in 5:5 and πίστις in 5:6d—determine the parallelism between the B (5:5) and the B' (5:6d) elements. The only occurrences in this unit of "neither/nor" (οὔτε) in 5:6a, 6c establish the parallelism between the C (5:6a) and the C' (5:6c) elements. Finally, the only occurrence in Galatians of the expression "counts for anything" in 5:6b serves as the unparalleled D element at the pivotal center of this chiastic unit.

12. The Flesh Is Opposed to the Spirit Whose Fruit Includes Faith (5:14–26)

If we live by the Spirit, the Spirit let us also follow

A ¹⁴For all the law is fulfilled in one statement, namely, "You shall *love* your neighbor as yourself" (Lev 19:18). ¹⁵But if you go on biting and devouring one another [ἀλλήλους], beware that you are not consumed by one another [ἀλλήλων]. ¹⁶But I say, walk by the Spirit and you will not bring to an end the desire [ἐπιθυμίαν] of the flesh. ¹⁷For the flesh desires [ἐπιθυμεῖ] against the Spirit, and the Spirit against the flesh, for these are opposed to one another [ἀλλήλοις], so that you may not do the things you want. ¹⁸But if you are led by the Spirit, you are not under the law.

> B ¹⁹The works of the flesh are [ἐστιν] evident, whatever is [ἐστιν] sexual immorality, impurity, licentiousness, ²⁰idolatry, sorcery, hostilities, enmities, strife, jealousy, rages, rivalries, dissensions, factions, ²¹ᵃenvies, drunkenness, orgies, and similar things,

C ²¹ᵇwhich things I warn [προλέγω] you,

C' ²¹ᶜas I warned before [προεῖπον],

B' ²¹ᵈthat those who practice such things will not inherit the kingdom of God! ²²But the fruit of the Spirit is [ἐστιν] love, joy, peace, patience, kindness, generosity, faith, ²³humility, self-control; such things the law is [ἐστιν] not against.

A' ²⁴Those who belong to Christ Jesus have crucified the flesh with its passions and desires [ἐπιθυμίαις].²⁵If we live by the Spirit, the *Spirit* let us also follow. ²⁶Let us not become conceited, provoking one another [ἀλλήλους], envying one another [ἀλλήλοις].

The verb "you shall love" (ἀγαπήσεις) at the beginning of this unit in 5:14 recalls the noun "love" (ἀγάπης) at the end of the preceding unit in 5:13. These successive references to love function as the transitional terms linking the eleventh (5:1–13) to the twelfth (5:14–26) unit.

An A-B-C-C'-B'-A' chiastic pattern secures the integrity and distinctness of this twelfth unit (5:14–26). Several linguistic occurrences constitute the parallelism between the A (5:14–18) and the A' (5:24–26) elements: the only occurrences in this unit of "one another" (ἀλλήλους in 5:15, 26, ἀλλήλων in 5:15, and ἀλλήλοις in 5:17, 26); and of references to "desire" (the noun "desire" [ἐπιθυμίαν] in 5:16, the verb "desires" [ἐπιθυμεῖ] in 5:17, and the noun "desires" [ἐπιθυμίαις] in 5:24). The only occurrences in this unit of the verb "are/is" (ἐστιν) in 5:19 (twice) and 5:22 (twice) determine the parallelism between the B (5:19–21a) and the B' (5:21d–23) elements. The only occurrences in this unit of the verb "warn/warn before"—"I warn" (προλέγω) in 5:21b and "I warned before" (προεῖπον) in 5:21c—establish the parallelism between the C (5:21b) and the C' (5:21c) elements at the pivotal center of this chiastic unit.

13. The Grace and Peace of Our Lord Jesus Christ to the Brothers (6:1–18)

For neither circumcision is anything nor uncircumcision but only a new creation

A ¹Brothers [ἀδελφοί], if indeed a person is overtaken by some wrongdoing, you who are Spiritual [πνευματικοί] correct such a one in a *Spirit* [πνεύματος] of humility, looking to yourself, so that you also may not be tempted. ²Bear [βαστάζετε] the burdens of one another and thus you will completely fulfill the law [νόμον] of Christ [Χριστοῦ]. ³For if anyone thinks he is something when he is nothing, he is deceiving himself. ⁴Let each one examine the work of himself, and then he will have a reason to boast [καύχημα] with regard to himself alone [μόνον] and not with regard to the other. ⁵For each one will bear [βαστάσει] his own load. ⁶Let the one who is being instructed in the word share with the one instructing in all good things. ⁷Do not be led astray; God [θεός] is not mocked, for a person will reap only what he sows, ⁸because the one sowing to the flesh of himself from the flesh will reap destruction, but the one who sows to the Spirit [πνεῦμα] from the Spirit [πνεύματος] will reap life eternal.

> B ⁹ᵃLet us not lose heart in doing what is commendable, for in due time [καιρῷ] we will reap,
>
> C ⁹ᵇif we do not give up.
>
> B' ¹⁰So then while we have time [καιρόν], let us work the good for all, and especially for those who are members of the household of the faith.

A' ¹¹See with what large letters I am writing to you in my own hand! ¹²As many as want to make a good showing in the flesh, these are forcing you to be circumcised, only [μόνον] that for the cross of Christ [Χριστοῦ] they may not be persecuted. ¹³For those who are circumcised do not keep the law [νόμον] themselves but they want you to be circumcised, so that they may boast [καυχήσωνται] in your flesh. ¹⁴But as for me, may I never boast [καυχᾶσθαι] except in the cross of our Lord Jesus Christ [Χριστοῦ], through which the world has been crucified to me and I to the world. ¹⁵For neither circumcision is anything nor uncircumcision but only a new creation!

¹⁶And as many as will follow this rule, peace and mercy upon them, that is upon the Israel of God [θεοῦ]. ¹⁷From now on let no one cause me troubles, for I bear [βαστάζω] the marks of Jesus in my body. ¹⁸The grace of our Lord Jesus Christ [Χριστοῦ] with your spirit [πνεύματος], brothers [ἀδελφοί]. Amen!

The word "Spirit" (πνεύματος) near the beginning of this unit in 6:1 recalls "Spirit" (πνεύματι) toward the end of the preceding unit in 5:25. These successive occurrences of the noun "Spirit" serve as the transitional terms linking the twelfth (5:14–26) to the thirteenth (6:1–18) unit.

Introduction

An A-B-C-B'-A' chiastic pattern secures the integrity and distinctness of this thirteenth unit (6:1-18). Several linguistic occurrences constitute the parallelism between the A (6:1-8) and the A' (6:11-18) elements: the only occurrences in this unit of "brothers" (ἀδελφοί) in 6:1 and 18; of references to "Spirit" ("Spiritual" [πνευματικοί] in 6:1, "Spirit" [πνεύματος] in 6:1, 8, and 18, and "Spirit" [πνεῦμα] in 6:8); of the verb "bear" ("bear" [βαστάζετε] in 6:2, "will bear" [βαστάσει] in 6:5, and "I bear" [βαστάζω] in 6:17); of "law" (νόμον) in 6:2 and 13; of "Christ" (Χριστοῦ) in 6:2, 12, 14, and 18; of references to boasting (the noun "reason to boast" [καύχημα] in 6:4, the verb "they may boast" [καυχήσωνται] in 6:13, and the infinitive "boast" [καυχᾶσθαι] in 6:14); of "only" (μόνον) in 6:4 and 12; and of "God" (θεός in 6:7 and θεοῦ in 6:16).

The only occurrences in this unit of "time"—καιρῷ in 6:9a and καιρόν in 6:10—determine the parallelism between the B (6:9a) and B' (6:10) elements. And the only occurrence in Galatians of the expression "if we do not give up" in 6:9b serves as the unparalleled C element at the pivotal center of this chiastic unit.

THE MACROCHIASTIC STRUCTURE OF GALATIANS

Having illustrated the sequence of the various microchiastic structures operative in the thirteen distinct units of Galatians, I will now indicate how these thirteen units form an A-B-C-D-E-F-G-F'-E'-D'-C'-B'-A' macrochiastic structure unifying and organizing the entire letter.

A: The *Grace* and *Peace* of *Our Lord Jesus Christ* from All the *Brothers* (1:1-10)

A': The *Grace* and *Peace* of *Our Lord Jesus Christ* to the *Brothers* (6:1-18)
   The first and last occurrences in Galatians of the terms "grace" (1:3, 6; 6:18), "peace" (1:3; 6:16), and "brothers" (1:2; 6:1, 18), as well as the only occurrences in Galatians of the expression "our Lord Jesus Christ" (1:3; 6:14, 18), secure the parallelism between the opening A (1:1-10) and the closing A' (6:1-18) units within the macrochiastic structure of Galatians.

B: I Did Not Consult with *Flesh* and Blood before Preaching the *Faith* (1:11-24)

B': The *Flesh* Is Opposed to the Spirit Whose Fruit Includes *Faith* (5:14-26)

The parallelism between the B (1:11–24) and the B' (5:14–26) units is characterized by the first occurrence in Galatians of the term "flesh" (1:16) in the B unit and the most occurrences (five) of "flesh" (5:16, 17 [twice], 19, 24) in any unit of Galatians in the B' unit. These units also contain the first and penultimate occurrences of the term "faith" in Galatians—πίστιν in 1:23 and πίστις in 5:22.

C: *Freedom* from *Circumcision* for Worship in accord with the *Truth* (2:1–14)

C': The *Truth* of *Freedom* from *Circumcision* to Serve One Another (5:1–13)

The first and last occurrences of the terms "freedom" (2:4; 5:1, 13 [twice]) and "truth" (2:5, 14; 5:7) in Galatians, as well as the first six occurrences of the term "circumcision" (2:7, 8, 9, 12; 5:6, 11) in Galatians provide the parallelism between the C (2:1–14) and the C' (5:1–13) units.

D: I Live by Faith in the *Son* of God (2:15–21)

D': We Are Children with the *Son* of the Free Woman (4:21–31)

The first occurrence in Galatians of the expression "Son of God" (2:20) and the last four occurrences in Galatians of the term "son" (4:22, 30 [thrice]) indicate the parallelism between the D (2:15–21) and the D' (4:21–31) units.

E: Have You Suffered So Many Things *in Vain*? (3:1–5)

E': I Fear Lest Somehow *in Vain* I Labored for You (4:8–20)

The only occurrences in Galatians of the adverb "in vain" (εἰκῇ) in 3:4 (twice) and 4:11 provide the parallelism between the E (3:1–5) and the E' (4:8–20) units.

F: Christ *Redeemed* Us from the Curse of the Law (3:6–16)

F': That the Son of God Might *Redeem* Those Under the Law (4:1–7)

The only two occurrences in Galatians of forms of the verb "redeem"—"Christ redeemed [ἐξηγόρασεν] us" in 3:13 and "that he might redeem [ἐξαγοράσῃ]" in 4:5—indicate the parallelism between the F (3:6–16) and the F' (4:1–7) units.

G: Baptized into Christ, with Christ You Have Clothed Yourselves (3:17–29)

Introduction

The G (3:17–29) unit functions as the unparalleled central and pivotal unit within the macrochiastic structure of Galatians. This unit contains the only occurrences in Galatians of the verbal forms "you were baptized" (ἐβαπτίσθητε) and "you have clothed yourselves" (ἐνεδύσασθε) in 3:27.

OUTLINE OF THE MACROCHIASTIC STRUCTURE OF GALATIANS

A: 1:1–10: The *Grace* and *Peace* of *Our Lord Jesus Christ* from All the *Brothers*

  B: 1:11–24: I Did Not Consult with *Flesh* and Blood before Preaching the *Faith*

    C: 2:1–14: *Freedom* from *Circumcision* for Worship in accord with the *Truth*

      D: 2:15–21: I Live by Faith in the *Son* of God

        E: 3:1–5: Have You Suffered So Many Things *in Vain*?

          F: 3:6–16: Christ *Redeemed* Us from the Curse of the Law

            G: 3:17–29: Baptized into Christ, with Christ You Have Clothed Yourselves

          F': 4:1–7: That the Son of God Might *Redeem* Those Under the Law

        E': 4:8–20: I Fear Lest Somehow *in Vain* I Labored for You

      D': 4:21–31: We Are Children with the *Son* of the Free Woman

    C': 5:1–13: The *Truth* of *Freedom* from *Circumcision* to Serve One Another

  B': 5:14–26: The *Flesh* Is Opposed to the Spirit Whose Fruits Include *Faith*

A': 6:1–18: The *Grace* and *Peace* of *Our Lord Jesus Christ* to the *Brothers*

PRELIMINARY INDICATIONS OF WORSHIP FOR LIFE AS A KEY THEME OF GALATIANS

As indicated above, the subtitle chosen for this study, *Worship for Life by Faith in the Crucified and Risen Lord*, expresses what I am proposing as a key theme and concern of Galatians. I will now present an introductory overview of the preliminary indications that "worship for life," with "worship" including both liturgical and ethical worship and with "life" including both present and future, eschatological life, serves as a key theme that organizes and unifies the entire letter to the Galatians.

Galatians begins and ends with acts of epistolary worship with an orientation to eternal life, thus framing the entire letter within a context of worship for life. Paul begins the letter with an assertion that he is an apostle "through Jesus Christ and God the Father who raised him from the dead" (1:1), and thus to eternal life. Paul addresses the letter to "the churches of Galatia" (1:2), assemblies of Christian believers gathered to hear the letter in the context of their communal worship.[8] He then prays that they receive grace and peace "from God our Father and the Lord Jesus Christ" (1:3). The grace and peace are benefits coming from the risen Lord "who gave himself for our sins" (1:4a), which prevent proper worship, "that he might free us from the present evil age" (1:4b), and thus enable us to worship for the life of the future, eschatological age initiated by his resurrection. Paul then leads his audience in an act of doxological worship of the God who raised Jesus, as he exclaims, "to whom be the glory for the ages of the ages. Amen!" (1:5). The members of the audience are invited to add their own exuberant "amen!"[9]

As he brings the letter to a close, Paul prays that the grace of our risen Lord Jesus Christ be with "your spirit, brothers. Amen!" (6:18). This provides the Galatian audience with a final reminder of how their human "spirit" has been transformed by the divine "Spirit" of God's Son, which they have received as a grace through their faith (3:2, 5, 14; 4:6). This Spirit

---

8. According to BDAG, 303, the word "church" (ἐκκλησία) often refers to a specific Christian assembly or gathering "ordinarily involving worship."

9. Paul "closes the sentence with the word *amên*, an exclamation by which worshipers are invited to participate in a blessing, a prayer, or a doxology. Taken as a whole, then, vv 3–5 do not merely extend Paul's greetings. They have the effect of evoking the setting of worship ... We may assume that Paul brings the doxology from its usual liturgical setting into this epistolary introduction in order to make clear that the reading of this letter belongs properly to the context of worship" (Martyn, *Galatians*, 87, 91).

Introduction

has empowered them to offer proper worship to God, not by undergoing the Jewish ritual of circumcision but by their faith in Christ. Paul's final prayer recalls how the one who "sows" to the Spirit by the way he lives, will "reap" life eternal from the Spirit (6:8). The solemn "Amen!" that concludes the letter invites the audience to add their final assenting confirmation to the epistolary worship for life. It reverberates with the exuberant "Amen!" that concluded the letter's initial act of doxological worship of the God who raised our Lord Jesus Christ to eternal life (1:5). This literary inclusion formed by the letter's introductory (1:3–5) and concluding acts of worship (6:18) places the entire letter within a context of worship for life.[10]

These preliminary indications that "worship for life by faith in the crucified and risen Lord" expresses a chief theme and concern of Galatians will be further explained, developed, and confirmed by the remainder of my exegetical investigation into the chiastic structures of Galatians in the chapters to follow.

SUMMARY

There are thirteen distinct units in Galatians, with each exhibiting its own microchiastic structure.

These thirteen units operate as a macrochiastic structure with six pairs of parallel units and with the pivot of the entire macrochiastic structure occurring as the unparalleled central G unit in 3:17–29.

Paul's letter to the Galatians was heard by its various audiences in the "churches of Galatia" (1:2) within a setting of communal worship. It begins and ends with epistolary acts of worship (1:3–5; 6:18) inviting the members of the audience to participate with Paul by adding their own "Amen!" (1:5; 6:18) to his. These acts of epistolary worship provided preliminary indications that worship (both liturgical and ethical) for life (both present and future eternal) is a main theme and thrust of Galatians. More specifically, the subtitle, *Worship for Life by Faith in the Crucified and Risen Lord*, expresses a prominent and primary purpose of Galatians.

---

10. For a brief treatment of Galatians as a ritual of worship, see Heil, *Letters of Paul*, 64–74; on worship in Galatians, see also Borchert, *Worship*, 123–29. For a broader treatment of worship in the Pauline letters, see Costa, *Worship*. See also Fredriksen, "Question of Worship," 175–201.

2

Galatians 1:1–10

THE GRACE AND PEACE OF OUR LORD JESUS CHRIST FROM ALL THE BROTHERS

Glory to God who raised from the dead Jesus Christ who gave himself for our sins

A ¹Paul, an apostle *not* from *human beings* nor through a *human being* but through Jesus Christ and God the Father who raised him from the dead, ²and all the brothers with me, to the churches of Galatia,

    B ³*grace* to you and peace from God our Father and the Lord Jesus Christ, ⁴who gave himself for our sins, that he might free us from the present evil age according to the will of our God and Father,

    C ⁵to whom be the glory for the ages of the ages. Amen!

    B' ⁶I am amazed that you are so quickly turning away from the one who called you in the *grace* of Christ for a different gospel,

A' ⁷*not* that there is another, but there are some who are troubling you and want to distort the gospel of Christ. ⁸But even if we or an angel from heaven should preach to you a gospel other than the gospel we preached to you, let him be accursed! ⁹As we have said before, and now I say again, if anyone is preaching to you a gospel other than the one you received, let him be accursed! ¹⁰Am I now trying to gain the approval of *human beings* or of God? Or am I seeking to please *human beings*? If I were still pleasing *human beings*, I would *not* be a slave of Christ!¹

1:1–2 (A): Paul, an apostle through Jesus Christ, to the churches of Galatia

Paul begins the letter by boldly asserting that his authority as an apostle has a divine rather than human origin and agency. He accentuates the divine authority of his apostleship with an emphatic double denial. He is an apostle not from a community of human beings, nor from any individual human being, but through Jesus Christ and God the Father, who raised him from the dead (1:1). This implies that Jesus Christ has a divine status as one whom God raised from the realm of the dead into a heavenly, eternal life. His resurrection signals the beginning of the expected general resurrection of the dead to life and thus inaugurates the eschatological age.² From the beginning of the letter, then, Paul has established that he is an apostle with a message of the good news that, in raising Jesus Christ from the dead, God has initiated the end time with an implicit promise of a new and eternal life after death. This reference to the resurrection hints that the letter to follow will be concerned with how things have changed and how lives are to be lived in this new and final age.³

Although Paul is the primary sender of the letter, it is also sent by "all the brothers with me" (1:2a), that is, all his and his audience's fellow Christian believers from wherever, which is not specified, he is sending the letter.⁴ This implies that, as a believing community who are with Paul, they agree with what Paul will say in the letter. It further enhances his authority as an apostle and the significance of the letter, as sent and endorsed by

---

1. For the establishment of Gal 1:1–10 as a chiasm, see chapter 1 of this book.

2. "Resurrection *is* life being given to the dead, as the death/life lexicon in Paul broadly demonstrates (Rom 4:17; 6:4; 14:9; 1 Cor 15:45)" (Boakye, *Death and Life*, 80; emphasis original).

3. "The resurrection signifies that the new age has dawned (cf. Isa 26:19; Ezek 37:1–14; Dan 12:1–3), in which God will fulfill all his saving promises to Israel and to the entire world. One of the major themes of the letter emerges here" (Schreiner, *Galatians*, 75). Paul "alludes here to what will become the key theological argument of the letter: in Christ, God has inaugurated a new age in salvation history, a situation that 'changes everything'" (Moo, *Galatians*, 69).

4. Regarding the term "brother," Beutler notes: "The prevailing sense in Paul is that of *fellow Christians*" ("ἀδελφός," 1.30; emphasis original).

a community of fellow believers. Paul and all the brothers with him are sending the letter to "the churches of Galatia" (1:2b), that is, to worshiping communities of fellow believers in various locations most likely within the region of southern Galatia, probably in the cities of Pisidian Antioch, Lystra, Iconium, and Derbe (cf. Acts 13–14).[5] Galatians is thus a circular letter intended to be read and heard by various "churches," that is, audiences of believing "brothers" gathered together in a context of communal worship.[6]

1:3–4 (B): He gave himself for our sins to free us from the present evil age

Paul's opening greeting affirms that, as believers, the Galatians have already received grace and peace "from God our Father and the Lord Jesus Christ" (1:3), implicitly because of God raising Jesus Christ from the dead. It progresses from a reference to God "the" Father to God "our" Father, and from Jesus Christ to the (risen) "Lord" Jesus Christ (1:1), with the implication that, as "our" Father, God can also raise believers from the dead.[7] It also serves as a prayer for the Galatians to continue to experience this grace and peace, especially during and after their listening to the letter. That the Lord Jesus Christ "gave himself for our sins" (1:4a) complements the reference to his resurrection by God the Father with a reference to his self-sacrificial and expiatory death as the source of the grace and peace.[8] And that he might

---

5. For some rather speculative reconstructions of the historical and social context of Galatians, see, for example, Nanos, *Irony*; Elliott, *Cutting Too Close*; Elmer, *Paul*; Hardin, *Galatians*; Kahl, *Galatians*. For a critique that such historical reconstructions disregard historical plausibility, see Chester, "Paul and Galatian Believers," 64–65. For a recent discussion and defense of the southern Galatia location for the churches to whom the letter is sent, see John, *Galaterbrief*, 133–59. He also critiques theories of outside influences on Galatians, such as emperor worship or other forms of pagan worship, and concludes that the problems Paul addresses in the letter are an inner ecclesial phenomenon (212).

6. "Doubtless Paul's messenger went to each Galatian city, assembling the church in that place, so that in the context of worship the members could hear Paul's letter as though it were one of his sermons" (Martyn, *Galatians*, 86). "The churches of Galatia can be addressed even when they are not actually in assembly, though the letter will undoubtedly be read and thus heard in the meetings (for worship and fellowship) of the Galatian Christians" (De Boer, *Galatians*, 27).

7. On the title "Lord" as an indication of the divinity of Jesus Christ in Paul's letters, see Capes, *Divine Christ*.

8. Paul "conjoins God the Father and the Lord Jesus Christ closely together in the provision of this grace and peace" (Moo, *Galatians*, 71).

"free" or "rescue" (ἐξέληται) us from the present evil age, according to the will of our God and Father (1:4b), confirms that his death and resurrection initiates a new age with a promise of life after death, a new age of freedom from the sins that prevent the proper worship of God as our Father.[9]

1:5 (C): To God our Father be the glory for the ages of the ages

At the pivotal center of this chiastic unit, Paul exemplifies the proper worship of God as our Father, as he leads his audience in an act of doxological worship of God our Father, "to whom be the glory for the ages of the ages. Amen!" (1:5). That this acknowledgment of glory is "for the ages of the ages [αἰῶνας τῶν αἰώνων]," that is, forever, stands in contrast to the present evil "age [αἰῶνος]" (1:4), which has implicitly come to an end with the death and resurrection of the Lord Jesus Christ, so that it will not last forever.[10] The members of the audience, as a "church" gathered for worship (1:2), reminded that their sins—which prevented their proper worship—have been expiated and that they have been freed from the present evil age oriented to death rather than life, are invited to join Paul in this doxological worship by adding their own exuberant and assenting "Amen!"[11] Paul's initial act of worship at the beginning of his letter, oriented to the life that comes from God as our Father, sets the tone for the whole letter. It indicates that proper worship for life is a main concern and the intended outcome for the letter to follow.

---

9. "Christ's mission of rescue was undertaken *in order that he might set us free*. Paul personified the Present Age as a sinister slave master holding humanity hostage" (Lyons, *Galatians*, 54; emphasis original). "Paul confesses that it is by Christ's self-offering that persons may be delivered out of the 'present age of evil' and into the new age that God has promised—the age signaled by the resurrection of Jesus Christ from the dead" (Bryant, *Risen Crucified Christ*, 147).

10. "Praise and glory should go to God forever and ever for what God accomplished in Christ . . . In short there should be eternal praises for the eternal life wrought by God in Christ" (Witherington, *Grace in Galatia*, 77).

11. Regarding "amen" here, Lyons (*Galatians*, 55) notes: "Within the worship setting in which it was first read, this was an invitation to the assembled Galatian congregations to give verbal affirmation."

1:6 (B'): Turning away from the grace of Christ for a different gospel

After the unparalleled central and pivotal C element (1:5) of this chiastic unit, the Galatians hear a chiastic progression from the prayer greeting of "grace to you" (1:3) in the B element to "in the grace of Christ" (1:6) in the B' element. After leading the Galatians in an act of doxological worship of the God who raised Christ from death to life, Paul begins to chastise them as he expresses his amazement that they are so quickly turning away from the God who called them in the "grace" or "gift" (χάριτι) of Christ, who "gave" (δόντος) himself in death to expiate our sins (1:4), for a different gospel (1:6). They are turning away for a gospel different than the one Paul has just enunciated as the gospel of the Christ whom God raised from death to life (1:1) and who set us free from the present evil age by his death for our sins (1:4). This gospel, with its promise of eternal life after death, is the source of the grace and peace (1:3) for which the Galatians are to join Paul in worshiping God as our Father (1:5), who called them in the grace of the Christ to whom he gave eternal life after death.

1:7–10 (A'): If I were pleasing human beings, I would not be a slave of Christ

The A' element (1:7–10) of this chiastic unit forms a chiastic pattern in itself:

a) ⁷*not* that there is another, but there are some who are troubling you and want to distort the gospel of Christ.

    b) ⁸But even if we or an angel from heaven should *preach* to you a *gospel other than* the *gospel* we *preached* to you, *let him be accursed*!

        c) ^{9a}As we have *said before*,

        c') ^{9b}and now I *say* again,

    b') ^{9c}if anyone is *preaching* to you a *gospel other than* the one you received, *let him be accursed*!

a') ¹⁰Am I now trying to gain the approval of human beings or of God? Or am I seeking to please human beings? If I were still pleasing human beings, I would *not* be a slave of Christ!

At the center of this chiastic subunit is a pivot of parallels involving the only occurrences in this subunit of forms of the verb "say." As "we have said before [προειρήκαμεν]" (1:9a) progresses to "and now I say [λέγω] again" (1:9b). There is a progression of parallels involving the only occurrences in this subunit of the verb "to preach the gospel," of the phrase "other than," and of the expression "let him be accursed." "But even if we or an angel from heaven should preach to you a gospel [εὐαγγελίζηται] other than [παρ' ὅ] the gospel we preached [εὐηγγελισάμεθα] to you, let him be accursed [ἀνάθεμα ἔστω]" (1:8) progresses to "if anyone is preaching to you a gospel [εὐαγγελίζεται] other than [παρ' ὅ] the one you received, let him be accursed [ἀνάθεμα ἔστω]" (1:9c). Finally, parallels involving the only occurrences in this subunit of "not" progress from "not [οὐκ] that there is another" (1:7) to "I would not [οὐκ] be a slave of Christ" (1:10).

After strongly affirming that there is no other gospel, Paul refers to some who are troubling the Galatians and want to distort the one and only gospel of Christ (1:7). This reference to the "gospel of Christ" resonates with and develops the "grace of Christ" in which God called the Galatians (1:6). The "gospel" of Christ is the good news about the "grace" or "gift" of Christ—that Christ "gave" himself for our sins in a self-sacrificial death to free us from the present evil age (1:4) and that God the Father gave or graced to Christ eternal life by raising him from the dead (1:1).

If Paul or the brothers with him or even an angel from heaven should preach to the Galatians a gospel other than the one preached to them, "let him be accursed [ἀνάθεμα ἔστω]" (1:8), that is, condemned by God and thus deprived of the life God has made possible by raising Christ from the dead.[12] With a progression from "as *we* have said before" (1:9a) to "and now *I* say again" (1:9b), Paul emphatically reiterates and elaborates that if anyone, especially anyone of those who are troubling the Galatians and wish to distort the gospel of Christ (1:7), is preaching to them a gospel other than the gospel of Christ they received from Paul, "let him be accursed" by God (1:9c). If anyone who preaches a gospel different than the gospel of Christ is to be accursed by God, then surely the Galatians who are turning away to a different gospel are risking being likewise condemned by the God who called them in the grace of Christ (1:6). This would contradict their doxo-

---

12. "Paul does not need literally to identify it as *God's* curse, for in the world of Greek religions the term *anathêma* denotes something 'set up' (*anatetheimenon*) in the holy precincts, and therefore set apart from the profane orb, so that the god can either receive and bless it or—more often—curse and destroy it . . . Both the Greek and the Israelite know that a human being does not truly have the power to curse something. The most one can do is to deliver it to God, so that, in accordance with his own purposes, God can curse it" (Martyn, *Galatians*, 114; emphasis original).

logical worship of God our Father (1:5) for the grace of Christ, the grace of the life made possible by the resurrection of Christ to life from the dead.

Paul then prompts the Galatians to admit that he is trying to gain the approval of and seeking to please God rather than human beings (1:10), recalling that his being an apostle for the gospel of Christ did not come from human beings (1:1). As Paul asserts, if he were still pleasing human beings, he would *not* be a slave of Christ (1:10), recalling that there is *not* any other gospel than the gospel of Christ (1:7). That Paul is an obedient "slave" (δοῦλος) of Christ stands in ironic contrast to Christ "freeing" us from the present evil age (1:4). This implies that such freedom paradoxically makes it possible for Paul and the Galatians, for whom he is providing a model here to be "slaves" who serve the risen Christ in the life of the new age, rather than being enslaved to the evil and death of the present age.[13] That Paul and his audience are to be "slaves" who try to please Christ as an object of their ethical worship complements their doxological worship directed to God our Father (1:5), who raised Christ to life (1:1) and according to whose will Christ gave himself for our sins (1:4), thus enabling us to worship for life.

SUMMARY ON GALATIANS 1:1-10

Paul has established that he is an apostle with a message of the good news that in raising Jesus Christ from the dead God has initiated the end time with an implicit promise of a new and eternal life after death (1:1). This reference to the resurrection hints that the letter to follow will be concerned with how things have changed and how lives are to be lived in this new and final age.

Galatians is a circular letter intended to be read and heard by various "churches," that is, audiences of believing "brothers" gathered together in a context of communal worship (1:2).

---

13. "Galatians is characterized by a number of emphatic references to slavery and freedom. Slavery was a central mark of the past, the period before the advent of Christ, the period that still exists anomalously as 'the present evil age' (1:4). Freedom, by contrast, characterizes existence in Christ (4:3-7; 5:1). It presents a striking paradox, then, that Paul should here characterize himself, the messenger of the new liberation, as a slave" (Martyn, *Galatians*, 140). "As Christ's slave, Paul is completely subservient to his master, and yet he has found a freedom which only obedience to Christ can bring" (Matera, *Galatians*, 48).

That the Lord Jesus Christ "gave himself for our sins" (1:4a) complements the reference to his resurrection by God the Father with a reference to his self-sacrificial and expiatory death as the source of grace and peace for the Galatians (1:3). And that he might free us from the present evil age according to the will of our God and Father (1:4b) confirms that his death and resurrection initiates a new age with a promise of life after death, a new age of freedom from the sins that prevent the proper worship of God as our Father. Paul's initial act of doxological worship at the beginning of his letter (1:5), oriented to the life that comes from God as our Father, sets the tone for the whole letter. It indicates that proper worship for life is a main concern and the intended outcome for the letter to follow.

The Galatians are turning to a gospel different (1:6) than the one Paul has enunciated as the gospel of the Christ whom God raised from death to life (1:1) and who set us free from the present evil age by his death for our sins (1:4). If anyone who preaches a gospel different than the gospel of Christ is to be accursed by God (1:8–9), then surely the Galatians, who are turning away to a different gospel, are risking being likewise condemned by the God who called them in the grace of Christ (1:6). This would contradict their doxological worship of God our Father (1:5) for the grace of Christ, the grace of the life made possible by the resurrection of Christ to life from the dead.

That Paul and his audience are to be "slaves" who try to please Christ (1:7–10) as an object of their ethical worship complements their doxological worship directed to God our Father (1:5), who raised Christ to life (1:1) and according to whose will Christ gave himself for our sins (1:4), thus enabling us to worship for life.

3

Galatians 1:11–24

I DID NOT CONSULT WITH FLESH AND BLOOD BEFORE PREACHING THE FAITH

They were glorifying in me God

A ¹¹For I want you to know, brothers, that *the gospel preached* by me is not according to a human being. ¹²For I did not receive it nor was I taught it from a human being, but through a revelation of Jesus *Christ*. ¹³For you heard of my former conduct in Judaism, that beyond measure I was *persecuting* the *church* of God and trying to *destroy* it, ¹⁴and I was advancing in Judaism beyond many contemporaries in my race, being far greater a zealot for my ancestral traditions. ¹⁵But when the one who set me apart from my mother's womb and called me through his grace was pleased ¹⁶to reveal his Son *in me*, so that I might *preach the gospel* about him among the gentiles, I did not immediately consult with flesh and blood,

> B ¹⁷nor did I go up to Jerusalem to those who were apostles before me, rather I went away into Arabia and then returned to Damascus. ¹⁸*Then* after three years I did go up to Jerusalem to visit Cephas and I remained with him fifteen days. ¹⁹But I did not see any other of the apostles except James the brother of the Lord.

C ^{20}What things I am writing to you, behold, before God I am not lying.

B' ^{21}*Then* I went into the regions of Syria and Cilicia.

A' ^{22}But I was unknown personally to the *churches* of Judea that are in *Christ*. ^{23}They were only hearing that "the one who once was *persecuting* us is now *preaching the gospel* about the faith he once tried to *destroy*." ^{24}So they were glorifying *in me* God.[1]

1:11–16 (A): God was pleased to reveal his Son in Paul

The A element (1:11–16) of this chiastic unit forms a chiastic pattern in itself:

a) ^{11}For I want you to know, brothers, that *the gospel preached* by me is not according to a human being. ^{12}For I did not receive it nor was I taught it from a human being, but through a *revelation* of Jesus Christ.

b) ^{13a}For you heard of my former conduct *in Judaism*,

c) ^{13b}that beyond measure I was persecuting the church of God and trying to destroy it,

b') ^{14}and I was advancing *in Judaism* beyond many contemporaries in my race, being far greater a zealot for my ancestral traditions.

a') ^{15}But when the one who set me apart from my mother's womb and called me through his grace was pleased ^{16}*to reveal* his Son in me, so that I might *preach the gospel* about him among the gentiles, I did not immediately consult with flesh and blood.

Paul's statement "that beyond measure I was persecuting the church of God and trying to destroy it" (1:13b) serves as the unparalleled central and pivotal element of this chiastic subunit. Chiastic parallels progress from "in Judaism" in 1:13a to "in Judaism" in 1:14, and from "the gospel preached" and "revelation" in 1:11–12 to "reveal" and "preach the gospel" in 1:15–16.

In addressing the Galatians as "brothers" (1:11a), Paul acknowledges that they are fellow Christian believers like the "brothers" with him (1:2). Paul wants them to know that the gospel preached by him—that is, the gospel of Christ (1:7)—is not "according" (κατά) to a human being (1:11b). This implies that it is "according" (κατά) to the will of God (1:4). It recalls

1. For the establishment of Gal 1:11–24 as a chiasm, see chapter 1 of this book.

and reinforces not only that Paul is not trying to gain the approval of or seeking to please human beings (1:10), but that he is an apostle not from human beings nor through a human being (1:1). The gospel Paul preaches has a divine origin and authority, for he did not receive it, nor was he taught it by a human being, but through God's revelation of Jesus Christ (1:12).[2] God revealed to Paul that Christ was raised from the dead (1:1) to life after dying for our sins to free us from the present evil age (1:4). This message of the divine gift of life after death serves as a central characterization of the gospel Paul preaches.

The Galatians heard of Paul's former conduct in Judaism, that beyond measure he was persecuting the church of God and trying to destroy it (1:13). This refers to the universal church into which Paul has incorporated the churches of Galatia (1:2) through his preaching of the gospel to them. Paul was advancing in Judaism beyond many of his Jewish contemporaries, being far greater a zealot for his ancestral traditions (1:14). But God set Paul apart in his mother's womb and "called" him through his "grace" (1:15), that he might preach the gospel among the gentiles (1:16).[3] It was through his preaching of the gospel to the gentile Galatians that God "called" them in the "grace" of Christ, but they are now turning away from this gospel (1:6). That God was pleased to "reveal" his Son "in me" (1:16a) reinforces and confirms that Paul's gospel was through God's "revelation" of Jesus Christ (1:12).[4] But when Paul was called by God, he did not immediately consult

---

2. "Christ is the object of God's revelatory act. And Paul's receipt of the gospel is the result" (Martyn, *Galatians*, 144).

3. This alludes to Isa 49:1, 6, where God "called" the name of the servant of the Lord from his "mother's womb" and promised to make him a light to the gentiles. It also alludes to Jer 1:5, where God tells Jeremiah that before he formed him in the "womb" he knew him and appointed him to be a prophet to the gentiles.

4. Regarding the phrase "in me" (ἐν ἐμοί) in 1:16a, De Boer notes: "Paul wants the Galatians to understand that 'the *apokalypsis* of Jesus Christ' (1:12c), whereby 'God was pleased to reveal [*apokalypsai*] his Son in me" (1:16a), means that God entered into the life of Paul, the persecutor of God's church and an extremely zealous, law-observant Pharisee, in order to bring that manner of life to a complete and irrevocable end" (*Galatians*, 93). Paul's "choice to use ἐν here is likely intended to denote that the revelation of God's Son had a transformative power 'in' his very being" (Moo, *Galatians*, 104). "According to 1:12, the *gospel* came through a revelation of Jesus Christ. In 1:16, *Jesus himself* is revealed 'in' Paul. These two statements point to one revelatory moment—*the unveiling of the risen Jesus was the unveiling of the gospel*" (Boakye, *Death and Life*, 84; emphases original). See also Fee, *Jesus the Lord*, 108.

with "flesh and blood" (1:16), that is, with human beings. This emphasizes the divine origin and authority of the gospel he preaches.[5]

1:17–19 (B): The apostle Paul is independent of other apostles

The B element (1:17–19) of this chiastic unit forms a chiastic pattern in itself:

a) ¹⁷ᵃnor *did I go up to Jerusalem* to those who were *apostles* before me,

    b) ¹⁷ᵇrather I went away into Arabia and then returned to Damascus.

a') ¹⁸Then after three years *I did go up to Jerusalem* to visit Cephas and I remained with him fifteen days. ¹⁹ But I did not see any other of the *apostles* except James the brother of the Lord.

Paul's statement that "rather I went away into Arabia and then returned to Damascus" (1:17b) serves as the unparalleled central and pivotal element of this chiastic subunit. Chiastic parallels progress from "nor did I go up to Jerusalem" and "apostles" (1:17a) to "I did go up to Jerusalem" and "apostles" (1:18–19).

That Paul did not immediately go up to Jerusalem further indicates his separation from the Judaism in which he had been zealously advancing (1:14). For Paul, Jerusalem has now become a center for the church of God.[6] He distanced himself from those who were apostles before him by instead going into Arabia and then returning to Damascus (1:17), which, in contrast to Jerusalem, was the city central to his revelation of Christ raised from the dead (cf. Acts 9:1–22; 22:5–16; 26:12–20).[7] It was not until three years later that Paul did go up to Jerusalem to visit Cephas (Peter), a leading apostle in Jerusalem (cf. Acts 1:15; 2:14, 37–38; etc.), but he remained with him only fifteen days (1:18).[8] He did not see any other of the apostles

---

5. "The idiom *flesh and blood* follows Jewish precedent as a reference to *human beings* in contrast to God" (Lyons, *Galatians*, 84; emphases original).

6. "In short, for Paul the word 'Jerusalem' is dominantly a metonym for the Jerusalem *church*" (Martyn, *Galatians*, 169; emphasis original).

7. "The mention of his return to Damascus confirms the record of Acts (9:3; 22:6; 26:12f) that it was at or near Damascus that he was confronted by the risen Christ" (Bruce, *Epistle to the Galatians*, 96).

8. Paul "did not see Peter for three years after his conversion, and when he did see him, the time was relatively short. Both temporal references, then, underline the independence of Paul's gospel" (Schreiner, *Galatians*, 110).

except James the brother of the Lord (1:19), another leader of the Jerusalem community (cf. Acts 12:17; 15:13; 21:18). This underlines that Paul was an apostle with a divine authority based on God's revelation to him of the risen Christ, a divine authority independent of those who were apostles before him.

1:20 (C): Before God I am not lying

Paul emphatically and solemnly assures the Galatians of the truth of what he is writing to them in the letter they are now hearing, gathered together in the presence of God in a context of worship, as he declares, "Before God I am not lying" (1:20).[9] Paul is not lying before the God who was pleased to reveal his Son in Paul that he might preach the gospel about him among the gentiles (1:15-16). Paul is not now lying before the God whose church he once persecuted (1:13), the God whose approval he is trying to gain (1:10). Paul is not lying before God our Father, a giver of grace and peace to the Galatians (1:3), since according to the will of our God and Father the Lord Jesus Christ gave himself for our sins, that he might free us from the present evil age (1:4). And Paul is not lying before the God who raised Jesus Christ from the dead and through whom Paul is an apostle (1:1).

1:21 (B'): Then I went into the regions of Syria and Cilicia

Paul's report that he went into the regions of Syria and Cilicia (1:21) after his brief stay in Jerusalem (1:18-19) further distances him from those who were apostles before him (1:17) and further underlines his independence of human authority as an apostle with divine authority from the God who raised Jesus Christ from the dead to life (1:1).[10]

---

9. "This solemn oath is another indication that the letter will be read aloud in the context of a worship service, and thus in the presumed presence of God" (De Boer, *Galatians*, 99). "The vehement solemnity with which Paul calls God to witness that he is not lying implies that another account of the matter was current and might have reached the Galatian converts—an account which represented him as having gone to Jerusalem to receive from those who were apostles before him the authority to exercise his own ministry" (Bruce, *Epistle to the Galatians*, 102).

10. "Paul's point is to make clear that he was not in Jerusalem during this time" (Witherington, *Grace in Galatia*, 124). "Paul delineates his itinerary with care to defend the independence of his gospel" (Schreiner, *Galatians*, 111). "His purpose remains clear: to show how little contact he had with the Jerusalem apostles so that no one can accuse

GALATIANS 1:11-24

1:22-24 (A'): Glorifying God in Paul now preaching the gospel about the faith

Paul was unknown personally to the churches of Judea that are in Christ (1:22). This further separates Paul, not only from the Jerusalem church, but from the members of the various churches in its vicinity. They were only hearing that the Paul who once was "persecuting" them is now preaching the gospel about the faith he once tried to "destroy" (1:23). This reinforces Paul's report that beyond measure he was "persecuting" the church of God and trying to "destroy" it (1:13). Paul's preaching inspired them to a doxological worship of God. They were glorifying "in me" God (1:24), who was pleased to reveal his Son "in me" (1:16), because Paul was now preaching the gospel about the faith that acknowledges and receives the grace and peace (1:3) that come from God raising Jesus Christ from the dead (1:1) after he gave his life for our sins to free us from the present evil age (1:4).[11] Having led the Galatians to give glory to God for this new life (1:5), Paul implicitly invites the Galatian churches to join the Judean churches in glorifying God for Paul's gospel about this new life, rather than turning away from it (1:6).

SUMMARY ON GALATIANS 1:11-24

The gospel Paul preaches has a divine origin and authority, for he did not receive it, nor was he taught it by a human being, but through God's revelation of Jesus Christ (1:12). God revealed to Paul that Christ was raised from the dead (1:1) after he gave his life for our sins to free us from the present evil age (1:4). This message of life after death serves as a central characterization of the gospel Paul preaches.

God set Paul apart from his mother's womb and "called" him through his "grace" (1:15), that he might preach the gospel among the gentiles (1:16). It was through his preaching the gospel to the gentile Galatians that God "called" them in the "grace" of Christ, but they are now turning away from this gospel (1:6). That God was pleased to "reveal" his Son "in me" (1:16a)

---

him of having learned his gospel from them (v. 12)" (Moo, *Galatians*, 111).

11. Regarding "in me" in 1:24, "Paul has used the same phrase in 1:16a and it there means 'in my manner of life earlier in Judaism.' Here the phrase may have an analogous meaning: Paul's *new* manner of life as the apostle of Christ to the Gentiles" (De Boer, *Galatians*, 103; emphasis original).

reinforces and confirms that Paul's gospel was through God's "revelation" of Jesus Christ (1:12).

Paul's report that he went into the regions of Syria and Cilicia (1:21) after his brief stay in Jerusalem (1:18–19) further distances him from those who were apostles before him (1:17) and further underlines his independence of human authority as an apostle with divine authority from the God who raised Jesus Christ from the dead (1:1).

Paul's preaching inspired the churches of Judea to a doxological worship of God. They were glorifying "in me" God (1:24), who was pleased to reveal his Son "in me" (1:16), because Paul was now preaching the gospel about the faith that acknowledges and receives the grace and peace (1:3) that come from God's raising Jesus Christ from the dead (1:1) after he gave his life for our sins to free us from the present evil age (1:4). Having led the Galatians to give glory to God for this new life (1:5), Paul implicitly invites the Galatian churches to join the Judean churches in glorifying God about this new life, rather than turning away from it (1:6).

4

Galatians 2:1-14

FREEDOM FROM CIRCUMCISION FOR WORSHIP IN ACCORD WITH THE TRUTH

God shows no partiality

A ¹Then after fourteen years I again went up to Jerusalem with *Barnabas*, taking Titus along also. ²I went up according to a revelation, and I presented to them the *gospel* that I proclaim among the gentiles, but privately to those of repute, lest somehow for no purpose I might be running or had run. ³Yet not even Titus, who was with me, although being a Greek, was forced to be circumcised. ⁴But because of the false brothers secretly brought in, who slipped in to spy on our freedom that we have in Christ Jesus, that they might enslave us, ⁵to them not even for a moment did we yield to the subjection, so that the *truth* of the *gospel* might remain with you.

    B ⁶ᵃBut to those who were reputed to be something—what they once were means *nothing* to me;

        C ⁶ᵇGod does not show partiality to a human being—

    B' ⁶ᶜthose of repute made me add *nothing*.

A' ⁷On the contrary, seeing that I had been entrusted with the *gospel* of the uncircumcision, just as Peter of the circumcision, ⁸for the one who worked in Peter for an apostolate of the circumcision worked also in me for the gentiles, ⁹and recognizing the grace given to me, James and Cephas and John, who were reputed to be pillars, gave me and *Barnabas* their right hands in fellowship, that we would go to the gentiles, and they to the circumcision. ¹⁰Only that we might remember the poor, the very thing I also was eager to do. ¹¹But when Cephas came to Antioch, I opposed him to his face, because he was clearly wrong. ¹²For until certain people came from James, he had been eating with the gentiles; but when they came, he drew back and separated himself, fearing those of the circumcision. ¹³And the rest of the Jews also joined with him in this hypocrisy, so that even *Barnabas* was led astray with them in the hypocrisy. ¹⁴But when I saw that they were not acting rightly with the *truth* of the *gospel*, I said to Cephas in front of all, "If you, although being a Jew, are living like a gentile and not like a Jew, how can you force the gentiles to live like Jews?"[1]

2:1–5 (A): That the truth of the gospel might remain with you

The A element (2:1–5) of this chiastic unit forms a chiastic pattern in itself:

a) ¹Then after fourteen years I again went up to Jerusalem with Barnabas, taking Titus along also. ²I went up according to a revelation, and I presented to them the *gospel* that I proclaim among the gentiles, but privately to those of repute, lest somehow for no purpose I might be running or had run. ³Yet *not even* Titus, who was with me, although being a Greek, was forced to be circumcised.

    b) ⁴ᵃBut because of the false brothers *secretly brought in*,

        b') ⁴ᵇwho *slipped in* to spy on our freedom that we have in Christ Jesus, that they might enslave us,

a') ⁵to them *not even* for a moment did we yield to the subjection, so that the truth of the *gospel* might remain with you.

At the center of this chiastic subunit is a pivot of parallels involving the only occurrences in this subunit of alliterative and synonymous terms: "Secretly brought in [παρεισάκτους]" (2:4a) pivots to "slipped in [παρεισῆλθον]" (2:4b). Chiastic parallels progress from "gospel" in 2:2 and "not even" in 2:3 to "not even" and "gospel" in 2:5.

---

1. For the establishment of Gal 2:1–14 as a chiasm, see chapter 1 of this book.

The first element (2:1–3) of this chiastic subunit forms a chiastic pattern in itself:

[a] ¹Then after fourteen years I again went up to Jerusalem with Barnabas, taking *Titus* along also. ²ᵃI went up according to a revelation, and I presented to them the gospel that I proclaim among the gentiles, but privately to those of repute,

[b] ²ᵇlest somehow for no purpose I might *be running*

[b'] ²ᶜor *had run*.

[a'] ³Yet not even *Titus*, who was with me, although being a Greek, was forced to be circumcised.

At the center of this chiastic subunit is a pivot of parallels from "be running" in 2:2b to "had run" in 2:2c. Chiastic parallels progress from "Titus" in 2:1 to "Titus" in 2:3.

Further distancing himself from the leaders of the Jerusalem church, Paul reports that it was not until fourteen years later that he again went up to Jerusalem with Barnabas and Titus, two of his coworkers (2:1).[2] He went up according to a "revelation" (2:2a), which resonates with the "revelation" to him of the risen Christ (1:12) through which God was pleased to "reveal" his Son in Paul (1:15–16). Paul presented privately to those of repute (2:2a), presumably including Cephas and James (1:18–19), the gospel of Christ he proclaims among the gentiles, as this is what God called him to do (1:15–16). His intention in presenting was to have them assure him that, in preaching the gospel, he was not "running" (2:2b) or "had run" (2:2c) to no purpose.[3] Yet not even Titus, who was with Paul for this private consultation, although being a Greek, was forced by these Jewish leaders to be circumcised (2:3). This implies that the gospel Paul proclaims among the gentiles does not require them to be circumcised to be part of God's people.

---

2. "The fourteen-year interval before traveling again to Jerusalem underscores the independence of Paul's gospel" (Schreiner, *Galatians*, 119). "In Acts, Barnabas, a Jewish Christian from Cyprus, is depicted as Paul's mentor, introducing him to 'the apostles' in Jerusalem... Titus, who (strangely) is nowhere mentioned in Acts, was undoubtedly an important figure in Paul's mission. In 2 Corinthians he plays a crucial role in Paul's relationship with the Corinthian church and the collection for Jerusalem" (De Boer, *Galatians*, 107–8).

3. Martyn, *Galatians*, 192: "'running' is a widespread metaphor for exerting oneself strenuously." See also BDAG, 1015.

The Jewish leaders, then, have implicitly assured Paul that he was indeed "running" on the right track.[4]

But some "false brothers," those who only pretended to be fellow believers, sneaked into this private consultation with the Jewish leaders to spy on the freedom that true believers have in Christ Jesus, that they might enslave "us"—Paul, his coworkers, and all believing gentiles (2:4).[5] This refers to the freedom from the requirement (which Paul considers an enslavement) that gentiles, such as Titus, be circumcised. And it accords with the freedom from the present evil age inaugurated by the death and resurrection of Jesus Christ (1:1, 4). But not even for a moment did Paul and his coworkers yield to this subjection, which would be an enslavement contradicting their freedom. This was so that the truth of the gospel, namely that Christ has freed gentiles from this enslaving subjection and brought them into a proper relationship with God, might remain with "you"—the Galatians (2:5), Paul's true believing "brothers" (1:11), as well as all gentile believers.[6]

2:6a (B): Those reputed to be something

But what those Jerusalem leaders who were reputed to be something once were now means nothing to Paul (2:6a). This further separates Paul from the Jerusalem leaders and underlines his independence from human beings and thus the divine authority of his gospel and apostleship.

---

4. "As the test case, Titus established the essential point of Paul's gospel: Gentiles were not required to become Jews to be Christians. Thus, Paul's missionary efforts were not 'in vain' (v. 2)" (Lyons, *Galatians*, 107).

5. A "false brother" (ψευδάδελφος) is "one who pretends to be a fellow-believer, but whose claim is belied by conduct toward fellow-believers" (BDAG, 1096). The false brothers "professed to be Christians, but they did not live as if the new age had already dawned in Christ" (Lyons, *Galatians*, 113).

6. "The freedom/slavery contrast points to the fulfillment of God's eschatological promises in Christ... Those who live under the old age of the law are enslaved, whereas those who are in Christ live in the new era in which God's saving promises are being fulfilled" (Schreiner, *Galatians*, 125). "The particular aspect of the 'truth of the gospel' in view here is its power both to bring Gentiles into relationship with God and to maintain them in that relationship right up through the judgment day" (Moo, *Galatians*, 130).

2:6b (C): God does not show partiality to a human being

In this context, Paul's assertion that God does not show partiality to a human being (2:6b) has a double application. God has not shown partiality in calling human beings to be apostles. He has revealed the risen Christ to both the apostle Paul and those who were apostles before him. And God shows no partiality in the sense that he is not partial to and does not favor circumcised Jewish human beings over uncircumcised gentile human beings.

2:6c (B'): Those of repute made Paul add nothing

That the status of those reputed to be something means "nothing" to Paul (2:6a) progresses to those of repute making Paul add "nothing" (2:6c) to the gospel he preaches. This means that Paul did not have to add a requirement that gentile believers need to be circumcised to be in the same relationship with God as circumcised Jews.[7]

2:7-14 (A'): Uncircumcised Gentiles cannot be forced to live like circumcised Jews

The A' element (2:7-14) of this chiastic unit forms a chiastic pattern in itself:

   a) ⁷On the contrary, *seeing* that I had been entrusted with the *gospel* of the uncircumcision, just as Peter of the *circumcision*, ⁸for the one who worked in Peter for an apostolate of the *circumcision* worked also in me for the *gentiles*, ⁹and recognizing the grace given to me, *James* and *Cephas* and John, who were reputed to be pillars, gave me and *Barnabas* their right hands in fellowship, that we would go to the *gentiles*, and they to the *circumcision*.

      b) ¹⁰Only that we might remember the poor, the very thing I also was eager to do.

   a') ¹¹But when *Cephas* came to Antioch, I opposed him to his face, because he was clearly wrong. ¹²For until certain people came from *James*, he had been eating with the *gentiles*; but when they came, he drew back and

---

7. Paul "has made clear that the issue at this consultation was the 'truth of the gospel,' especially here, its essentially gracious nature. The Jerusalem apostles did nothing to interfere with that understanding of the gospel" (Moo, *Galatians*, 133).

separated himself, fearing those of the *circumcision*. ¹³And the rest of the Jews also joined with him in this hypocrisy, so that even *Barnabas* was led astray with them in the hypocrisy. ¹⁴But when I *saw* that they were not acting rightly with the truth of the *gospel*, I said to *Cephas* in front of all, "If you, although being a Jew, are living like a *gentile* and not like a Jew, how can you force the *gentiles* to live like Jews?"

At the center of this chiastic subunit (2:7–14) is the only occurrence in Galatians of the statement: "Only that we might remember the poor, the very thing I also was eager to do" (2:10). Chiastic parallels progress from "seeing" in 2:7 to "I saw" in 2:14; from "gospel" in 2:7 to "gospel" in 2:14; from "circumcision" in 2:7, 8 and 9 to "circumcision" in 2:12; from "gentiles" in 2:8 and 9 to "gentiles" in 2:12 and 14 and "gentile" in 2:14; from "James" in 2:9 to "James" in 2:12; from "Cephas" in 2:9 to "Cephas" in 2:11 and 14; and from "Barnabas" in 2:9 to "Barnabas" in 2:13.

The first element (2:7–9) of this chiastic subunit forms a chiastic pattern in itself:

[a] ⁷On the contrary, seeing that I had been entrusted with the gospel of the uncircumcision, just as Peter of the *circumcision*, ⁸for the one who worked in Peter for an apostolate of the *circumcision* worked also in me *for the gentiles*,

    [b] ⁹ᵃand recognizing the grace *given* to me,

        [c] ⁹ᵇJames and Cephas and John, who were reputed to be pillars,

    [b'] ⁹ᶜ*gave* me and Barnabas their right hands in fellowship,

[a'] ⁹ᵈthat we would go *to the gentiles*, and they to the *circumcision*.

At the center of this chiastic subunit (2:7–9) is the only occurrence in Galatians of the expression: "James and Cephas and John, who were reputed to be pillars" (2:9b). Chiastic parallels progress from "given" in 2:9a to "gave" in 2:9c; from "circumcision" in 2:7 and 8 to "circumcision" in 2:9d; and from "for the gentiles" in 2:8 to "to the gentiles" in 2:9d.

Not only did those of repute at Jerusalem not make Paul add anything to his gospel (2:6c), but they realized that Paul had been and still is "entrusted" (perfect tense) by God (divine passive) with the gospel of the "uncircumcision" (gentiles), thus including Paul's audience of Galatian churches, just as Peter (Cephas) had been entrusted by God with the gospel of the "circumcision" (Jews; 2:7).⁸ For the God who worked in Peter for an apostolate of the circumcision worked in Paul for the gentiles (2:8), illustrating how God shows no partiality (2:6c).⁹ Corresponding to their recognizing the grace "given" to Paul by God (cf. 1:15), James, Cephas, and John—who were reputed to be "pillars," the main leaders of the Jerusalem church—"gave" to Paul and Barnabas their right hands in fellowship, confirming their partnership that Paul and Barnabas would go to the gentiles and they to the circumcision (2:9).¹⁰ But they requested that Paul and Barnabas (and, by implication, the gentiles) "remember" with their financial support the poor members of the Jerusalem church, which Paul was eager to do (2:10).¹¹

The last element (2:11–14) of this chiastic subunit forms a chiastic pattern in itself:

[a] ¹¹But *when Cephas* came to Antioch, I opposed him to his face, because he was clearly wrong. ¹²For until certain people came from James, he had been eating with the *gentiles*; but *when* they came, he drew back and separated himself, fearing those of the circumcision.

[b] ¹³ᵃAnd the rest of the Jews also *joined* with him *in* this *hypocrisy*,

[b'] ¹³ᵇso that even Barnabas was led astray with them in the *hypocrisy*.

---

8. "Paul does not speak of two different gospels in content but of two different cultures in which the one gospel was proclaimed ... Paul believed that Peter preached the same gospel he did" (Schreiner, *Galatians*, 128). "Paul's preaching to Gentiles would require that he make clear to them that the gracious nature of the gospel means that they should not be circumcised or put themselves under the law of Moses. Peter, on the other hand, while also making clear to a Jewish audience the gracious nature of the gospel, would not necessarily bring up circumcision or the law in the same manner" (Moo, *Galatians*, 134).

9. "In 2:7b-8, Paul twice refers to Cephas as Peter. He does so nowhere else. Four times elsewhere in Galatians he uses Peter's Aramaic nickname 'Cephas' instead (1:18; 2:9, 11, 14) ... Paul assumes that the Galatians will understand that 'Peter' is a nickname meaning 'Rock,' and that it is the Greek translation of 'Cephas.' The first mention of Cephas in 1:18 already suggests that the Galatians were familiar with the name" (De Boer, *Galatians*, 120–21).

10. "The pillars in Paul's account, however, each offered to Paul and Barnabas not so much the right hand of friendship or agreement as that 'of partnership.' The Greek word *koinonia*, often translated 'fellowship,' means 'sharing' or 'participation.' Here the sharing involves 'partnership': joint and equal participation in the work of God (2:7-8)" (De Boer, *Galatians*, 124).

11. "Perhaps the Jerusalem leaders requested no more than prayer. But they more likely implicitly requested economic support (see Heb 13:7), using a euphemism" (Lyons, *Galatians*, 121–22).

[a'] ¹⁴But *when* I saw that they were not acting rightly with the truth of the gospel, I said to *Cephas* in front of all, "If you, although being a Jew, are living like a *gentile* and not like a Jew, how can you force the *gentiles* to live like Jews?"

The pivotal center of this chiastic subunit contains the only occurrences in Galatians of terms expressing "hypocrisy." "Joined in hypocrisy" (συνυπεκρίθησαν) in 2:13a pivots to "hypocrisy" (ὑποκρίσει) in 2:13b. Chiastic parallels progress from "when" in 2:11 and 12 to "when" in 2:14; from "Cephas" in 2:11 to "Cephas" in 2:14; and from "gentiles" in 2:12 to "gentile" in 2:14 and "gentiles" in 2:14.

The truth of the gospel Paul preached had ramifications for the worship that took place in and through the meals shared by believers, which had a sacred character and included the eucharistic celebration of the Lord's Supper.[12] Paul reports to the Galatians an incident that occurred in Antioch in which Cephas (Peter) was clearly wrong regarding the corporate worship that took place within the meals shared by Jewish and gentile believers (2:11). Until certain people came to Antioch from James in Jerusalem, Peter used to "eat with," that is, share meal fellowship with, the gentile believers. But when these people, who advocated that gentiles must be circumcised and thus become Jewish, arrived, Peter began to draw back and "separated" (ἀφώριζεν) himself—a technical cultic term—from this kind of worship (2:12). The rest of the Jews followed Peter in this hypocrisy, and even Barnabas was led astray in the hypocrisy, which amounted to a cultic "separation" of themselves from the meal fellowship of "eating with," and thus worshiping with, gentile believers (2:13).[13]

---

12. "In sum, the Christian sacred meals reflected in the NT and other very early Christian texts likely were varied in what was done and in what they meant for the participants. But in all cases, Jesus was the central figure for whom and with whom thanks were offered to God, and the meal itself was a central feature of Christian corporate worship across various circles of the Christian movement. Further, as a group meal, there was an emphasis on the solidarity of those who partook; it was a corporate action and not that of individuals in some private act of devotion" (Hurtado, "Worship," 922–23).

13. "ἀφωρίζω became a technical term for the dissolution of cultic community (Gal 2:12). Peter *separated* himself *from* table fellowship between Gentile and Jewish Christians and held the Lord's Supper for the Jewish Christians separately when the 'visitors' from James arrived" (Kellermann, "ἀφωρίζω," 1.184; emphases original). "The Jerusalem church, truly observant of the Law, held its common meals—including the Eucharist—in accordance with the Jewish food laws . . . In the Antioch church, however, the meals—again including the Eucharist—were arranged by an adjustment on the part of the members who were Jews by birth. At least by implication, the food laws were declared to be

But when Paul saw that they were not behaving correctly with the truth of the gospel, which includes freedom from the requirement that gentile believers be circumcised (2:3–5), he rebuked Peter in front of all: "If you, being a Jew, are living like a gentile and not like a Jew, how can you force gentiles to live like Jews [ἰουδαΐζειν]?" (2:14).[14] Peter was "living like a gentile" in the sense that he was not observing the Jewish food laws when sharing meal fellowship, which included the Eucharist, with gentile believers. This implies that the truth of the gospel includes freedom not only from the requirement for gentile believers to become Jewish but from any requirement for gentile believers to observe Jewish food laws to share eucharistic meals with them. It thus reinforces Paul's implicit appeal for the Galatians not to turn away from the truth of the gospel of Christ as preached by Paul for a different gospel (1:6). The Galatian believers have been freed from any need to live like Jews to engage in the worship of the eucharistic Lord's Supper with any other community of believers.[15]

SUMMARY ON GALATIANS 2:1–14

Not even Titus, although being a Greek, was forced by the Jewish leaders to be circumcised (2:3). This implies that the gospel Paul proclaims among the gentiles does not require them to be circumcised to be part of God's people. Not for a moment did Paul and his coworkers yield to a subjection, which would be an enslavement contradicting their freedom, requiring that gentile believers need to be circumcised. This was so that the truth of the gospel, namely that Christ has freed gentiles from this enslaving subjection

---

essentially a matter of no consequence in the church . . . Since the Eucharist was part of the common meal, Peter's withdrawal from the latter brought with it his withdrawal from the former. He has now separated himself from the Gentile members, as they eat the Lord's Supper" (Martyn, *Galatians*, 232–33).

14. "The repetition of the phrase 'the truth of the gospel' reveals that the imposition of food laws on the Gentiles by Peter cannot be differentiated from the attempt to force Titus to be circumcised. For Paul the gospel itself was at stake, for in effect Peter was requiring the Gentiles to observe the food laws to be saved" (Schreiner, *Galatians*, 146). "The word Ἰουδαΐζειν is a significant term which occurs nowhere else in the NT, meaning to adopt Jewish customs and practices, which would include sabbath observance, observing food laws, and even being circumcised" (Witherington, *Grace in Galatia*, 159).

15. "Paul viewed the sharing of meals between Jewish and Gentile believers as a critical indication of the status of the Gentiles within the people of God. For this reason, celebration of the Lord's Supper was probably one aspect of the sharing of meals that was involved in the Antioch dispute" (Moo, *Galatians*, 151).

and brought them into a proper relationship with God, might remain with "you"—the Galatians (2:5), Paul's true believing "brothers" (1:11), as well as all gentile believers.

Paul's assertion that God does not show partiality to a human being (2:6b) has a double application. God has not shown partiality in calling human beings to be apostles. He has revealed the risen Christ to both the apostle Paul and those who were apostles before him. And God shows no partiality in the sense that he is not partial to and does not favor circumcised Jewish human beings over uncircumcised gentile human beings.

The truth of the gospel includes freedom, not only from the requirement for gentile believers to become Jewish, but from any requirement for gentile believers to observe Jewish food laws to share eucharistic meals with them (2:11–14). This reinforces Paul's implicit appeal for the Galatians not to turn away from the truth of the gospel of Christ as preached by Paul for a different gospel (1:6). The Galatian believers have been freed from any need to live like Jews to engage in the worship of the eucharistic Lord's Supper with any other community of believers.

5

Galatians 2:15–21

I LIVE BY FAITH IN THE SON OF GOD

Christ lives in me

A ¹⁵We are Jews by nature and not sinners from the gentiles. ¹⁶Yet knowing that a human being is not justified from works of the *law* but through *faith* in Jesus *Christ*, even we have believed in *Christ* Jesus, that we may be justified from *faith* in *Christ* and not from works of the *law*, because from works of the *law* will not be justified any flesh [cf. Ps 143:2]. ¹⁷But if seeking to be justified in *Christ* we ourselves have also been found to be sinners, is *Christ* then an agent of sin? Of course not!

B ¹⁸ᵃFor if those things I tore down *I am* again *building up*,

B' ¹⁸ᵇthen that I myself am a transgressor *I am confirming*.

A' ¹⁹For I myself through the *law* to the *law* died, so that I might live for God. I have been crucified with *Christ*. ²⁰Yet I live, no longer I, but *Christ* lives in me; insofar as now I live in flesh, in *faith* I live, that (faith) in the Son of God who loved me and gave himself up for me. ²¹I do not reject the grace of God; for if through the *law* is justification, then to no purpose *Christ* died![1]

---

1. For the establishment of Gal 2:15–21 as a chiasm, see chapter 1 of this book.

2:15–17 (A): We may be justified by God from faith in Christ

The A element (2:15–17) of this chiastic unit forms a chiastic pattern in itself:

a) ¹⁵We are Jews by nature and not *sinners* from the gentiles.

    b) ¹⁶ᵃYet knowing that a human being is not justified *from works of the law*

        c) ¹⁶ᵇbut through *faith* in Jesus Christ,

            d) ¹⁶ᶜeven we have believed in Christ Jesus,

        c') ¹⁶ᵈthat we may be justified from *faith* in Christ

    b') ¹⁶ᵉand not *from works of the law*, because *from works of the law* will not be justified any flesh (cf. Ps 143:2).

a') ¹⁷But if seeking to be justified in Christ we ourselves have also been found to be *sinners*, is Christ then an agent of sin? Of course not!

The expression, "even we have believed in Christ Jesus" (2:16c), unparalleled within this chiastic subunit, serves as its pivotal central element. Chiastic parallels progress from "faith" in 2:16b to "faith" in 2:16d; from "from works of the law" in 2:16a to "from works of the law" (twice) in 2:16e; and from "sinners" in 2:15 to "sinners" in 2:17.

Paul speaks for himself, Peter, and all Jewish Christians in asserting that "we are Jews by nature and not sinners from the gentiles" (2:15). Being Jews "by nature" (φύσει) refers to the Jewish mode and habit of life as governed by the divine morality of the Mosaic law.[2] Jews are not "sinners" from the gentiles—those who do not live in observance of the moral and cultic expectations of the Mosaic law, and thus are unable to practice authentic liturgical or ethical worship of the one true God.[3]

Yet Jewish Christians know that a human being, whether a Jew by nature or a sinner from the gentiles, is not justified by God (divine passive)

---

2. "'By nature' is to be preferred to 'by birth' . . . it denoted 'by virtue of what something happens to be' or that which is modal because of habit" (Boakye, *Death and Life*, 102n35).

3. A "sinner" (ἁμαρτωλός) is one whose behavior or activity "does not measure up to standard moral or cultic expectations" (BDAG, 51). "Paul is almost certainly using ἁμαρτωλοί from the typical Jewish perspective that viewed Gentiles as by definition 'excluded from citizenship in Israel and foreigners to the covenants of the promise, without hope and without God in the world' (Eph 2:12) . . . Paul uses the language in this traditional sense only to debunk it" (Moo, *Galatians*, 156).

from works of the Mosaic law (2:16a). To be "justified" (δικαιοῦται) refers to God's recognition that one is presently just or righteous in his relationship to God with the expectation of being found just in the final divine judgment and thus rewarded with divine eternal life rather than condemned to an eternal death. Being presently justified by God means one can begin to live the new life now enabled by the resurrection of Jesus Christ from the dead (1:1) in accord with the future eternal life in and through one's cultic and ethical worship.[4] But one is not justified by practicing any of the works or commandments prescribed by the Mosaic law, including circumcision, the Jewish food regulations, or the Jewish days for worship.[5]

Rather, a human being is justified by God "through faith in Jesus Christ" (2:16b).[6] This means that one is now justified by God through believing or trusting in God's implicit promise of eternal life for human beings by raising Jesus Christ from the dead (1:1). Such "faith" (πίστις) entails accepting the freely given "grace" (χάρις) of Christ (1:6) available after, as an act of grace, he "gave" himself for our sins to free us from the mortality of the present evil age according to God's will (1:4), so that we believers may already live the new life of the future and final age. And this grace is proclaimed in the gospel of Christ (1:7), the word that invites such faith, the gospel the Galatians are turning away from for a different gospel (1:6).[7]

---

4. "Since Paul views God's justifying action in close connection with the power of Christ's resurrection, there is sometimes no clear distinction between the justifying action of acquittal and the gift of new life through the Holy Spirit as God's activity in promoting uprightness in believers" (BDAG, 249). Being justified or rectified "will be shown to operate as a revivifying moment by which believers are imbued with the resurrected life of Jesus, through Spirit, who possesses them on the grounds of faith in Jesus . . . the rectified life given by Messiah embodies an inclusive community ethic" (Boakye, *Death and Life*, 95).

5. "The term 'works of law' most likely refers to all the works prescribed by the Mosaic law" (Schreiner, *Galatians*, 161).

6. For the view that πίστις Χριστοῦ for Paul means not "faith (or faithfulness) of Christ" (subjective genitive) but "faith in Christ" (objective genitive), see Dunn, "Faith," 417–19; Silva, "Galatians," 789–90; Schreiner, *Galatians*, 163–66; Moo, *Galatians*, 38–48; Hunn, "Πίστις in Galatians 5.5–6," 477–83. The phrase πίστις Χριστοῦ "should be understood with a more sophisticated hermeneutical nuance. For the believers' faith is in Christ's faithful death and resurrection in accordance with the divine plan" (Boakye, *Death and Life*, 105).

7. Faith is "right in the center of Paul's theological thinking, where he takes over the general Christian meaning of the acceptance of the proclamation of God's salvation activity in Christ. Thus faith always comes from the word itself . . . If God has acted for salvation once and for all in Christ's cross, then the human response can only consist in obedient acceptance, in trust in God's χάρις, and in receiving this gift with and in

Paul emphasizes that even "we" Jewish Christians, who by nature try to observe the works prescribed by the Mosaic law, have believed in Christ Jesus (2:16c) as the one whom God raised from the dead to life. Thus, Jewish Christians have believed that they may be justified by God from faith in Christ (2:16d), and not from works of the law, because from works of the law "will not be justified [δικαιωθήσεται] any flesh" (2:16e; cf. Ps 143:2).[8] That God will not justify any flesh—any human being whether Jew or gentile—from works of the law reinforces how divine justification is totally dependent upon accepting the divine grace of a new life by believing in the Christ God raised from the dead to life. By referring to human beings (cf. 2:16a) as "flesh" (σάρξ), Paul points to their weakness and mortality in the present evil age from which Christ freed them (1:4) for a new life by being justified through faith in the risen Christ.[9]

But if in seeking to be justified by believing in Christ rather than by doing the works of the Mosaic law, "we" Jewish Christians have also been found before God to be sinners, like the sinners from the gentiles (2:15), it is absurd to think that Christ would then be an agent or cause of sin (2:17), since both Jews and gentiles were sinners all along.[10] And indeed this would contradict Christ's expiatory, salvific death when he gave himself for our sins to free us from the present evil age (1:4). When they sought to be justified by believing in Christ, Jewish Christians recognized that they were sinners, since they, like the gentiles, did not and could not accomplish the works of the law to be justified by God. But they found forgiveness and

---

a life lived from within the gift itself. Thus πίστις belongs together with χάρις" (Barth, "πίστις," 3.95). "Χάρις views the event of initiation from God's perspective, but that event is described from the human perspective as 'faith'... The word χάρις was naturally suited to describing that element of salvation already received in the present" (Berger, "χάρις," 3.459).

8. The appeal to Ps 143:2 "lends to Paul's statement a distinctly eschatological force... Although the future form δικαιωθήσεται could be understood as a generalizing use of the tense, a reference to the future judgment is most likely... the phrasing in the psalm itself (both the Hebrew and the Greek) clearly indicates the finality of the divine judgment" (Silva, "Galatians," 791).

9. The word "flesh" in 2:16e "emphasizes human fallenness and weakness" (Schreiner, *Galatians*, 167).

10. "The word 'found' (εὑρέθημεν) has a legal and forensic meaning, denoting one's standing before God as Judge and Lord of all. It refers to the verdict pronounced by the Divine Judge, whether one is 'found' to be guilty or innocent. Both Peter and Paul as Jews were found to be 'sinners' (ἁμαρτωλοί), so that before God they occupied the same status as 'sinners from the Gentiles' (ἐξ ἐθνῶν ἁμαρτωλοί, 2:15)" (Schreiner, *Galatians*, 168).

2:18 (B-B'): If what I tore down I am building up, I confirm that I am a transgressor

Shifting from speaking in the first-person plural as a representative of all Jewish Christians (2:15–17) to speaking in the first-person singular, Paul presents himself as the individual Jewish Christian apostle with whom the Galatians are to identify.[11] He says that if those things (that is, the provisions or works of the law) that "I" tore down, "I" am again building up, then that "I myself" (ἐμαυτόν) am a "transgressor" (παραβάτην) of the law "I" am confirming (2:18).[12] But, of course, Paul is not building up again the provisions or works of the law, and thus not requiring the Galatians to be circumcised, and so Paul is not confirming that he is a transgressor of the law, which in fact the death and resurrection of Christ has now abrogated and replaced as the means to be justified by God.[13]

2:19–21 (A'): In faith I live, the faith in the Son of God

The A' element (2:19–21) of this chiastic unit forms a chiastic pattern in itself:

a) [19a]For I myself *through the law* to the law *died,*

---

11. "The 'I' makes it easier for the Galatians to identify with what Paul is saying here and to take warning from it" (Moo, *Galatians,* 166).

12. "For Paul now to rebuild what he had torn down would be to revert to that old attitude, where such table-fellowship as he enjoyed at Antioch would make him not simply an involuntary 'sinner' like the Gentiles, but a conscious lawbreaker (that 'transgressor' [παραβάτης] meant 'transgressor of the law' would be self-evident—cf. the use of the word elsewhere in the NT, Rom. ii. 25, 27 and James ii. 9, 11). For Paul now to be asked to accept that his whole life as a Christian, in its outreach to Gentiles, was one long act of transgression, which put him beyond the pale of God's acceptance, was an impossible contradiction of what the gospel meant" (Dunn, *Epistle to the Galatians,* 143).

13. "Thus, if Paul is now rebuilding (reinstituting) the things (the works of the law) he earlier tore down (abrogated), he is indeed what the followers of the circumcision party in Antioch claimed he was: a transgressor of the law, for he would then once again be placing himself under the law's authority. But since Paul is *not* building the law up again, he cannot be a transgressor of it. If the law is now irrelevant for justification (v. 16), so also are transgressions of that law . . . a believer in Christ has been decisively separated from the law" (De Boer, *Galatians,* 158; emphasis original).

b) ¹⁹ᵇso that I might *live* for God.

c) ¹⁹ᶜI have been crucified with Christ.

b') ²⁰Yet I *live*, no longer I, but Christ *lives* in me; insofar as now I *live* in flesh, in faith I *live*, that (faith) in the Son of God who loved me and gave himself up for me.

a') ²¹I do not reject the grace of God; for if *through the law* is justification, then Christ to no purpose *died*!

The only occurrence in Galatians of the expression "I have been crucified with Christ" (2:19c) serves as the pivotal central element of this chiastic subunit. Chiastic parallels progress from "live" in 2:19b to "live" in 2:20 (thrice) and "lives" in 2:20, and from "through the law" and "died" in 2:19a to "through the law" and "died" in 2:21.

Paul is not building up again the works of the law and thus not confirming that "I myself" (ἐμαυτόν) am a transgressor of the law (2:18), for "I myself" (ἐγώ) "through the law to the law died" (2:19a).¹⁴ With the emphatic "I myself," Paul is speaking not only personally about himself but also paradigmatically as a representative of all believers.¹⁵ "Through the law" recalls and abbreviates that not "from works of the law" but "through faith in Jesus Christ" is one justified by God (2:16). Through faith, then, the believer has "died" to the law since it does not justify anyone before God for a life from and for God. Consequently, "I" (meaning Paul), as a Jewish Christian and as representing every believer, "died" to the Mosaic law, since it is not a way to be justified for a future eternal life with God and not a way to be justified to live presently a life pleasing to God and thus to practice proper cultic and ethical worship of God. Every individual Galatian believer, because of being justified through faith in Jesus Christ (2:16), should likewise realize that "I" have "died" to the law.¹⁶

---

14. "The explicit first person singular pronoun, ἐγώ, *I*, is noteworthy . . . Greek subject pronouns are usually emphatic. Orally, such an '*I*' should be stressed or translated *I myself*" (Lyons, *Galatians*, 158; emphases original). "The juxtaposition of 'through the law' and 'to the law' (especially in the Greek, where νόμου and νόμῳ are right next to each other) is deliberately paradoxical—even provocative" (Moo, *Galatians*, 168).

15. "'I' is used representatively. Paul speaks, not merely as a believer in general, but as a Jewish Christian, though what he says about dying to the law applies by implication to all believers" (Schreiner, *Galatians*, 170). See also Adewuya, *Holiness*, 89.

16. "When Paul therefore claims that he has 'died to the law,' he means that he has been released from the binding authority of the law of Moses . . . how wrong for Jewish Christians, and by extension Gentile Christians such as the Galatians, to try to be

Paul, and every believer he is representing, through the law to the law "died" (2:19a), so that "I might live" to and/or for God (2:19b).[17] That "I might live" (ζήσω) "for God" means to live one's present life in a way pleasing to God through cultic and ethical worship. Paul pointed out to Peter that although he is a Jew, "you are living" (ζῇς) like a gentile (2:14), referring to Peter's practice of sharing eucharistic meal fellowship with believing gentiles, a form of ritual worship meant to please God. For the believer to live "to God" means to live oriented to the implicit promise of future eternal life because God raised Jesus Christ from the dead (1:1) to eternal life. Living to God includes the doxological worship of glorifying God (1:5), since according to the will of God the Lord Jesus Christ gave himself for our sins, that he might free us from the mortality of the present evil age for an eternal life (1:4).[18]

In asserting that "I have been crucified with Christ" (2:19c), Paul again speaks for himself and every believer. Everyone who believes in Christ is not only justified (2:16) but crucified by God (divine passives), meaning that the believer has been united with the death of the Christ God raised to life (1:1) after he was crucified.[19] As a verb in the perfect tense, "I have been crucified with" (συνεσταύρωμαι) denotes not only that the believer has been crucified with Christ in the past when beginning to believe, but also continues to be crucified with Christ while living within the realm of mortality in this present evil age. But through his crucifixion, with which believers have been and still are being united, Christ gave himself for our sins to free us from the mortality of this present evil age (1:4) for life in the

---

justified in terms of the law (v. 16)" (Moo, *Galatians*, 168–69).

17. "In short, the death and resurrection of Christ has put to death all old means of trying to live or obtain life, here or hereafter, and has offered a new means of life and living" (Witherington, *Grace in Galatia*, 190). That "I might live to/for God" (θεῷ ζήσω) "may signify both that the believer now finds salvific life 'in relationship to God' and that the believer enters a new life that has God as its focus" (Moo, *Galatians*, 170).

18. "The antithetical contrast between life and death employs biological imagery to identify the same reality described in forensic imagery in Gal 2:17 and 21. That is, 'to be justified in Christ' (v. 17) is to *live for God*" (Lyons, *Galatians*, 159; emphasis original). "In the context of Galatians, 'life to God' has begun; employing a phrase that Jewish and Christian writers utilised to depict resurrection reaffirms that Paul saw rectification and resurrection as connected" (Boakye, *Death and Life*, 108).

19. Paul's being crucified with Christ expresses "a very personal way of speaking about what Christ did for believers through his crucifixion. His death meant their death, which alone can lead to their being raised to a new life" (Fee, *Pauline Christology*, 222–23).

new and final age inaugurated by his death and resurrection.[20] As believers who have been and still are being crucified with Christ, and so have died to the law (2:19a), the Galatians should not be turning away from the gospel of Christ (1:6–7) for a gospel advocating their circumcision and practice of the law.[21]

As having been and still being crucified with the Christ (2:19c) God raised from the dead (1:1), Paul and every believer yet lives. But the life a believer lives is not animated and directed by oneself, but by the risen Christ "who lives in me" (2:20a).[22] "I," Paul and every believer, still live "in flesh," that is, in the realm of the mortality of the present evil age (1:4), the realm in which not any "flesh" will be justified and thus given life from works of the law (2:16). But while "I live in flesh, in faith I live" (2:20b),[23] that faith of accepting the grace of a new life given by the Son of God who loved "me" and "gave" himself up for "me" (2:20c).[24] Here Paul makes personal for every believer, especially every Galatian believer, that Christ "gave" himself for "our" sins, that he might free "us" from the mortality of the present evil age (1:4). Living by faith in the Son of God and accepting the grace of a new

---

20. "When Paul says he has been 'crucified with Christ,' he also means that he has been rescued from the present evil age" (De Boer, *Galatians*, 161). "The perfect form of συνεσταύρωμαι emphasizes the continuing state of the subject of the verb: 'I am in the state of being crucified with Christ.'... To be 'crucified with Christ,' then, does not mean that believers undergo a metaphorical 'crucifixion' similar to Christ's actual crucifixion but that believers are regarded by God as having hung on the cross with Christ. The imagery is intended to highlight a decisive and total transfer from one state to another" (Moo, *Galatians*, 170–71).

21. "Paul's salvation provides a paradigm for all his readers, even (esp.) the gentile Galatians who do not have a prior relationship to Jewish law that they could die to.... If Paul went so far as to die to the law, the gentile Christians should not be adopting it.... Paul is also presenting himself as a paradigm of the person who has been (or is being) rescued from the present evil age by Christ, who gave himself for him (2:20; cf. 1:4). Paul has died. Paul has been crucified to the world (6:14). Paul is the person radically connected to God and Christ, not to this age and the world" (Oakes, *Galatians*, 95).

22. "That Paul may speak of Christ's crucifixion and follow this statement up with 'Christ lives' demonstrates the immediacy of the risen Christ in Paul's reckoning of his own rectification. The risen Christ lives in Paul. The former Paul no longer lives—the newly created apostle has new life flowing through him, and this new life is the resurrected Messiah" (Boakye, *Death and Life*, 118).

23. Note the chiastic word order that juxtaposes "in flesh" with "in faith": (a) "I live [ζῶ]" (b) "in flesh [ἐν σαρκί]," (b') "in faith [ἐν πίστει]" (a') "I live [ζῶ]."

24. "The 'flesh' in 2:20b is the sphere of what is mortal (susceptible to death) and weak (vulnerable to disease) ... The life Paul 'now' lives in this sphere—as a believer in Christ, as an apostle, and after his death to the law—he lives 'in faith'" (De Boer, *Galatians*, 162).

life from the risen Christ who "lives in me" means that "I might live to and for God" (2:19b), and thus by faith worship God in this present life in the realm of mortal flesh in view of an eternal life with the risen Christ.

Paul expects every believer to be able to say with him, "I do not reject the grace of God" (2:21a). Every Galatian believer, particularly, whom God called in the "grace" of the Christ God raised from the dead (1:1), should not reject the "grace" of God for a different gospel (1:6). The Galatian believer should not reject the "grace" God gave Paul to go to the gentiles with a gospel not requiring their circumcision (2:9), the "grace" through which God called him (1:15) to proclaim God's Son to the gentiles (1:16). And every believer should not reject the "grace" that comes from God our Father and the Lord Jesus Christ (1:3), who, as an act of grace, "gave" himself up for Paul and every believer (2:20) when he "gave" himself for our sins, that he might free us from the mortality of the present evil age (1:4) for new life.[25]

If "through the law," rather than through faith in Jesus Christ (1:16), is justification by God for new life, then to no purpose Christ died (2:21b). But "I" and every believer in Christ "through the law" to the law "died" to be justified to live to and for God (2:19ab), the purpose for which Christ "died." This sums up the gospel of Christ, which is being distorted by those troubling the Galatians and misleading them to turn to a different gospel (1:6–7), one that requires them to be circumcised and thus be justified through the law. The Galatians rather should not reject the gospel of Christ and the grace of God (2:21a) by which the risen Christ lives in them as believers (2:20), so that they may live a new life to and for God. The Galatian believers need not observe the Mosaic law by being circumcised and practicing the Jewish food regulations to properly worship God for life in the present evil age and for life in the age to come, the age that began when God raised Jesus Christ from the dead to a new and eternal life.[26]

---

25. "The self-giving of Christ (2:20), a manifestation of God's own free and unconstrained giving, is at root a matter of grace" (Moo, *Galatians*, 173).

26. "Galatians 2:20–21 then forms a tight argument from the necessity of Christ's self-giving death, a point on which all Christians presumably agree, to the impossibility of there being an alternative sufficient route to righteousness, namely, the law" (Oakes, *Galatians*, 96).

SUMMARY ON GALATIANS 2:15–21

That God will not justify any flesh—any human being, whether Jew or gentile—from works of the law reinforces how divine justification is totally dependent upon accepting the divine grace of a new life by believing in the Christ God raised from the dead to life (2:16). By referring to human beings as "flesh," Paul points to their weakness and mortality in the present evil age from which Christ freed them by his sacrificial death (1:4) for a new life by being justified through faith in the risen Christ.

When they sought to be justified by believing in Christ, Jewish Christians recognized that they were sinners, since they, like the gentiles, did not and could not accomplish the works of the law to be justified by God. But they found forgiveness and freedom from their sins by believing in Christ to live a new life in this final age inaugurated by the death and resurrection of Jesus Christ (2:15–17).

Paul is not building up again the provisions or works of the law, and thus not requiring the Galatians to be circumcised, and so Paul is not confirming that he is a transgressor of the law, which in fact the death and resurrection of Christ has now abrogated and replaced as the means to be justified by God (2:18).

Paul, and every believer he is representing, through the law to the law "died" (2:19a), so that "I might live" to and/or for God (2:19b). That "I might live for God" means to live one's present life in a way pleasing to God through cultic and ethical worship. Paul pointed out to Peter that, although he is a Jew, "you are living" like a gentile (2:14), referring to Peter's practice of sharing eucharistic meal fellowship with believing gentiles, a form of ritual worship meant to please God. For the believer to live "to God" means to live oriented to the implicit promise of future eternal life because God raised Jesus Christ from the dead (1:1) to eternal life. Living to God includes the doxological worship of glorifying God (1:5), since according to the will of God the Lord Jesus Christ gave himself for our sins, that he might free us from the mortality of the present evil age for an eternal life (1:4).

As having been and still being crucified with the Christ (2:19c) God raised from the dead (1:1), Paul and every believer yet lives. But the life a believer lives is not animated and directed by oneself, but by the risen Christ "who lives in me" (2:20a). "I," Paul and every believer, still live "in flesh," that is, in the realm of the mortality of the present evil age (1:4), the realm in which not any "flesh" will be justified and thus given life from works of the law (2:16). But while "I live in flesh, in faith I live" (2:20b), that faith of accepting the grace of a new life given by the Son of God who loved "me" and "gave" himself up for "me" (2:20c). Here Paul makes personal for every believer, especially every Galatian believer, that Christ "gave" himself for "our" sins, that he might free "us" from the mortality of the present evil age (1:4). Living by faith in the Son of God and accepting the grace of a new life from the risen Christ who "lives in me" means that "I might live to and for God" (2:19b), and thus by faith worship God in this present life in the realm of mortal flesh in view of an eternal life with the risen Christ.

If "through the law," rather than through faith in Jesus Christ (1:16), is justification by God for new life, then to no purpose Christ died (2:21b). But "I" and every believer in Christ "through the law" to the law "died" to be justified to live to and for God (2:19ab), the purpose for which Christ "died." This sums up the gospel of Christ, which is being distorted by those troubling the Galatians and misleading them to turn to a different gospel (1:6–7), one that requires them to be circumcised and thus be justified through the law. The Galatians, rather, should not reject the gospel of Christ and the grace of God (2:21a) by which the risen Christ lives in them as believers (2:20), so that they may live a new life to and for God. The Galatian believers need not observe the Mosaic law by being circumcised and practicing the Jewish food regulations to properly worship God for life in the present evil age and for life in the age to come, the age that began when God raised Jesus Christ from the dead to a new and eternal life.

6

Galatians 3:1–5

HAVE YOU EXPERIENCED SO MANY THINGS IN VAIN?

You received the Spirit from the hearing of faith

A ¹O foolish Galatians! Who has bewitched you, before whose eyes Jesus Christ was publicly proclaimed as crucified? ²This only I want to learn from you: *from works of the law* did you receive the *Spirit* or *from the hearing of faith*? ³Are you so foolish? Having begun with the *Spirit*, now with the flesh are you ending?

    B ⁴ᵃHave you experienced so many things *in vain*?

    B' ⁴ᵇIf indeed it has been *in vain*.

A' ⁵Does then the one supplying you the *Spirit* and working mighty deeds among you do so *from works of the law* or *from the hearing of faith*?[1]

3:1–3 (A): Beginning with the Spirit, are you now ending with the flesh?

The A element (3:1–3) of this chiastic unit forms a chiastic pattern in itself:

---

1. For the establishment of Gal 3:1–5 as a chiasm, see chapter 1 of this book.

a) ¹O *foolish* Galatians! Who has bewitched you, before whose eyes Jesus Christ was publicly proclaimed as crucified? ²ᵃThis only I want to learn from you:

b) ²ᵇ*from* works of the law

c) ²ᶜdid you receive the Spirit

b') ²ᵈor *from* the hearing of faith?

a') ³Are you so *foolish*? Having begun with the Spirit, now with the flesh are you ending?

The expression "did you receive the Spirit" (3:2c), unparalleled within this chiastic subunit, serves as its pivotal central element. Chiastic parallels progress from "from" in 3:2b to "from" in 3:2d and from "foolish" in 3:1 to "foolish" in 3:3.

After addressing his audience as "foolish Galatians,"² Paul asks who has "bewitched" (ἐβάσκανεν) them, with a connotation of placing them under a deceptive spell by the gaze of the "evil eye" (3:1a).³ The question of "who" (τίς) has bewitched them recalls and resonates with Paul's assertion that if "anyone" (τίς) "is preaching to you a gospel other than the one you received, let him be accursed!" (1:9). The singular "who" generalizes and/or individualizes the reference to "some" (τινές) "who are troubling you and wish to distort the gospel of Christ" (1:7).⁴ Paul's chastising address and provocative question to the Galatians reinforce his amazement that they are so quickly turning away from the one who called them in the grace of Christ for a different gospel (1:6). Before the very eyes of the Galatians, Paul publicly proclaimed to them Jesus Christ as crucified (3:1b). This recalls that Paul and every believer has been crucified with Christ (2:19). The perfect tense "crucified" (ἐσταυρωμένος) connotes a continuing effect—crucified in the past, the risen Christ now presently lives in every believer (2:20).⁵

---

2. "Foolish" (ἀνόητοι) "suggests failure to use one's powers of perception rather than natural stupidity" (Burton, *Galatians*, 143).

3. "The verb Paul uses, βασκαίνω, means 'to exert an evil influence through the eye' (BDAG, 171.1); we might say, 'to bewitch with the "evil eye"' . . . While it is unlikely that Paul means to say that the Galatians are under a spell cast by a sorcerer, his choice of this word does suggest that the Galatians' turnaround in their thinking can only be explained by recourse to an evil spiritual influence" (Moo, *Galatians*, 181). See also Wendt, "Galatians 3:1," 369–89.

4. "This singular is either generic (generalizing) or refers indirectly to a leading figure among the new preachers in Galatia" (De Boer, *Galatians*, 170).

5. "Christ's ongoing life is as the Crucified One . . . Paul's preaching, then, was not

Paul's next question reminds the Galatians that not from works of the law did they receive the divine Spirit but from the hearing of faith (3:2). "Not from works of the law" recalls that no human being will be justified "from works of the law" but "from faith in Christ" (2:16). Their reception of the life-giving Spirit was part of the grace of their being justified by God for a new life.[6] The risen Christ lives in every believer (2:20) by the gift of the Spirit.[7] The "hearing of faith" refers to the Galatians' hearing of Paul's public proclamation of the gospel about Jesus Christ as crucified (3:1). This hearing inspired their faith in Christ (cf. Rom 10:16–17). Consequently, from faith they were justified and received the life-giving divine Spirit of the crucified but risen Christ, which empowers them to live to and for God (Gal 2:19) as the people of God through their cultic and ethical worship.[8]

With "so" (οὕτως) in the emphatic first position, Paul intensifies his chastisement of the Galatians by asking if they really are *so* foolish (3:3a).[9] If, having begun their Christian lives with the Spirit as justified believers, are they now trying with the flesh rather than with the Spirit to bring it to completion (3:3)? The reference to "flesh" here carries a provocative double meaning. First, it somewhat sarcastically refers to the cutting of the flesh of the foreskin involved in the ritual of circumcision that the Galatians are being "bewitched" to undergo (3:1).[10] But, second and primarily, it refers to their returning to a life dominated by the mortality and weakness of the human flesh in this present evil age (1:4), after having been set free by the

---

about a Christ whose death had no significance (2:21). Neither was his proclamation about a Christ that no longer lived (1:1, 3, 10, 16; 2:20). Rather, Paul's clear public pronouncement—which the Galatians accepted—was of the living Jesus Christ who had been crucified and who now lives as the Crucified Christ" (Bryant, *Risen Crucified Christ*, 151–52).

6. "Having the Spirit was the irrefutable evidence that one had been 'justified' (Gal 2:16)" (Lyons, *Galatians*, 174).

7. "Paul's 'but Christ lives in me' most likely is a kind of shorthand for 'Christ by his Spirit lives in me' . . . in Paul's view Christ indwells his people by his Spirit" (Fee, *God's Empowering Presence*, 374).

8. "Since the Galatians have the Spirit, they are clearly Christians and belong to the people of God; hence, circumcision and observing the law are not required to belong to his people" (Schreiner, *Galatians*, 182).

9. BDAG, 742; Moo, *Galatians*, 183–84.

10. "In view of Gal 6:12–13, 'flesh' here is most probably a pointed reference to circumcision, the act whereby the fleshly foreskin of the penis is removed: 'For those who are wanting to make a good showing in the *flesh*, these are putting pressure on you to practice circumcision . . . they are wanting you to practice circumcision in order that they boast in your *flesh*'" (De Boer, *Galatians*, 177; emphases original).

crucified Christ from this old age for a life dominated by the divine life-giving Spirit of the risen Christ in the new age.[11] They would thus be trying to live to and for God (2:19) through their worship within the realm of the human flesh by doing the works of the law rather than within the realm of the divine Spirit as believers in Christ.[12]

3:4 (B-B'): Has it been in vain that you have experienced so many things?

After asking if the Galatians have experienced so many things in vain (3:4a), Paul suggests that perhaps, and hopefully, it has not been in vain (3:4b). In the emphatic first position in the sentence, "so many things" (τοσαῦτα) refers to the many remarkable things that the Galatians have experienced when they heard Paul's public proclamation of Jesus Christ as crucified—they heard Paul's public proclamation of Christ as crucified, they came to believe, were justified, and received the gift of the Spirit (3:1–3).[13] "In vain" (εἰκῇ) connotes "to no purpose" and suggests that, if the Galatians are going to end with the flesh by having themselves circumcised and practicing the works of the law (3:3), then they are denying the purpose for which Christ died (2:21); namely, so that they, as believers, might live to and for God (2:19). But they have not yet ended with the flesh, and Paul hopes that the many remarkable things they experienced indeed have not been in vain.[14]

11. "The opposition between the Spirit and flesh represents the eschatological contrast between this age and the age to come (cf. 1:4), with the flesh representing the old age and the Spirit the age to come. The age to come has penetrated this present evil age, and hence it does not make sense for the Galatians to turn back to the old age now that the new has arrived" (Schreiner, *Galatians*, 184).

12. "The concern that Paul expresses in this verse reaches to the rhetorical heart of Galatians. The Galatian Christians have started well; they have received the Spirit and have been justified by their faith in Christ, a gift of God's grace. But the agitators have come on the scene, arguing that people can go free in the judgment only if they add to their faith the 'works of the law.' Paul seeks to persuade the Galatians not to buy into this scheme: as they began, with the Spirit and with faith, so they must continue" (Moo, *Galatians*, 185).

13. For the meaning of "so many remarkable things" for τοσαῦτα, see BDAG, 1012. Regarding "so many things" (τοσαῦτα), "the word order puts the τοσαῦτα in the emphatic first position, referring to what has just been said in vv. 2–3" (Fee, *God's Empowering Presence*, 387).

14. Paul "seemed to assume that they were not beyond recovery ... he was confident that his letter would succeed in persuading them to see the error of their ways and to return to the truth of the gospel" (Lyons, *Galatians*, 179). "The last clause of v. 4 expresses

GALATIANS

3:5 (A'): God supplies the Spirit and works mighty deeds for those who believe

With his final question in this unit, Paul impresses upon the Galatians that God continues to supply them with the Spirit and works mighty deeds among them, not from works of the law, but from the hearing of faith (3:5). The preeminent context for the supplying of the Spirit and working of mighty deeds among the Galatian believers would seem to be their communal worship.[15] God supplies them with the Spirit in the form of various spiritual gifts or charisms that they exercise as part of their liturgical worship. The "mighty deeds" (δυνάμεις) would probably include the miraculous healings that take place within the context of their communal worship.[16] Not only did the Galatians first receive the gift of the Spirit, not from works of the law but from their faith (3:2), but they continue to experience various gifts of the Spirit for their communal worship, not from the works of the law but from their faith in Christ. Thus, Paul reminds the Galatians that God continues to supply them, as believers, with the Spirit, enabling them to work mighty deeds as they live to and for God (2:19) in and through their worship.

SUMMARY ON GALATIANS 3:1-5

Not from works of the law, but from faith, the Galatians were justified and received the life-giving divine Spirit of the crucified but risen Christ, which

---

the hope that what the Galatian Christians have experienced of the Spirit may not actually have been for nothing. Paul is deeply concerned about the situation, but he would not be writing the letter if he thought it was hopeless. By adding the clause, he causes the Galatians to share his hope and his concern" (De Boer, *Galatians*, 180).

15. "If the Galatians' past experience of the Spirit is not enough to convince them that their relationship to God is based on faith alone, Paul will try one more time—this time appealing to their ongoing life in the Spirit as a community of worshipping believers" (Fee, *God's Empowering Presence*, 387).

16. "Here δυνάμεις is used comprehensively of the manifestations of the Spirit's power; in 1 Cor. 12:10, 28f., it is used of one group of such manifestations . . . Even when δυνάμεις constitute one group of manifestations alongside others, they should not be too rigidly demarcated from those others; healings, for example, although separately mentioned, were one form of mighty work. But when the word is used comprehensively, as it is here, it no doubt includes several of the manifestations separately listed in 1 Cor. 12" (Bruce, *Epistle to the Galatians*, 151).

empowers them to live to and for God (2:19) as the people of God through their cultic and ethical worship (3:1–2).

Paul asks the Galatians if, having begun their Christian lives with the Spirit as justified believers, they are now trying with the flesh rather than with the Spirit to bring it to completion (3:3). The reference to "flesh" here carries a provocative double meaning. First, it somewhat sarcastically refers to the cutting of the flesh of the foreskin involved in the ritual of circumcision that the Galatians are being "bewitched" to undergo (3:1). But second and primarily, it refers to their returning to a life dominated by the mortality and weakness of the human flesh in this present evil age (1:4), after having been set free by the crucified Christ from this old age for a life dominated by the divine life-giving Spirit of the risen Christ in the new age. They would thus be trying to live to and for God (2:19) through their worship within the realm of the human flesh by doing the works of the law, rather than within the realm of the divine Spirit as believers in Christ.

If the Galatians are going to end with the flesh by having themselves circumcised and practicing the works of the law (3:3), then they are denying the purpose for which Christ died (2:21)—namely, so that they, as believers, might live to and for God (2:19). But they have not yet ended with the flesh, and Paul hopes that the many remarkable things they experienced in coming to faith and receiving the Spirit indeed have not been in vain (3:4).

Not only did the Galatians first receive the gift of the Spirit not from works of the law, but from their faith (3:2), but they continue to experience various gifts of the Spirit for their communal worship, not from the works of the law, but from their faith in Christ (3:5). Thus, Paul reminds the Galatians that God continues to supply them, as believers, with the Spirit, enabling them to work mighty deeds as they live to and for God (2:19) in and through their worship.

7

Galatians 3:6–16

CHRIST REDEEMED US FROM THE CURSE OF THE LAW

The just one from faith will live

A ⁶Just as *Abraham* "believed God and it was credited to him as justification" [Gen 15:6], ⁷recognize then that those from faith, these are sons of *Abraham*. ⁸And the scripture, foreseeing that from faith God would justify *the gentiles*, foretold the gospel to *Abraham*, saying, "In you will be blessed all *the gentiles*" [Gen 12:3; 18:18]. ⁹So those from faith are blessed with the believing *Abraham*.

    B ¹⁰For as many as are from works of the law are under a *curse*, for it is written, "*Cursed is everyone* who does not remain in all the things written in the book of the law, to do them" [Deut 27:26].

        C ¹¹And that by the law no one is justified before God is clear, for "the just one from faith *will live*" [Hab 2:4].

        C' ¹²But the law is not from faith, rather, "the one who does these things *will live* by them" [Lev 18:5].

    B' ¹³Christ redeemed us from the *curse* of the law having become for us a *curse*, for it is written, "*Cursed is everyone* who hangs on a tree" [Deut 21:23],

A' ¹⁴that to *the gentiles* the blessing of *Abraham* might come in Christ Jesus, that the promise of the Spirit we might receive through faith. ¹⁵Brothers, as a human being I speak, that even a covenant ratified by a human being no one rejects or amends. ¹⁶Now to *Abraham* were spoken the promises and to his descendant; it does not say, "And to descendants," as referring to many but as referring to one, "And to your descendant" [Gen 12:7; 13:15; 17:8; 22:17; 24:7], who is Christ.[1]

3:6-9 (A): Those from faith are blessed with the believing Abraham

The A element (3:6-9) of this chiastic unit forms a chiastic pattern in itself:

a) ⁶Just as *Abraham* "believed God and it was credited to him as justification" [Gen 15:6], ⁷recognize then that those from faith, these are sons of *Abraham*. ⁸ᵃAnd the scripture, foreseeing that from faith God would justify the gentiles, foretold the gospel to *Abraham*,

b) ⁸ᵇsaying, "In you will be *blessed* all the gentiles" [Gen 12:3; 18:18].

b') ⁹ᵃSo those from faith are *blessed*

a') ⁹ᵇwith the believing *Abraham*.

At the center of this chiastic subunit is a pivot of parallels from "blessed" in 3:8b to "blessed" in 3:9a. Chiastic parallels progress from "Abraham" in 3:6, 7 and 8a to "Abraham" in 3:9b.

The scriptural statement that Abraham "believed" God and it was credited to him (by God) as "justification" (3:6; cf. Gen 15:6) serves as a foundational foreshadowing for the previous assertion that we have "believed" in Christ Jesus that we may be justified by faith in Christ (2:16), so that not through the law is "justification" (2:21). Based on this scriptural quotation, the Galatians are to recognize that they, as "those from faith," are sons of Abraham (3:7), implying that they are entitled to inherit the blessing God gave to Abraham.[2] The scripture that says in Abraham all the gentiles will be blessed (3:8b; cf. Gen 12:3; 18:18) with justification, foresee-

---

1. For the establishment of Gal 3:6–16 as a chiasm, see chapter 1 of this book.
2. Contra Trick (*Abrahamic Descent*), who limits the "sons" of Abraham to believing Jews. "Among the likely factors leading him to speak of 'sons' (υἱοί) is the way his argument will relate to inheritance" (Oakes, *Galatians*, 105). The expression "sons of Abraham" likely "denotes people who belong to Abraham and hence participate in his blessing" (Moo, *Galatians*, 197).

ing that from faith God would justify the gentiles, "foretold the gospel" to Abraham (3:8a).³ This means that Abraham already received the "gospel" of Christ (1:7), with its promise of eschatological life for those justified by faith, an implied consequence of the gospel that God raised Jesus Christ from the dead (1:1) to new life. As "those from faith," with the believing Abraham, the Galatians are blessed with justification (3:9) for new life.⁴

3:10 (B): Cursed is everyone who does not do all the works of the law

Paul's statement that as many as are "from works of the law" are under a curse (3:10a) recalls not only that not "from works of the law" did the Galatians receive the Spirit (3:2, 5), but that "from works of the law" no human being will be justified by God (2:16). Those "from works of the law" are under a curse, since, according to scripture, "Cursed is everyone who does not remain in all the things written in the book of the law, to do them" (3:10b; cf. Deut 27:26).⁵ Thus, Paul warns the Galatians that everyone who fails to do all the works of the law is cursed rather than blessed by God, like Abraham (3:8–9), with God's gift of justification for eschatological life.

3:11 (C): By the law no one is justified before God, for the just one from faith will live

That by the law no one is justified before God (cf. 2:16) is clear, for "the just one from faith will live" (3:11; cf. Hab 2:4). In the Galatian context, this scriptural quotation has a double meaning.⁶ It promises that one who

---

3. "Paul's claim that the scripture 'announced the gospel ahead of time' (προευηγγελίσατο; the verb occurs only here in Biblical Greek) is striking because he usually connects the gospel firmly to the new era of salvation history inaugurated by Christ's death and resurrection" (Moo, *Galatians*, 199).

4. "Genesis 12:3 promised that all nations would be blessed in Abraham and in Gal 3:8 Paul explains that this blessing becomes a reality when Gentiles are justified by faith. Hence, Paul draws the conclusion here that those who believe enjoy the same blessing that the believing Abraham did" (Schreiner, *Galatians*, 195).

5. "'Those who are from works of the law' are those who derive their identity from observance of the law and thus live on the basis of such observance" (De Boer, *Galatians*, 198).

6. "The form of Paul's quotation also leaves open the question of how to integrate the prepositional phrase ἐκ πίστεως into the sentence. Most of the English versions and interpreters attach the following phrase to the verb: 'the one who is righteous will live by faith.' But it is also possible that it should be construed with δίκαιος: 'the one who is

is justified or just from faith (not law) will live a future divine eternal life. And it asserts that the just one will live presently a life of worship from faith (not law). That the just one from faith "will live" (ζήσεται) a life of worship presently and for the future resonates with the life "I [every believer] live" (ζῶ) in flesh, in faith "I live" (ζῶ), that faith in the Son of God who loved me and gave himself up for me, so that "I live" (ζῶ), no longer I, but the risen Christ "lives" (ζῇ) in me (2:20). It recalls and reinforces that to the law "I died," so that "I might live" (ζήσω) for God presently and to God in view of future eternal life (2:19).[7] And that "will live" connotes a life of worship accords with "you are living" (ζῇς) as a reference to Peter sharing meal fellowship and thus worshiping with gentiles (2:14). As a just one, every Galatian believer is to live a life of worship from faith (not law) now to live eternally in the future.

3:12 (C'): The one who does the things of the law will live by them

But the law to which the Galatians are being attracted to observe is not from faith, as it is concerned with doing rather than believing, as indicated by yet another scriptural quotation: "the one who does these things will live by them" (3:12; cf. Lev 18:5). The one who does the works of the law will live a present life of worship in accord with them, and will live a future eternal life only by doing all of them. But everyone who does not do all the works of the law is cursed (3:10; cf. Deut 27:26) and thus will not live by doing them. Doing the things in the law does not justify one before God and thus cannot promise that one "will live [ζήσεται]" (3:12), rather, believing justifies one before God, so that the just one from faith "will live [ζήσεται]" (3:11) to and for God now and in the future (2:19).[8] The Galatians are to realize that they cannot gain justification before God and a life for and to

---

righteous by faith will live'" (Moo, *Galatians*, 206).

7. "We should observe as well that the words 'shall live' (ζήσεται) refer here to eternal life, not merely to life on earth" (Schreiner, *Galatians*, 209). "Righteousness by faith is for Paul so closely bound up with true life that the two terms—'righteousness' and 'life'—can in practice be used interchangeably (cf. v 21b)" (Bruce, *Epistle to the Galatians*, 162).

8. "In his citation of these OT passages, Paul uses a common exegetical technique, the interpretation of passages in Scripture on the basis of shared key words: Lev 18:5 uses a verb also found in Deut 27:26 ('to do') and another also found in Hab 2:4 ('to live')" (De Boer, *Galatians*, 206).

God now and in the future by doing the works of the law but only through faith.[9]

3:13 (B'): Christ redeemed us from the curse of the law having become for us a curse

Christ redeemed us from the curse of the law (3:13a), that is, the curse of having to do all the works of the law (3:10) to be justified for new life (3:12). Christ did this by becoming "for" (ὑπέρ) us a curse through his crucifixion on a tree in fulfillment of the scriptural quotation that "cursed is everyone who hangs on a tree" (3:13b; cf. Deut 21:23). This resonates with how Christ gave himself "for" (ὑπέρ) our sins through his crucifixion, that he might free us from the present evil age (1:4).[10] It reinforces how the life that "I" (every believer) live in flesh in this present evil age in faith "I" live, that faith in the Son of God who loved me and through his crucifixion gave himself up "for" (ὑπέρ) me, so that now the risen Christ lives in me (2:20).[11] Since, according to scripture, "cursed is everyone" who hangs on a tree, through his crucifixion on a tree Christ redeemed and set us free from the curse of the law, namely that, according to scripture, "cursed is everyone" who does not do all the things written in the book of the law.[12] By his crucifixion, Christ has enabled every believer to live to and for God now and in the future (2:19).

---

9. Paul uses the phrase "from faith" in 3:12 "as a way of contrasting clearly and directly what he is saying here about the law with what Hab. 2:4 says about gaining life: 'the righteous person will find life "through faith"; but the law is not a matter of "through faith"'" (Moo, *Galatians*, 208).

10. "The point of redemption language is that the saving death of Christ sets people free. Christ liberates, releases, and delivers them from whatever held them captive. Humanity's personified Captors included 'our sins' and 'the present evil age' (1:4)" (Lyons, *Galatians*, 194).

11. "The phrase 'having become a curse [i.e., accursed] for us' is evidently meant to call attention to the depth of Christ's love (2:20). He went so far as to share 'our' predicament of being under the law and its curse" (De Boer, *Galatians*, 211–12).

12. "Paul no doubt knows the original context of Deut. 21.22–23, and that in its original setting the saying was about the hanging of a corpse on a tree after execution, as a shaming device. However, Paul may also have known about the use of the text in early Judaism, for example in 11QTemple 64.6–13 where the language of this text is used to speak of execution on a tree, that is of crucifixion" (Witherington, *Grace in Galatia*, 239).

GALATIANS 3:6-16

3:14-16 (A'): That the promise of the Spirit we might receive through faith

The A' element (3:14-16) of this chiastic unit forms a chiastic pattern in itself:

- a) ¹⁴that to the gentiles the blessing of *Abraham* might come in Christ Jesus, that the *promise* of the Spirit we might receive through faith.

    - b) ¹⁵ªBrothers, as a *human being* I speak,

    - b') ¹⁵ᵇthat even a covenant ratified by a *human being* no one rejects or amends.

- a') ¹⁶Now to *Abraham* were spoken the *promises* and to his descendant; it does not say, "And to descendants," as referring to many but as referring to one, "And to your descendant" [Gen 12:7; 13:15; 17:8; 22:17; 24:7], who is Christ.

At the center of this chiastic subunit is a pivot of parallels from "human being" in 3:15a to "human being" in 3:15b. Chiastic parallels progress from "Abraham" in 3:14 to "Abraham" in 3:16 and from "promise" in 3:14 to "promises" in 3:16.

Christ redeemed us from the curse of the law through his crucifixion (3:13) "that to the gentiles the blessing of Abraham might come in Christ Jesus" (3:14a). The blessing of Abraham here refers to the gentiles being justified by God from faith (3:8-9), that is, believing in the God who raised Christ Jesus from the dead (1:1) to new life. The Abrahamic blessing of justification came to the gentiles, so that the promise of the Spirit "we" (all believers) might "receive" through faith (3:14b). This reinforces Paul's point that the Galatians "received" the Spirit from the hearing of faith (3:2, 5). The "promise of the Spirit" refers not to the promised Spirit, but to the promise of eschatological life that believers receive by being justified through faith and that the Spirit will bring to fulfillment.[13] The promise, then, accords

---

13. "The 'blessing of Abraham' is not simply 'justification by faith.' Rather, it points toward the eschatological life now available to Jews and Gentiles alike, effected through Christ's death, but realized through the dynamic ministry of the Spirit—and all of this by faith" (Fee, *God's Empowering Presence*, 395). In Gal 3:14 "the blessing of Abraham is identified with justification, and the Spirit functions as the evidence of receiving the blessing and the means of perpetuating the blessing" (Lee, *Blessing of Abraham*, 210). The "Spirit," strictly speaking then, is not the "promise" itself, *contra* Thiessen, *Gentile Problem*, 130-31.

with the scriptural promise that the just one from faith "will live" (3:11) not only presently but eternally.

Addressing the Galatians again as "brothers" (cf. 1:11), that is, fellow believers, and speaking as a human being, Paul implies that if no one rejects or amends a covenant ratified by a human being (3:15) then surely not a covenant ratified by God. In a covenant ratified by God, to Abraham was spoken (by God, divine passive) the promises and to his descendant (3:16a). This does not refer to many descendants but only to one, who is Christ (3:16b). That "to Abraham" God spoke the promises and to his descendant recalls that the scripture foretold the gospel "to Abraham," when it promised that in Abraham (and implicitly in his descendant) all the gentiles will be blessed (3:8) with justification (3:6, 14a) for present and future life (3:11). The "promises," then, include the promise of being blessed with justification by faith and the promise that one justified from faith "will live" (3:11).[14] This reinforces that the Galatians have been blessed with justification and received the promise of life to be realized by the Spirit (3:14) through their faith in the God who raised Christ from the dead (1:1) to eternal life.[15]

SUMMARY ON GALATIANS 3:6–16

The scripture that says in Abraham all the gentiles will be blessed (3:8b; cf. Gen 12:3; 18:18) with justification (3:6–7), foreseeing that from faith God would justify the gentiles, and thus the Galatians, "foretold the gospel" to Abraham (3:8a). This means that Abraham already received the "gospel" of Christ (1:7), with its promise of eschatological life for those justified by faith, an implied consequence of the gospel that God raised Jesus Christ from the dead (1:1) to new life. As "those from faith," with the believing Abraham, the Galatians are blessed with justification (3:9) for new life.

Those "from works of the law" are under a curse, since, according to scripture, "Cursed is everyone who does not remain in all the things written in the book of the law, to do them" (3:10b; cf. Deut 27:26). Thus, Paul

---

14. "'The promises' lose the specificity that they had in Genesis and become a term that relates to the benefits brought by the gospel" (Oakes, *Galatians*, 119).

15. "The Abrahamic promise will be realized in one sole heir, Messiah—*this life is manifest in his resurrection—this is the meaning of Gal 3:16*. It is this risen life which animates Paul, a life in him by faith (Gal 2:20). *That life predicted by Habakkuk, which comes from faith, is thus understood as the resurrected life of Messiah* (Gal 3:1; Hab 2:4)" (Boakye, *Death and Life*, 158; emphases original).

warns the Galatians that everyone who fails to do all the works of the law is cursed rather than blessed by God, like Abraham (3:8–9), with God's gift of justification for eschatological life.

That by the law no one is justified before God (cf. 2:16) is clear, for "the just one from faith will live" (3:11; cf. Hab 2:4). In the Galatian context, this scriptural quotation has a double meaning. It promises that one who is justified or just from faith (not law) will live a future divine eternal life. And it asserts that the just one will live presently a life of worship from faith (not law). That the just one from faith "will live" a life of worship presently and for the future resonates with the life "I [every believer] live" in flesh, in faith "I live," that faith in the Son of God who loved me and gave himself up for me, so that "I live," no longer I, but the risen Christ "lives" in me (2:20). It recalls and reinforces that to the law "I died," so that "I might live" for God presently and to God in view of future eternal life (2:19). And that "will live" connotes a life of worship accords with "you are living" as a reference to Peter sharing meal fellowship and thus worshiping with gentiles (2:14). As a just one, every Galatian believer is to live a life of worship from faith (not law) now to live eternally in the future.

Doing the things in the law does not justify one before God and thus cannot promise that one "will live" (3:12), rather, believing justifies one before God, so that the just one from faith "will live" (3:11) to and for God now and in the future (2:19). The Galatians are to realize that they cannot gain justification before God and a life for and to God now and in the future by doing the works of the law, but only through faith.

Since, according to scripture, "cursed is everyone" who hangs on a tree (3:13; cf. Deut 21:23), through his crucifixion on a tree Christ redeemed and set us free from the curse of the law—namely, that, according to scripture, "cursed is everyone" who does not do all the things written in the book of the law (3:10). By his crucifixion, Christ has enabled every believer to live to and for God now and in the future (2:19).

Christ redeemed us from the curse of the law through his crucifixion (3:13) "that to the gentiles the blessing of Abraham might come in Christ Jesus" (3:14a). The blessing of Abraham here refers to the gentiles being justified by God from faith (3:8–9), that is, believing in the God who raised Christ Jesus from the dead (1:1) to new life. The Abrahamic blessing of justification came to the gentiles, so that "we" (all believers) might "receive" the promise of the Spirit through faith (3:14b). This reinforces Paul's point that the Galatians "received" the Spirit from the hearing of faith (3:2, 5). The "promise of the Spirit" refers not to the promised Spirit, but to the promise of eschatological life that believers receive by being justified through faith and that the Spirit will bring to fulfillment. The promise, then, accords with the scriptural promise that the just one from faith "will live" (3:11) not only presently but eternally.

That "to Abraham" God spoke the promises and to his descendant (3:16) recalls that the scripture foretold the gospel "to Abraham," when it promised that in Abraham (and implicitly in his descendant) all the gentiles will be blessed (3:8) with justification (3:6, 14a) for present and future life (3:11). The "promises," then, include the promise of being blessed with justification by faith and the promise that one justified from faith "will live" (3:11). This reinforces that the Galatians have been blessed with justification and received the promise of life to be realized by the Spirit (3:14) through their faith in the God who raised Christ from the dead (1:1) to eternal life.

8

Galatians 3:17–29

BAPTIZED INTO CHRIST, WITH CHRIST YOU HAVE CLOTHED YOURSELVES

All of you are one in Christ Jesus

A ¹⁷This then I am saying: The law that came after four hundred and thirty years does not annul a covenant previously ratified by God so as to remove the *promise*. ¹⁸For if from the law is the *inheritance*, it is no longer from a *promise*, but to *Abraham* through a *promise* God graciously gave it. ¹⁹Why then the law? It was added for the sake of transgressions, until would come the descendant to whom the *promise* was made, ordered through angels at the hand of an intermediary. ²⁰But an intermediary is not of one, yet God is one. ²¹Is the law then against the *promises* of God? Of course not! For if a law had been given that was able to give life, then justification would indeed be from the law. ²²But the scripture confined all things under sin, that the *promise* from faith in Jesus Christ might be given to those who believe.

B ²³Before faith came we were held in custody under the law, confined for the faith that was about to be revealed, ²⁴so that the law became our *guardian* until Christ, that from faith we might be justified.

B' ²⁵But now that faith has come, we are no longer under a *guardian*.

A' ²⁶For all of you through faith are sons of God in Christ Jesus. ²⁷For as many of you as into Christ were baptized, with Christ you have clothed yourselves. ²⁸There is neither Jew nor Greek, there is neither slave nor free, there is not male and female, for all of you are one in Christ Jesus. ²⁹And if you are of Christ, then you are a descendant of *Abraham*, *heirs* according to the *promise*.[1]

3:17–22 (A): The promise of life from faith in Jesus Christ

The A element (3:17–22) of this chiastic unit forms a chiastic pattern in itself:

a) ¹⁷This then I am saying: The *law* that came after four hundred and thirty years does not annul a covenant previously ratified by God so as to remove the *promise*. ¹⁸For if from the *law* is the inheritance, it is no longer from a *promise*, but to Abraham through a *promise* God graciously gave it. ¹⁹ᵃWhy then the *law*? It was added for the sake of transgressions, until would come the descendant to whom the *promise* was made,

  b) ¹⁹ᵇordered through angels at the hand of an *intermediary*.

  b') ²⁰But an *intermediary* is not of one, yet God is one.

a') ²¹Is the *law* then against the *promises* of God? Of course not! For if a *law* had been given that was able to give life, then justification would indeed be from the *law*. ²²But the scripture confined all things under sin, that the *promise* from faith in Jesus Christ might be given to those who believe.

At the center of this chiastic subunit is a pivot of parallels from "intermediary" in 3:19b to "intermediary" in 3:20. Chiastic parallels progress from "law" in 3:17, 18 and 19a to "law" in 3:21 (thrice) and from the noun "promise" in 3:17 and 18 (twice) and the verb "promise was made" in 3:19a to "promises" in 3:21 and "promise" in 3:22.

Reinforcing that a covenant ratified by God no one rejects or amends (3:15–16), Paul asserts that the law that came four hundred and thirty years later does not annul a covenant previously ratified by God so as to remove its promise of eschatological life (3:17).[2] For if from the law is

---

1. For the establishment of Gal 3:17–29 as a chiasm, see chapter 1 of this book..

2. "The Mosaic covenant, which was enacted 430 years after the Abrahamic covenant, cannot invalidate or supersede the provisions of that covenant" (Schreiner, *Galatians*, 230).

the inheritance of eschatological life, it is no longer from a promise, but God graciously gave it to Abraham through a promise (3:18), as well as to Abraham's descendant, Christ (3:16), who inherited God's promise of eschatological life when God raised him from the dead (1:1) to eternal life.[3] The law was added for the sake of transgressions, until would come the descendant, Christ (3:16), to whom the promise of inheriting eschatological life was made (3:19a). The law was ordered (by God) through angels at the hand of an intermediary (Moses; 3:19b). But an intermediary is not of "one" (ἑνός), yet God is "one [εἷς]" (3:20). This develops and reinforces that the one God made the promise of inheriting eschatological life to Abraham's "one" (ἑνός) descendant, who is Christ (3:16).[4]

The law is certainly not against the "promises" of God (3:21a), the "promises" spoken to Abraham and to his descendant, Christ (3:16), particularly the promise of being blessed, through believing, with justification/righteousness (3:6-8, 14)—the purpose for which Christ died (2:21)—and the promise of eschatological life to be realized by the Spirit (3:14). For if a law had been given that was able to give eschatological life, being justified/made righteous for that life would indeed be from the law (3:21b).[5] But the scripture, according to which everyone who does not do all the things in the law is cursed (3:10), confined all things under sin, that the promise of eschatological life from faith in Jesus Christ might be given to those who believe (3:22). As among those who believe, then, the Galatians have been given the promise of eschatological life from their faith in Jesus Christ, who gave himself for our sins, that he might free us from the present evil age

---

3. "In the OT, the 'inheritance' is usually identified with the land (e.g., Gen. 28:4; Deut. 1:39); for Paul (and for other NT authors), the 'inheritance' is Christ himself and all the blessings Christ provides his people" (Moo, *Galatians*, 231). "To speak of an inheritance, then, is another way of describing the possession of eschatological salvation" (Schreiner, *Galatians*, 232).

4. On the "descendant" (σπέρμα) of Abraham as the one who "will inherit" (κληρονομήσει) God's promise, see Gen 12:7; 15:3-4 (LXX).

5. "Paul is arguing from the effect ('to bestow life') to the cause ('righteousness'): if a law had been given that could impart life, then righteousness, which is the prior condition of life, would have come from keeping the law" (Fung, *Epistle to the Galatians*, 163). "To be justified (by faith) is to receive life (by faith); δικαιοσύνη, which often means righteousness which *leads* to life, can become simply the equivalent of 'life'" (Bruce, *Epistle to the Galatians*, 180; emphasis original). "Theologically, then, justification is tantamount to eschatological new life, since the former necessarily secures or effects the latter" (De Boer, *Galatians*, 233). "Only through the promise arrangement that God entered into with Abraham and that requires faith in response can righteousness/eschatological life be found" (Moo, *Galatians*, 239).

(1:4) for eschatological life in the new and final age inaugurated by the resurrection of Jesus Christ from the dead (1:1) to eternal life.

3:23-25 (B-B'): The law became our guardian, but we are no longer under a guardian

Before faith "came," faith in Jesus Christ (3:22)—the descendant who would "come," to whom the promise of eschatological life was made (3:19)—we were held in custody under the law (3:23a), the law that was not able to give eschatological life (3:21).[6] We were confined, though, for the faith that was about to be "revealed" (3:23b), recalling that God was pleased to "reveal" his Son to Paul (1:16) as the Christ God raised from the dead (1:1) to eschatological life, the focus of our faith. The law, then, became only our "guardian" (παιδαγωγός) until Christ came, that from faith in the risen Jesus Christ we might be justified (3:24), since by the law no one is justified before God (3:11).[7] But we are no longer held in custody under the law as our "guardian" now that faith has come (3:25). Thus, not from the law but from faith in the risen Jesus Christ, the Galatians and all who believe have been given the promise of inheriting eschatological life (3:18, 21-22).[8]

---

6. "After 3:10 and 3:13-14, and in contrast to 2:16, the first-person plural ('we') in this passage is probably inclusive of Gentiles as well as Jews. Paul may perhaps have Jews particularly in view, at least in the first instance, but if so he uses their situation 'under the law' to be representative of the situation of all humankind (cf. 3:10-14; 4:5)" (De Boer, *Galatians*, 238).

7. "Despite the English cognate pedagogue, the παιδαγωγός was not a teacher . . . a modern counterpart might combine the job descriptions of a bodyguard, school bus driver, crossing guard, safety officer, vice principal, nanny, and chaperone . . . The παιδαγωγός played a role in ancient childrearing that was preventive and protective. It was neither parental nor permanent. It was neither entirely positive nor negative. Like the law, the παιδαγωγός had an essential, but transitional and transient, role. He assured that children survived their childhood to become responsible adults" (Lyons, *Galatians*, 218). "The παιδαγωγός was the personal slave-attendant who accompanied the freeborn boy wherever he went . . . During the boy's minority the παιδαγωγός imposed a necessary restraint on his liberty until, with his coming of age, he could be trusted to use his liberty responsibly" (Bruce, *Epistle to the Galatians*, 182).

8. "These three verses [3:23-25] further illuminate Paul's understanding of faith and the law in Galatians. He first introduced these terms in 2:16, and what was implicit there and in the intervening verses about both 'faith' and the 'law' becomes explicit here" (De Boer, *Galatians*, 238).

3:26–29 (A'): You are a descendant of Abraham, heirs according to the promise

The A' element (3:26–29) of this chiastic unit forms a chiastic pattern in itself:

- a) [26]For all of *you are* through faith sons of God *in Christ Jesus*. [27]For as many of you as into *Christ* were baptized, with *Christ* you have clothed yourselves.

    - b) [28a]*There is neither* Jew nor Greek, *there is neither* slave nor free,

    - b') [28b]*there is not* male and female,

- a') [28c]for all of *you are* one *in Christ Jesus*. [29]And if you are of *Christ*, then *you are* a descendant of Abraham, heirs according to the promise.

At the center of this chiastic subunit is a pivot of parallels from "there is neither" (οὐκ) in 3:28a (twice) to "there is not" (οὐκ) in 3:28b. Chiastic parallels progress from "you are" in 3:26 to "you are" in 3:28c and 29; from "in Christ Jesus" in 3:26 to "in Christ Jesus" in 3:28c; and from "Christ" in 3:27 (twice) to "Christ" in 3:29.

With "all" in an emphatic first position, Paul stresses that *all* his Galatian audience "through faith" are sons of God "in Christ Jesus" (3:26). This recalls that, to the gentiles, the blessing of Abraham (justification [3:8–9]) might come "in Christ Jesus," that all who believe the promise of eschatological life (3:11), to be realized by the Spirit, might receive "through faith" (3:14).[9] It means that the Galatians and all who believe are not only "sons" of Abraham (3:7) but "sons" of God, along with Christ Jesus as the "Son" of God (1:16; 2:20), the one descendant of Abraham to whom was spoken the promises (3:16, 19) of justification and eschatological life. And it thus implies that, as "sons" of God, all who believe are also descendants of Abraham, along with Christ and in line then for the inheritance of eschatological life (3:18).

"For as many as" are from works of the law are under a curse to do all of them (3:10). But "for as many as" into Christ were baptized, with Christ they have clothed themselves (3:27).[10] Believers who were baptized into Christ in an act of communal worship that ritualizes their faith in Christ

---

9. That these are the only occurrences in Galatians of the phrase "through faith" (διὰ τῆς πίστεως) enhances the connection between 3:14 and 3:26.

10. That these are the only occurrences in Galatians of the phrase "as many as" (ὅσοι γάρ) enhances the connection between 3:10 and 3:27.

have clothed themselves with Christ, in implicit contrast to the ritual act of circumcision, which places one under the curse of doing all the works of the law.[11] That all baptized believers have metaphorically and sacramentally "clothed" themselves with Christ corresponds to every individual believer having died to the law and having been crucified with Christ, so that the risen Christ now lives in each believer (2:19–20).[12] Just as clothing identifies and unites with its wearer, so the risen Christ identifies and unites with all believers baptized into Christ so that they have clothed themselves with the risen Christ who lives in them.[13] The sacrament of baptism, then, plays an essential role in the worship for life by faith in the crucified and risen Lord Jesus Christ.[14]

Baptized believers who have clothed themselves with Christ (3:27) are so united with Christ and one another that ethnic, social, and gender dualities, which would otherwise divide them, now no longer matter: "There is neither Jew nor Greek, there is neither slave nor free, there is not male and female, for all of you are one in Christ Jesus" (3:28).[15] That "all of you" believers are one "in Christ Jesus" reinforces that "all of you" are, through faith, sons of God "in Christ Jesus" (3:26). And that all believers are "one"

---

11. "Christian water-and-Spirit baptism replaces the mark of Jewish circumcision" (Taylor, "Baptism," 394).

12. "Clothing's function as an object of societal symbolism allows it to serve as a symbol of life itself" (Matthews, "Clothe Oneself," 696).

13. "As a garment tends to be identified with its wearer, so Christ becomes one with Christians... As Paul speaks of believers' union with Christ's death and life (cf. Gal. 2.20) and then refers to the baptized believers' having put on Christ (3.27), his audience probably understands this concept of clothing with Christ as indicating that they have been unified with Christ in his death and life" (Kim, *Significance of Clothing Imagery*, 118–19).

14. "In Galatians, Paul does not explain much about baptism, but the idea of it representing Christ's death and new life would clearly tie very well into the letter's motif of sharing in Christ's crucifixion and new life (2:19–20; 5:24; 6:14–15, 17)" (Oakes, *Galatians*, 130–31). "Baptism reenacts the burial and resurrection of Christ, allowing believers to participate in the drama of salvation with him. Baptism dramatizes the spiritual reality of appropriating the life-giving benefits of Christ's atoning death" (Lyons, *Galatians*, 229).

15. For a discussion of how the unity of these three pairs of distinctions express a cosmopolitan ideal, that is, that all people were fundamentally connected and could all live in a unified society, see Neutel, *Cosmopolitan Ideal*. "The point of the paradoxical assertion of the nonexistence of evidently continuing social polarities is that being in Christ brings oneness, unity, across these polarities" (Oakes, *Galatians*, 129). "As co-heirs of the promise of Abraham, Jews are not superior to Gentiles, those who are free are not more important than slaves, and men are not worth more than women" (Schreiner, *Galatians*, 258).

in Christ Jesus reaffirms their unity with Christ as the "one" descendant of Abraham (3:16). Consequently, believers who are "of Christ"—that is, those who are sons of God in Christ Jesus (3:26), clothed with Christ (3:27), and one in Christ Jesus (3:28)—are, along with Christ, a descendant of Abraham, "heirs" entitled to eschatological life according to the "promise" for it (3:29; cf. 3:11). This reasserts that if the "inheritance" for eschatological life is from the law, it is no longer from a "promise," but God graciously gave it to Abraham through a "promise" (3:18).[16]

SUMMARY ON GALATIANS 3:17-29

If from the law is the inheritance of eschatological life, it is no longer from a promise, but to Abraham through a promise God graciously gave it (3:18), and to Abraham's descendant, Christ (3:16), who inherited God's promise of eschatological life when God raised him from the dead (1:1) to eternal life. The law was added for the sake of transgressions, until would come the descendant, Christ (3:16), to whom the promise of inheriting eschatological life was made (3:19a). The law was ordered (by God) through angels at the hand of an intermediary (Moses; 3:19b). But an intermediary is not of "one," yet God is "one" (3:20). The one God made the promise of inheriting eschatological life to Abraham's "one" descendant, who is Christ (3:16).

The law became only our "guardian" until Christ came, that from faith in the risen Jesus Christ we might be justified (3:24), since by the law no one is justified before God (3:11). But we are no longer held in custody under the law as our "guardian" now that faith has come (3:25). Thus, the Galatians and all who believe have been given the promise of inheriting eschatological life, not from the law but from faith in the risen Jesus Christ (3:18, 21-22).

Believers who were baptized into Christ in an act of communal worship that ritualizes their faith in Christ have clothed themselves with Christ (3:27), in implicit contrast to the ritual act of circumcision, which places one under the curse of doing all the works of the law (3:10). That all baptized believers have metaphorically and sacramentally "clothed" themselves with Christ corresponds to every individual believer having died to the law

---

16. "Gentiles do not become members of Abraham's family, nor do they receive the inheritance, by observing the law. The inheritance is theirs by faith in Christ. The inheritance is secured by God's gracious promise, and hence it is received by faith alone" (Schreiner, *Galatians*, 259).

and been crucified with Christ, so that the risen Christ now lives in each believer (2:19–20). Just as clothing identifies and unites with its wearer, so the risen Christ identifies and unites with all believers baptized into Christ so that they have clothed themselves with the risen Christ who lives in them. The sacrament of baptism, then, plays an essential role in the worship for life by faith in the crucified and risen Lord Jesus Christ.

Believers who are "of Christ," that is, those who are sons of God in Christ Jesus (3:26), clothed with Christ (3:27), and one in Christ Jesus (3:28), are, along with Christ, a descendant of Abraham, "heirs" entitled to eschatological life according to the "promise" for it (3:29; cf. 3:11). This reasserts that if the "inheritance" for eschatological life is from the law, it is no longer from a "promise," but God graciously gave it to Abraham through a "promise" (3:18).

9

Galatians 4:1–7

THAT THE SON OF GOD MIGHT REDEEM THOSE UNDER THE LAW

You are sons gifted with the Spirit and thus heirs through God

A ¹I say then, for as long a time as the *heir* is a minor, he does not differ from a *slave*, though being the owner of all, ²but he is under managers and stewards until the date set by the *father*. ³So also we, when we were minors, we were *enslaved* under the elemental powers of the world. ⁴ᵃBut when the fullness of time had come, *God sent his Son*,

   B ⁴ᵇborn from a woman, born *under the law*,

   B' ⁵ᵃthat he might redeem those *under the law*,

A' ⁵ᵇthat we might receive sonship. ⁶And because you are sons, *God sent* the Spirit of his Son into our hearts, crying out, "Abba, *Father*!" ⁷So you are no longer a *slave* but a son, and if a son, also an *heir* through *God*.[1]

4:1–4a (A): When the fullness of time had come, God sent his Son

The A element (4:1–4a) of this chiastic unit forms a chiastic pattern in itself:

1. For the establishment of Gal 4:1–7 as a chiasm, see chapter 1 of this book.

a) ¹I say then, for as long a *time* as the heir is a minor, he does not differ from a slave, though being the owner of all, ²but he is under managers and stewards until the date set by the father.

b) ³ªSo also we, when *we were* minors,

b') ³ᵇ*we were* enslaved under the elemental powers of the world.

a') ⁴ªBut when the fullness of *time* had come, God sent his Son.

At the center of this chiastic subunit is a pivot of parallels from "we were" in 4:3a to "we were" in 4:3b. Chiastic parallels progress from "time" in 4:1 to "time" in 4:4a.

For as long a time as the "heir," recalling that the Galatians and all believers are "heirs" of eschatological life according to God's promise (3:29), is a minor, he does not differ from a slave, though he will eventually become the owner of the inheritance (4:1). But he is "under" managers and stewards "until" the date set by the father (4:2). This resonates with being "under" the law (3:23) as being "under" a guardian (3:25) "until" would come the descendant, Christ (3:16), to whom the promise was made (3:19).² So also "we"—Paul, the Galatians, and all believers—when we were minors "under" managers and stewards, and the law as a guardian, we were enslaved "under" the elemental powers of the world (4:3).³ Being "under" these evil and demonic elemental powers corresponds to being "under" the curse of doing all the law (3:10), which, in effect, means being "under" the power of sin (3:22).⁴ But when the fullness of "time" had come, that is, the date ending the "time" before the inheritance (4:2), God sent his Son (4:3a), Christ, the descendant to whom the promise of eschatological life was made (3:16, 19).

---

2. That these are the only occurrences in Galatians of the conjunction "until" (ἄχρι) enhances the connection between 3:19 and 4:2.

3. According to BDAG, 946, "the elemental powers of the world" (τὰ στοιχεῖα τοῦ κόσμου) in Gal 4:3 refers to "transcendent powers that are in control over events in this world." Paul does not "*equate*" being under the elements with being under the law, but speaks "in terms of close *association*" (Arnold, "Returning to the Domain," 68; emphases original). "If 'the elements of the world' include a reference to demonic powers, Paul may be saying that demons have used the law (because of human sin) to enslave human beings" (Schreiner, *Galatians*, 269n22).

4. "Paul clearly sees the elements ruling during the period in which the Mosaic law was in force. The use of the 'under' (ὑπό) phrase calls to mind the other references to the law in Galatians (see 3:10, 22–23, 25; 4:2, 4–5, 21; 5:18). They lived under slavery, so that to be under the law is to be under the power of sin" (Schreiner, *Galatians*, 269).

4:4b-5a (B-B'): That the Son of God might redeem those under the law

God sent his divine Son (4:4a), born from a woman, and thus as a human being,[5] born under the law (4:4b), that he might "redeem" those under the law (4:5a), and thus free all of us who were enslaved under the demonic elemental powers of the world (4:3b). This develops and reinforces the assertion that Christ "redeemed" and thus freed us from the curse of having to do all the law (3:10) by becoming for us a curse by his crucifixion (3:13), after which God raised him from the dead (1:1) to eternal life.[6] It resonates with the assertion that the Lord Jesus Christ gave himself over to a sacrificial death for our sins, that he might free us from the present evil age (1:4), which is still enslaved under the demonic elemental powers of the world, for a new, eschatological life. And it reminds the audience that every believer, who still lives in flesh, lives by faith "in the Son of God who loved me and gave himself up for me" (2:20), so that every believer might now live an eschatological life to and for God (2:19), as part of the people of God, through cultic and ethical worship.

4:5b-7 (A'): You are a son and an heir through God

The A' element (4:5b-7) of this chiastic unit forms a chiastic pattern in itself:

a) ⁵ᵇthat we might receive *sonship*. ⁶ᵃAnd because you are *sons*, *God* sent the Spirit of his *Son* into our hearts, crying out,

  b) ⁶ᵇ"Abba, Father!"

a') ⁷So you are no longer a slave but a *son*, and if a *son*, also an heir through *God*.

After "Abba, Father" in 4:6b as the unparalleled central and pivotal element of this chiastic subunit, chiastic parallels progress from "sonship"

---

5. Paul's mention that Christ was born from a woman "seems understandable only if one recognizes the presuppositional nature of Christ's preexistence ... that the sending word *presupposes* a prior existence that was not human" (Fee, *Pauline Christology*, 215; emphasis original).

6. That these are the only occurrences in Galatians of the verb "redeem" (ἐξαγοράζω) enhances the connection between 3:13 and 4:5.

in 4:5b, "sons" in 4:6a, and "Son" in 4:6a to "son" in 4:7 (twice); and from "God" in 4:6a to "God" in 4:7.

The Son of God redeemed those under the law (4:5a), that we believers might receive sonship (4:5b), which implies the right of inheritance. That we might "receive" (ἀπολάβωμεν) sonship resonates with the assertion that the promise of eschatological life to be realized by the Spirit we believers might "receive" (λάβωμεν) through faith (3:14).[7] And because "you"—the Galatians and all believers—are sons, God sent the Spirit of his Son into our hearts, crying out, "Abba, Father!" (4:6). That you are "sons" reinforces the assertion that all of you are through faith "sons" of God in Christ Jesus (3:26). The Spirit enables believers to address God in an act of filial worship as "Abba, Father," implicitly praising and thanking God as the "Father" (4:2) who sent his Son to redeem us (4:4–5).[8] This act of joyous laudatory worship thus complements the doxological worship of "our God and Father, to whom be glory for the ages of the ages. Amen!" (1:4–5).[9] It praises and thanks God for the grace and peace that come from God our "Father" (1:3), the "Father" who raised Jesus Christ from the dead (1:1) to eternal life.[10]

Every individual among the Galatians and all believers is no longer a "slave" (4:7), and thus no longer "enslaved" under the demonic elemental powers of the world (4:3b) or under the law (4:5a). That every believer is no longer a "slave" recalls that, while a minor, an heir does not differ from a "slave" (4:1). But now every believer is a son, and if a son, then an heir through God (4:7).[11] This makes explicit the implication that sonship

---

7. That Paul uses the compound verb ἀπολάβωμεν for "receive" in 4:5 accords with the Roman legal procedure of adoption, according to Burke, *Adopted into God's Family*, 88–89.

8. "Abba," a term for "Father" in Aramaic, was "used in prayer and in the family circle, taken over by Greek-speaking Christians as a liturgical formula" (BDAG, 1). See Mark 14:36; Rom 8:15. "In Gal 4:6, Paul described the Spirit's activity in the church gathered for worship" (Lyons, *Galatians*, 247). "The same Son whose death effected redemption and secured 'sonship' for them, now indwells them by his Spirit, 'the Spirit *of the Son*,' whom God sent forth as he had the Son himself. The ultimate evidence of this 'sonship' is their use of the Son's own address to the Father in prayer: *Abba*. Thus the 'sonship' motif, that goes back as far as 3:7, is brought to its ringing climax with this sentence" (Fee, *God's Empowering Presence*. 405; emphases original).

9. That the Spirit of God's Son exuberantly cries out in our hearts, "Abba, Father," indicates "an expression from the depths of a person full of heartfelt joy" (Witherington, *Grace in Galatia*, 291).

10. This serves as the final, climactic occurrence of "Father" in reference to God in Galatians (cf. 1:1, 3–4; 4:2, 6).

11. The phrase "through God" means "that God is the Creator, or bestower of the

includes the right of inheritance (4:5b). That every believer, as a son, is an "heir" reaffirms that believers are "heirs" of eschatological life according to the promise for it (3:29; cf. 3:11, 14). They are heirs through "God," the "God" who sent not only his Son to redeem those under the law (4:4-5a), but also the Spirit of his Son, enabling believers who have received sonship (4:5b), so that they are now heirs, to worship God as their "Father" (4:6) for the eschatological life God as their "Father" has entitled them to inherit (4:2).

SUMMARY ON GALATIANS 4:1-7

When we believers were minors "under" managers and stewards (4:1-2), with the law as a guardian (3:23-25), we were enslaved "under" the elemental powers of the world (4:3). Being "under" these evil and demonic elemental powers corresponds to being "under" the curse of doing all the law (3:10), which, in effect, means being "under" the power of sin (3:22). But when the fullness of "time" had come, that is, the date ending the "time" before the inheritance (4:2), God sent his Son (4:3a), Christ, the descendant to whom the promise of eschatological life was made (3:16, 19).

God sent his divine Son (4:4a), born from a woman, and thus as a human being, born under the law (4:4b), that he might "redeem" those under the law (4:5a), and thus free all of us who were enslaved under the demonic elemental powers of the world (4:3b). This develops and reinforces the assertion that Christ "redeemed" and thus freed us from the curse of having to do all the law (3:10) by becoming for us a curse by his crucifixion (3:13), after which God raised him from the dead (1:1) to eternal life. It resonates with the assertion that the Lord Jesus Christ gave himself over to a sacrificial death for our sins, that he might free us from the present evil age (1:4), which is still enslaved under the demonic elemental powers of the world, for a new, eschatological life. And it reminds the audience that every believer, who still lives in flesh, lives by faith "in the Son of God who loved me and gave himself up for me" (2:20), so that every believer might now live an eschatological life to and for God (2:19), as part of the people of God, through cultic and ethical worship.

The Spirit that God sent into our hearts enables us believers to address God in an act of filial worship as "Abba, Father" (4:6), implicitly praising and thanking God as the "Father" (4:2) who sent his Son to redeem us

---

inheritance" (Moo, *Galatians*, 271).

(4:4–5). This act of joyous laudatory worship thus complements the doxological worship of "our God and Father, to whom be glory for the ages of the ages. Amen!" (1:4–5). It praises and thanks God for the grace and peace that come from God our "Father" (1:3), the "Father" who raised Jesus Christ from the dead (1:1) to eternal life. That every believer, as a son, is an "heir" (4:7) reaffirms that believers are "heirs" of eschatological life according to the promise for it (3:29; cf. 3:11, 14). They are heirs through "God" (4:7), the "God" who sent not only his Son to redeem those under the law (4:4–5a), but also the Spirit of his Son, enabling believers who have received sonship (4:5b), so that they are now heirs, to worship God as their "Father" (4:6) for the eschatological life God as their "Father" has entitled them to inherit (4:2).

10

Galatians 4:8–20

I FEAR LEST SOMEHOW IN VAIN I LABORED FOR YOU

Become as I am because I also have become as you are

A ⁸Yet when not *knowing* God, you were slaves of things that by nature are not gods. ⁹But now recognizing God, or rather being recognized by God, how can you turn back *again* to the weak and destitute elemental powers? Do you *want* to be slaves of them all over *again*? ¹⁰You are observing days and months and seasons and years. ¹¹I fear for you lest somehow in vain I have labored for you.

  B ¹²ᵃBecome as *I* am,

  B' ¹²ᵇbecause *I also* have become as you are, brothers, I implore you.

A' ¹²ᶜYou did me no wrong. ¹³You *know* that it was because of a weakness of the flesh that I preached the gospel to you previously, ¹⁴and your trial in my flesh you did not despise or reject, but rather as the angel of God you received me, as Christ Jesus. ¹⁵Where then is your blessedness? For I testify to you that if possible, you would have torn out your eyes and given them to me! ¹⁶So have I become your enemy by telling you the truth? ¹⁷They are zealous for you but not commendably, rather they *want* to exclude you, that you may be zealous for them. ¹⁸It is always commendable to be zealous in a commendable way and not only when I am present with you.

¹⁹My children, for whom I *again* have birth pangs until Christ be formed in you! ²⁰I *want* to be present with you now and change my tone, for I am perplexed in you.¹

4:8–11 (A): You were enslaved to things that by nature are not gods

The A element (4:8–11) of this chiastic unit forms a chiastic pattern in itself:

a) ⁸Yet when not knowing God, *you were slaves* of things that by nature are not gods.

b) ⁹ᵃBut now *recognizing* God,

b') ⁹ᵇor rather being *recognized* by God,

a') ⁹ᶜhow can you turn back again to the weak and destitute elemental powers? Do you want *to be slaves* of them all over again? ¹⁰You are observing days and months and seasons and years. ¹¹I fear for you lest somehow in vain I have labored for you.

At the center of this chiastic subunit is a pivot of parallels from "recognizing" in 4:9a to "recognized" in 4:9b. Chiastic parallels progress from "you were slaves" in 4:8 to "to be slaves" in 4:9c.

Before the Galatians became Christian believers, they did not know God (4:8a), the God through whom now, as believers, they have become heirs of eschatological life (4:7). But before they became believers, "you were slaves" (ἐδουλεύσατε), serving and thus worshiping things that by nature are not gods (4:8b).² This likens their pre-Christian situation to their situation before they became heirs, when they were "enslaved" (δεδουλωμένοι) under the elemental powers of the world (4:3). Their slavery to things that are not gods, the demonic elemental powers of the world, implies their past involvement in the service of idolatrous rather than true worship.³ But now that they have become believers, freed by Christ from the present evil age

---

1. For the establishment of Gal 4:8–20 as a chiasm, see chapter 1 of this book.

2. "You were slaves" in Gal 4:8 means that actively "you served as slaves" (and thus worshiped) idols rather than passively "you were enslaved," as in 4:3. See BDAG, 259. "Paul uses the term ['to be a slave'] as a virtual synonym for 'worship'" (De Boer, *Galatians*, 272).

3. Galatians 4:8 "reflects widely shared Jewish assumptions about Gentile idolatry" (Lyons, *Galatians*, 254). "The fundamental error of unbelievers is their failure to know and praise and thank God . . . those who do not know God give worship to someone or something else instead of to the one and only true God" (Schreiner, *Galatians*, 277).

(1:4) and thus from their serving as slaves and worshiping things that are not gods, they have been enabled to serve in worship the true and living God, like Paul, as a "slave" (δοῦλος) of Christ (1:10).

That as believers the Galatians are now recognizing God (4:9a) resonates with their worship, as sons, of the true and living God as their Father (4:6). But they can so worship God only because they were first recognized by God (4:9b) when God sent the Spirit of his Son into their hearts, so that they are no longer slaves but sons and thus heirs (4:6-7) of eschatological life. If, by having themselves circumcised, they were to place themselves under the curse of the law (3:10), they would again be slaves of things that are not gods (4:8), serving and worshiping the weak and destitute elemental powers (4:9c) associated with the law (4:3-5).[4] They are already observing various times for worship, which suggests that they are beginning to observe the law (4:10).[5] And so, Paul fears that, in bringing them to faith in the gospel whereby the Spirit enabled them to worship the true and living God as their Father, he may have labored for them "in vain [εἰκῇ]" (4:11). This resonates with and reinforces how their experiences, after receiving the Spirit as believers rather than from works of the law (4:2), may have been "in vain [εἰκῇ]" (3:4).[6]

4:12ab (B-B'): They are to become like Paul who has become like them

Paul then implores the Galatians, as fellow believing "brothers" (cf. 1:11; 3:15), to become as "I" (ἐγώ) am (4:12a), because "I also" (κἀγώ) have

---

4. The "elemental powers" (στοιχεῖα) "were often associated with various forms of idolatrous worship in the ancient world" (Moo, *Galatians*, 277). "The στοιχεῖα are just as ineffectual for salvation as the law, which is unable to give life (3:21) ... In Paul's mind the observance of the law and the veneration of the στοιχεῖα are in some sense functionally and thus also conceptually equivalent" (De Boer, *Galatians*, 275).

5. "Since it is the law of Moses that the Galatians are being urged to adopt, the language undoubtedly has some reference to Jewish religious observances ... At the same time, however, it is striking that Paul's list of terms contains no 'technical' references to Jewish religious celebrations. Paul may therefore choose a rather vague way of referring to the Jewish observances to tie them as closely as possible to the 'elements' and perhaps also to the religious observances in the Galatians' pagan past" (Moo, *Galatians*, 278). In Gal 4:10, Paul "intentionally uses terms that cover both Jewish and pagan calendrical observances, for he wants the Galatians to realize that by turning to the law, they are going back to where they came from" (De Boer, *Galatians*, 276).

6. The fact that, in Galatians, "in vain" (εἰκῇ) occurs only in 3:4 and 4:11 enhances this connection.

become as "you" are (4:12b). The Galatians are to become like the Paul who, speaking as representative of every individual believer, declared that "I" (ἐγώ) through the law to the law died, so that he might live a life of worship to and for God; he has been crucified with Christ (2:19). Yet Paul lives, no longer "I" (ἐγώ), but Christ lives in him, so that he now lives an eschatological life by faith in the Son of God (2:20) rather than by works of the law.[7] And the fact that Paul has become as "you" (ὑμεῖς) are means that he has been united with all of "you" (ὑμεῖς) who are one in Christ Jesus (3:28c), "you" (ὑμεῖς) who are of Christ, and so heirs of eschatological life (3:29) as sons of God through faith (3:26) rather than through the law.[8] Paul thus impresses upon the Galatians that, since being a Jew or Greek no longer matters (3:28a), he as a Jew and they as Greeks now have begun to worship God for life, not according to the law, which is not able to give life (3:21), but according to their faith.[9]

4:12c–20 (A'): I again have birth pangs until Christ be formed in you

The A' element (4:12c–20) of this chiastic unit forms a chiastic pattern in itself:

a) ¹²ᶜYou did me no wrong. ¹³You know that it was because of a weakness of the flesh that I preached the gospel to you previously, ¹⁴and your trial in my flesh you did not despise or reject, but rather as the angel of God you received me, as *Christ* Jesus. ¹⁵Where then is your blessedness? For I testify to you that if possible, you would have torn out your eyes and given them to me! ¹⁶So have I become your enemy by telling you the truth?

b) ¹⁷ᵃThey *are zealous* for you but not *commendably,*

---

7. "Paul has already been writing about himself in a paradigmatic fashion . . . Such writing is most evident in 2:19–21, where much of what he has done or experienced is surely presented as a pattern for Christian life" (Oakes, *Galatians,* 145).

8. That "I" (ἐγώ) in Gal 4:12 is the next occurrence of this first person singular emphatic pronoun after 2:19–20, and that "you" (ὑμεῖς) in 4:12 is the next occurrence of this emphatic second person plural pronoun after 3:28–29, enhances these connections.

9. "The entreaty is patently paradoxical: Paul is asking the Galatians to become like him for the reason that he has already become like them! Since the context clearly indicates that Paul's entreaty functions as part of his campaign to keep the Galatians from becoming observers of the law, the sense appears to be as follows: 'Become and remain as I am now, free from the law, because I also have become as you are now, free from the law'" (De Boer, *Galatians,* 278).

c) ¹⁷ᵇrather they want to exclude you,

b') ¹⁷ᶜthat you *may be zealous* for them. ¹⁸ᵃIt is always *commendable to be zealous* in a *commendable* way

a') ¹⁸ᵇand not only when I am present with you. ¹⁹My children, for whom I again have birth pangs until *Christ* be formed in you! ²⁰I want to be present with you now and change my tone, for I am perplexed in you.

The statement "rather they want to exclude you" in 4:17b serves as the unparalleled central and pivotal element of this chiastic subunit. Chiastic parallels progress from "are zealous" and "commendably" in 4:17a to "may be zealous" in 4:17c, "commendable to be zealous" in 4:18a, and "commendable" in 4:18a. Finally, chiastic parallels progress from "Christ" in 4:14 to "Christ" in 4:19.

And the a' element (4:18b–20) of this chiastic subunit forms a chiastic pattern in itself:

[a] ¹⁸ᵇand not only when I am *present with you.*

[b] ¹⁹My children, for whom I again have birth pangs until Christ be formed in you!

[a'] ²⁰I want to be *present with you* now and change my tone, for I am perplexed in you.

The statement "My children, for whom I again have birth pangs until Christ be formed in you" (4:19) serves as the unparalleled central and pivotal element of this chiasm. Chiastic parallels progress from "present with you" in 4:18b to "present with you" in 4:20.

The Galatians did Paul no wrong (4:12c) when he first preached to them the gospel because of a physical weakness of his (4:13), which did not prevent them from welcoming him as though he were an angel of God, indeed as though he were Christ Jesus himself (4:14).¹⁰ This reinforces Paul's implicit exhortation for them not to turn to a different gospel (1:6), one that is a distortion of the gospel of Christ (1:7), even if he or an angel from

---

10. "Paul is not simply praising the Galatians' hospitality but also points out that they gave that hospitality because they perceived Paul and his message (if not Paul's body itself) as coming from God, as representing Christ" (Oakes, *Galatians*, 148). "Paul's sickness, however, was not a liability for the spread of the gospel. Rather, he considered it to be a *corollary* of Christ's sufferings. In other words, Paul did not think his diseases and suffering should be separated from his calling as an apostle. The weakness of Paul, manifested in sickness, was the pathway by which Christ's strength was manifested through him" (Schreiner, *Galatians*, 286; emphasis original).

heaven should preach it to them (1:8). Their welcoming of Paul as though he were Christ Jesus himself reminds them that because of Paul's preaching of the gospel about the faith (1:23) to them they became, through their faith, sons of God in Christ Jesus (3:26), united with Paul and all other believers, whether Jew or Greek, in Christ Jesus (3:28). Having become sons of God because of their welcoming of Paul, they were enabled not only to become like Paul (4:12), but through the Spirit of God's Son, to worship God as their Father (4:6) for the eschatological life they are now entitled to inherit as sons who are heirs through God (4:7).[11]

Paul then asks the Galatians where now is "your" blessedness (4:15a), that is, their previous welcoming of Paul as Christ Jesus himself despite "your" trial regarding Paul's physical weakness (4:14). Paul testifies to them that, if possible, they would have torn out their "eyes" and given them to Paul (4:15b) implicitly in gratitude for Paul publicly proclaiming Jesus Christ as crucified before their "eyes" (3:1).[12] So now have "I," the Paul whom they once welcomed as if he were Christ Jesus and who became like them so that "you are to become" (γίνεσθε) like him (4:12), "become" (γέγονα) their enemy by telling them the truth (4:16). Paul's telling them the "truth" refers to the "truth" of the gospel that gentiles have the freedom to not be circumcised (2:3-5) or observe the law, by which they would again become slaves of the demonic elemental powers (4:9). It reminds them of the "truth" of the gospel, according to which uncircumcised gentiles and circumcised Jews together may worship God (2:14) for the eschatological life to which all believers are entitled as sons and heirs through God (4:7).[13]

Those who are troubling the Galatians and "wanting" (θέλοντες) to distort the gospel of Christ (1:7) are zealous for them, but not commendably, as they "want" (θέλουσιν) to exclude them from worshiping as members of the people of God unless they are circumcised (4:17ab).[14] The

---

11. "Paul's reminder that the Galatians had welcomed him as if he were Christ himself subtly strengthens Paul's authority as Christ's apostle, and thus it also reinforces the entreaty in v. 12 for the Galatians to become as he is" (De Boer, *Galatians*, 281).

12. That the term "eyes" (ὀφθαλμούς) occurs in Galatians only in 3:1 and 4:15 enhances this connection. "The eyes in antiquity were considered the most precious of the body's parts, and so 'to tear out one's eyes for someone' is a graphic and significant idiom for going to the extreme for another's welfare" (Longenecker, *Galatians*, 193).

13. "The central component of this truth is not that the gospel has opened the way for Gentiles to be included (as important as that is), but that the gospel is offered freely by grace and is to be accepted and lived out by means of faith alone" (Moo, *Galatians*, 286).

14. "Paul's image of shutting out or exclusion probably reflects their agenda of wanting to impose the observance of the law on the Galatians, beginning with circumcision

Galatians may then be zealous for them by following their directions and having themselves circumcised (4:17c). In contrast, Paul is zealous for the Galatians in a commendable way, not only when he is present with them (4:18) but implicitly while he is writing this letter to them, in which he is zealously exhorting them not to turn to a different, distorted gospel (1:6-7).

Using a maternal metaphor, Paul demonstrates his zeal for the Galatians by now addressing them as his "children" for whom he again has "birth pangs" until Christ be formed in them (4:19).[15] The possibility that they may "want" to be slaves of the elemental powers "again" (4:9) has caused birth pangs "again" in the Paul who previously gave them birth by bringing them to faith in the gospel of Christ.[16] He "wants" to be present with them now to further demonstrate his zeal for them (4:18) and change his tone, for he is perplexed "in you [ἐν ὑμῖν]" (4:20) because Christ has not yet been formed "in you [ἐν ὑμῖν]" (4:19). This reinforces Paul's exhortation for them to become like him (4:12) in whom Christ has been formed to the extent that Paul has died to the law and been crucified with Christ (2:19), so that Christ lives "in me [ἐν ἐμοί]" (2:20). As believers in whom Christ has been formed by God (divine passive), so that Christ lives in them, they may worship and live to and for God (2:19) as sons and heirs of eschatological life through God (4:7).[17]

(cf. 5:2-4) . . . this pressure probably takes the form of telling the Galatians that apart from circumcision and further law observance, they remain excluded from membership in God's people, the offspring of Abraham" (De Boer, *Galatians*, 283).

15. For a discussion and interpretation of "the maternity of Paul" in Gal 4:19, see Gaventa, *Our Mother Saint Paul*, 29-39.

16. "The 'again' (πάλιν) in this clause shows that Paul thinks of his initial evangelization of the Galatians in these terms, as he proclaimed the gospel to them, hoping thereby to bring them to the 'new birth' or regeneration. There is an implicit rebuke, then, in Paul's claim that he feels himself to be back in that position, suffering such 'birth pains' all over again on their behalf" (Moo, *Galatians*, 289).

17. Christ is formed in believers as part of the grace of God. "The formation of Christ occurs as a gift, not as an achievement" (Gaventa, *Our Mother Saint Paul*, 37). "Paul speaks of the formation of Christ rather than the birth of the Galatians to call attention to the supernatural work of God. Paul is not only speaking of the Galatians individually, for the phrase 'in you' (ἐν ὑμῖν) also refers to the growth of the Galatians as a church" (Schreiner, *Galatians*, 289-90).

Galatians

SUMMARY ON GALATIANS 4:8-20

The fact that, as believers, the Galatians are now recognizing God (4:9a) resonates with their worship, as sons, of the true and living God as their Father (4:6). But they can so worship God only because they were first recognized by God (4:9b) when God sent the Spirit of his Son into their hearts, so that they are no longer slaves, but sons, and thus heirs (4:6-7) of eschatological life. If, by having themselves circumcised, they were to place themselves under the curse of the law (3:10), they would again be slaves of things that are not gods (4:8), serving and worshiping the weak and destitute elemental powers (4:9c) associated with the law (4:3-5). They are already observing various times for worship, which suggests that they are beginning to observe the law (4:10). So, Paul fears that, in bringing them to faith in the gospel whereby the Spirit enabled them to worship the true and living God as their Father, he may have labored for them "in vain" (4:11).

Paul implores the Galatians as fellow believing "brothers" (cf. 1:11; 3:15) to become as "I" am (4:12a), because "I also" have become as "you" are (4:12b). The Galatians are to become like the Paul who, speaking as representative of every individual believer, declared that "I" through and to the law died, so that he might live a life of worship to and for God; he has been crucified with Christ (2:19). Yet Paul lives; no longer "I," but Christ, lives in him, so that he now lives an eschatological life by faith in the Son of God (2:20) rather than by works of the law. And that Paul has become as "you" are means that he has been united with all of "you" who are one in Christ Jesus (3:28c), "you" who are of Christ, and so heirs of eschatological life (3:29) as sons of God through faith (3:26) rather than the law. Paul thus impresses upon the Galatians that, since being a Jew or Greek no longer matters (3:28a), he as a Jew and they as Greeks have now begun to worship God for life, not according to the law, which is not able to give life (3:21), but according to their faith.

Using a maternal metaphor, Paul demonstrates his zeal for the Galatians by addressing them as his "children," for whom he again has "birth pangs" until Christ be formed in them (4:19). The possibility that they may "want" to be slaves of the elemental powers "again" (4:9) has caused birth pangs "again" in the Paul who previously gave them birth by bringing them to faith in the gospel of Christ. He "wants" to be present with them now to further demonstrate his zeal for them (4:18) and change his tone, for he is perplexed "in you" (4:20) because Christ has not yet been formed "in you" (4:19). This reinforces Paul's exhortation for them to become like him

(4:12), in whom Christ has been formed, to the extent that Paul has died to the law and been crucified with Christ (2:19), so that Christ lives "in me" (2:20). As believers in whom Christ has been formed by God (divine passive), so that Christ lives in them, they may worship and live to and for God (2:19) as sons and heirs of eschatological life through God (4:7).

11

Galatians 4:21–31

WE ARE CHILDREN WITH THE SON OF THE FREE WOMAN

Drive out the slave woman and her son

A ²¹*Tell* me, you who want *to be* under the law, do you not listen to the law? ²²For it is written that Abraham *had* two *sons*, one from the *slave woman* and one from the *free woman*. ²³But the one from the *slave woman* was *born according to the flesh*, while the one from the *free woman* through the *promise*. ²⁴Which things are spoken about allegorically. For these *are* two covenants, one from Mount Sinai, *giving birth* for slavery; this *is* Hagar. ²⁵'The Hagar Sinai Mount *is* in Arabia, but corresponds to the present Jerusalem, for she is in slavery with her *children*. ²⁶But the Jerusalem above *is free*, and she *is* our mother. ²⁷ᵃFor it is written, "Rejoice,

    B ²⁷ᵇyou barren one *who does not give birth*;

        C ²⁷ᶜbreak forth and shout,

    B' ²⁷ᵈyou *who have no birth pangs,*

A' ²⁷ᵉbecause more are the *children* of the barren one than of the one *having a husband*" [Isa 54:1]. ²⁸But you, brothers, like Isaac, *are children* of the *promise*. ²⁹But just as then the one *born according to the flesh* persecuted the one according to the Spirit, so also now. ³⁰But what does the scripture say? "Drive out the *slave woman* and her *son*! For the *son* of the *slave woman* will not inherit with the *son*" [Gen 21:10] of the *free woman*. ³¹Therefore, brothers, we *are* not *children* of the *slave woman* but of the *free woman*.¹

4:21–27a (A): The Jerusalem above is free and she is our mother

The A element (4:21–27a) of this chiastic unit forms a chiastic pattern in itself:

a) ²¹Tell me, you who want to be under the law, do you not listen to the law? ²²*For it is written* that Abraham had two sons, one from the slave woman and one from the *free* woman. ²³But the one from the slave woman was born according to the flesh, while the one from the free woman through the promise. ²⁴ᵃWhich things are spoken about allegorically. For these are two covenants,

    b) ²⁴ᵇone from *Mount Sinai*, giving birth for *slavery*; this is *Hagar*.

    b') ²⁵The *Hagar Sinai Mount* is in Arabia, but corresponds to the present Jerusalem, for she is in *slavery* with her children.

a') ²⁶But the Jerusalem above is *free*, and she is our mother. ²⁷ᵃ*For it is written*, "Rejoice."

At the center of this chiastic subunit is a pivot of parallels from "Mount Sinai" in 4:24b to "Sinai Mount" in 4:25; from "slavery" in 4:24b to "slavery" in 4:25; and from "Hagar" in 4:24b to "Hagar" in 4:25. Chiastic parallels progress from "for it is written" in 4:22 to "for it is written" in 4:27a and from "free" in 4:22 to "free" in 4:26.

And the "a" element (4:21–24a) of this chiastic subunit forms a chiastic pattern in itself:

[a] ²¹Tell me, you who want to be under the law, do you not listen to the law? ²²ᵃFor it is written that Abraham had *two* sons,

    [b] ²²ᵇone from the *slave woman* and one from the *free woman*.

    [b'] ²³But the one from the *slave woman* was born according to the flesh, while the one from the *free woman* through the promise.

[a'] ²⁴ᵃWhich things are spoken about allegorically. For these are *two* covenants.

---

1. For the establishment of Gal 4:21–31 as a chiasm, see chapter 1 of this book.

At the center of this chiasm is a pivot of parallels from "slave woman" in 4:22b to "slave woman" in 4:23 and from "free woman" in 4:22b to "free woman" in 4:23. Chiastic parallels progress from "two" in 4:22a to "two" in 4:24a.

Paul addresses the Galatians as "you who want [θέλοντες] to be under the law" (4:21a). This recalls his previous question concerning whether "you want" (θέλετε) to be slaves again of the weak and destitute elemental powers associated with the law (4:9). That they want to be "under the law" reminds them that, before faith came, we believers were held in custody "under the law" (3:23). But God sent his Son, born "under the law" (4:4), that he might redeem those "under the law" (4:5) and thus free them from its slavery. Paul then asks the Galatians who want to be under the law as containing the commandments that enslave them, whether "you hear" (ἀκούετε), in the sense of "heed" or "obey," the law as scripture (4:21b).[2]

It is written in the law as scripture that Abraham had two sons, one (Ishmael) from the slave woman (Hagar) and one (Isaac) from the free woman (Sarah; 4:22; cf. Gen 16:1, 15; 21:3). The one from the slave woman was born according to the flesh, while the one from the free woman was born through the promise (4:23). The perfect tense of the verb "was born" (γεγέννηται) indicates a past event with a present relevance for the audience.[3] The son from the slave woman was born "according to the flesh," that is, a natural descent that is human, mortal, and earthly.[4] In stark contrast, the son from the free woman was born "through the promise," that is, a supernatural descent that is divine, immortal, and heavenly. "Through the promise" (δι' ἐπαγγελίας; cf. 3:18) resonates synonymously with the statement that the Galatians are no longer a slave but a son, and if a son, also an heir "through God [διὰ θεοῦ]" (4:7).[5] As a descendant of Abraham, along

---

2. "Paul mostly uses νόμος (law) to denote the body of commandments given by God to Israel through Moses; but in keeping with Jewish usage, he also uses the word in a 'canonical' sense, to denote the Pentateuch or sometimes the entire OT. The verb ἀκούω (hear) probably has the sense of . . . not just 'hearing' or 'listening' but also 'attentive hearing,' a 'listening that leads to understanding and obedience'" (Moo, *Galatians*, 297). See also Wright, *Communal Reading*, 164.

3. "Paul uses the perfect tense of the verb here (γεγέννηται, was born) to indicate that 'the OT event . . . still retains its (exemplary) meaning' (BDF §342.5)" (Moo, *Galatians*, 298). See also De Boer, *Galatians*, 293.

4. BDAG, 916.

5. The preposition "through" (διά) with the genitive in the phrase "through the promise" in 4:23 is the next occurrence of this preposition with the genitive after the phrase "through God" in 4:7, enhancing this connection. This connection is perhaps

with Christ (3:16), they are heirs of eschatological life according to God's promise for it (3:11, 29), foreshadowed by Abraham's son (Isaac) born through the promise.[6]

Paul is speaking allegorically about these two quite different women giving birth, for they represent two distinct covenants (4:24a).[7] One of the women is from Mount Sinai, giving birth for slavery; this is the slave woman (4:23), Hagar (4:24b). Her giving birth for "slavery" (δουλείαν) reinforces the association of the Mosaic law that originated from Mount Sinai with the weak and destitute elemental powers that the Galatians are in danger of "being slaves" (δουλεύειν) of again (4:9). Although the Hagar Sinai Mount is in Arabia, recalling that Paul previously went to Arabia in contrast to Jerusalem (1:17), it nevertheless corresponds to the present Jerusalem, portrayed as the mother of those under the law, for she is in slavery with her "children [τέκνων]" (4:25), whereas the Galatians are Paul's "children [τέκνα]" (4:19).[8] In addition, Jerusalem "is in slavery" (δουλεύει), further reinforcing the association of the law with slavery to the elemental powers (4:9), and with idolatry, recalling that "you," the Galatians before they knew God, "were slaves" (ἐδουλεύσατε) of things that by nature are not gods (4:8).[9]

---

the reason for the phrase "through the promise" rather than "according to the promise" (cf. 3:29). "The point is the miraculous nature of Isaac's begetting and birth. 'Through a promise' echoes the same phrase in 3:18 and means the same as 'through God' in 4:7" (De Boer, *Galatians*, 293).

6. "Isaac was born because God promised and not because natural, biological channels favoured. *His birth was effectively a revivification miracle.* As such, the promise of the Spirit is not initially the promise of countless descendants, but *the miraculous birth of Isaac* ... there is a strong ideological connection between 'promise' and 'life'" (Boakye, *Death and Life*, 138; emphases original).

7. According to De Boer, "the sense of the opening clause of v. 24 is this: 'These things are [now] being said [i.e., interpreted] allegorically [by me], for [in my view] these women are [i.e., represent] *two* covenants [not just one as the new preachers would have you believe]'" (*Galatians*, 295; emphasis original). See also Di Mattei, "Paul's Allegory," 102–22.

8. "The 'present' Jerusalem, then, is Paul's way of speaking of the Judaism of his day, a Judaism that continues to rely on the law and ignore or not give adequate place to Christ" (Moo, *Galatians*, 304). "'The present Jerusalem' must refer to the city itself, probably with particular reference to its identity as the Jewish center for festivals and other temple rituals" (Oakes, *Galatians*, 156–57).

9. "In 4:25-26 Paul uses the form Ἰερουσαλήμ, in contrast to the form Ἱεροσόλυμα (Jerusalem) that he used in 1:17, 18; 2:1, probably because the former has a more 'religious' connotation" (Moo, *Galatians*, 303n9).

Galatians

In contrast to the earthly "present" Jerusalem in slavery with her children (4:25), the heavenly, eschatological Jerusalem "above" is free, and she is the mother of us believers (4:26).[10] Believers then are children of the "free" Jerusalem that corresponds to the "free" woman whose son was born through the divine promise of eschatological life implicitly in the Jerusalem above (4:23).[11] "For it is written" with its focus on the "free" woman (4:22) progresses to "for it is written" with a focus on the "free" Jerusalem above who is the mother of believers. The scripture (Isa 54:1) exhorts her, and implicitly the believing children she corporately represents and personifies, including the Galatians, to engage in an act of exuberant and jubilant laudatory worship of God for the eschatological life promised to believers (3:11), as they are to "rejoice!" (4:27a).[12]

4:27b-d (B-C-B'): Break forth and shout with joy

The Jerusalem above, who is free and the mother of believers (4:26), is addressed as the barren one "who does not give birth [ἡ οὐ τίκτουσα]" (4:27b). This contrasts with the present Jerusalem, who "gave birth" (γεννῶσα) to slavery (4:24b) and is the mother who corresponds to the Hagar Sinai Mount in slavery with her children (4:25). People become children of this Jerusalem mother not by being born, but by believing. She, together with the children she represents and personifies, is to intensify her rejoicing (4:27a) by breaking out and shouting (4:27c) in joyful praise to God as an act of laudatory worship. This act of worship by believers for eschatological

---

10. "'The Jerusalem above' is therefore equivalent to 'the heavenly Jerusalem' (BDAG 471.3) or the 'new Jerusalem' and taps into a widespread OT and Jewish tradition. This tradition, especially prominent in apocalyptic, pictures the perfected eschatological Jerusalem to come as already existing in the heavenly sphere and anticipates the time when this city will be established on the earth" (Moo, *Galatians*, 304–5).

11. "The Jerusalem above" refers to "the new age now present in spatial terms and the anticipation of the full life of this new age now present in the church" (Lincoln, *Paradise*, 21). "Not the present Jerusalem, not the church located in that city, is 'our mother,' but rather Jerusalem above is, the church consisting of Jews and Gentiles free from the law. By using the possessive modifier 'our,' Paul indicates that the Jerusalem above is the mother of all believers, whether they be of Jewish or Gentile origin" (De Boer, *Galatians*, 302).

12. "Paul's quotation of Isa 54:1 may have been an implicit call for his auditors to rejoice in their part in its end-time fulfillment" (Lyons, *Galatians*, 288). "Therefore, the Gentiles of Galatia should exult with joy because they are the fulfillment of the promise; they are the true children of the Lord" (Schreiner, *Galatians*, 304).

life in the heavenly Jerusalem resonates with and complements not only the laudatory worship of God as Father (4:6), but also the doxological worship of God (1:5) for raising Jesus Christ from the dead to eschatological life in heaven (1:1).[13] Because of Paul's metaphorical "birth pangs" in bringing the Galatians to believe in the gospel of Christ (4:19), the Jerusalem above, as the metaphorical mother of believers, does not have "birth pangs" (4:27d).[14]

4:27e–31 (A'): We are children of the free woman

The A' element (4:27e–31) of this chiastic unit forms a chiastic pattern in itself:

- a) [27e]because more are the *children* of the barren one than of the one having a husband" [Isa 54:1]. [28]But you, *brothers*, like Isaac, are *children* of the promise.

  - b) [29a]But *just as then*

    - c) [29b]the one born *according to the flesh*

      - d) [29c]persecuted

    - c') [29d]the one *according to the Spirit*,

  - b') [29e]*so also now.*

- a') [30a]But what does the scripture say? "Drive out the slave woman and her son! For the son of the slave woman will not inherit with the son" [Gen 21:10] of the free woman. [31]Therefore, *brothers*, we are not *children* of the slave woman but of the free woman.

---

13. "Isaiah 54:1 is introduced to support Paul's argument in Gal 4:26, showing that the Gentile Christians in Galatia are the children of the Jerusalem above, for they are the children of the barren woman from whom no children were expected. Miraculously and supernaturally they have new life" (Schreiner, *Galatians*, 303–4). "It is no stretch at all, then, to think that Paul would have read Isa. 54:1 as a celebration of the new state of affairs brought about by the death and resurrection of Christ" (Moo, *Galatians*, 308).

14. On the "birth pangs" in 4:27d as an allusion to Paul's metaphorical "birth pangs" in 4:19 to refer to his gospel preaching as "giving birth" to his children, who, as believers, are children born for eschatological life in Jerusalem, see Eastman, *Recovering Paul's Mother Tongue*, 157. "Paul is convinced, of course, that the 'new Jerusalem,' representing the age to come, has come into being and that it is through his Spirit-empowered preaching of the gospel that this new Jerusalem is being populated . . . Paul's gospel-oriented reading of Isa. 54:1, in its context, convinces him that Sarah represents the new age, made available to humans by the life-giving gospel" (Moo, *Galatians*, 307).

The verb "persecuted" in 4:29c serves as the unparalleled central and pivotal element of this chiasm. Chiastic parallels progress from "children" in 4:27e and 28 to "children" in 4:31, and from "brothers" in 4:28 to "brothers" in 4:31. Finally, antithetical chiastic parallels progress from "just as then" in 4:29a to "so also now" in 4:29e and from "according to the flesh" in 4:29b to "according to the Spirit" in 4:29d.

The Galatians are to "rejoice" (4:27a) as an act of laudatory worship of God for eschatological life because, as believers they are among the "children" (τέκνα) of the barren one, the Jerusalem who is the free mother of believers (4:26), whose children are more than the one who has a husband (4:27e; cf. Isa 54:1). The one with a husband gave birth for slavery (4:24b) and is in slavery with her "children [τέκνων]" (4:25). But Paul again addresses the Galatians as "brothers" (cf. 1:11; 3:15; 4:12), his fellow believers, and assures them that they, like Isaac, who became a child through the "promise" (4:23), are "children" (τέκνα) of the "promise" (4:28) for new life.[15] This means that, as children who are believers and a descendant of Abraham, they are heirs of eschatological life according to the "promise" (3:29) for it (3:11). And it reinforces the exhortation for the Galatian believers, along with their free mother, the heavenly Jerusalem (4:26), to exuberantly and jubilantly "break forth and shout" (4:27c) in an act of laudatory worship of God for eschatological life.

Just as in the past the one born according to the flesh (Ishmael; cf. 4:23a), persecuted the one according to the Spirit (Isaac), who was born through the promise (4:23b) for a life that is brought about by the Spirit (cf. 3:14), so also now (4:29).[16] Paul thus interprets as persecutors those who are troubling the Galatians and want to distort the gospel of Christ (1:7) by

---

15. "This likeness includes both the means but perhaps also the outcome . . . in conjunction with the resurrection of Christ, he [God] gives life to people" (Moo, *Galatians*, 309). "The Isaiah 54 citation in Gal 4:27 reinforces the connection between life and freedom, *for it contextualizes Isaac's birth as an implicit revivification event*" (Boakye, *Death and Life*, 150; emphasis original).

16. "Isaac was born (or begotten) 'according to the Spirit,' which means virtually the same as 'through a promise' in v. 23. The link between the promise and the Spirit has already been made in 3:14" (De Boer, *Galatians*, 306). "The polarity between the Spirit and the flesh is stark. The Galatian Christians are part of the age to come. They have the Jerusalem above as their mother. They are men and women of the Spirit. Therefore, they must resist the blandishments of the Judaizers, who are spiritually dead and who want to impose the slavery of the law and circumcision on them" (Schreiner, *Galatians*, 305). "Paul declares in 4:29 that Isaac's birth was according to the Spirit; that is, *the Spirit brought Isaac to life*" (Boakye, *Death and Life*, 138; emphasis original).

being zealous for them to observe the works of the law (4:17, 21), including circumcision (cf. 2:12).[17] But the scripture (Gen 21:10) that once exhorted Abraham to drive out the slave woman (Hagar) and her son (Ishmael) is now exhorting the Galatians.[18] Since the son of the slave woman will not inherit with the son (Isaac) of the free woman (Sarah), the scripture is now exhorting the Galatians to drive out those persecuting them by requiring them to observe the works of the law and thus be in slavery to it (4:30).[19]

Addressing the Galatians again as "brothers" (cf. 4:28), his fellow believers, Paul asserts that we believers are not children of the slave woman but of the free woman (4:31). Believers are "children" (τέκνα) of the free woman in contrast to the son of the slave woman, who will not inherit with the son of the free woman (4:30), Isaac. Like Isaac, believers are "children" (τέκνα) of the promise (4:28), and thus those who will inherit eschatological life as heirs according to the promise (3:29) for it (3:11). By emphasizing that we believers are children of the "free" woman, Paul reinforces the scriptural exhortation for the Galatians, along with their mother, the Jerusalem who is "free" (4:26), to engage in the laudatory worship of God (4:27) for the eschatological life they will inherit as children of the heavenly Jerusalem. This complements the laudatory worship they can offer God as their Father (4:6), since they are no longer a slave but a son, and thus an heir, as a descendant of Abraham (3:29), with Christ (3:16), of eschatological life through God (4:7).[20]

---

17. "Paul is referring to the way the agitators are 'persecuting' the Gentiles in Galatia by trying to impose the burden of the law on them and suggesting that, if they do not submit, they will lose their position in the people of God" (Moo, *Galatians*, 310).

18. "Paul makes Sarah's words to Abraham into words of 'the Scripture' addressed to the Galatians in the present" (De Boer, *Galatians*, 307). This is contra Eastman ("Cast Out," 309-36), who claims that since the imperative "drive out" (ἔκβαλε) is singular, it cannot be addressed to the Galatians, but the context indicates otherwise. "Paul preserves the singular form of the OT text, perhaps simply because he is disinclined to change the text, perhaps because he wants to individualize the command: each of the Galatians is to take responsibility" (Moo, *Galatians*, 311).

19. "Did Paul mean that the new preachers (and their converts) were literally to be expelled from the Galatians churches? Apparently so, though he leaves it up to the Galatians. Perhaps the point is simply that the Galatians are to reject the message and the missionary efforts of the new preachers active in Galatia" (De Boer, *Galatians*, 308).

20. "The command to expel the slave woman and her child in v 30 . . . is not the climax or the main point of 4:21–5:1. Surely this is to be found in the call for the Galatians to celebrate their status as free children in 4:27" (Lyons, *Galatians*, 295).

SUMMARY ON GALATIANS 4:21–31

In contrast to the earthly "present" Jerusalem in slavery with her children (4:25), the heavenly, eschatological Jerusalem "above" is free, and she is the mother of us believers (4:26). Believers are then children of the "free" Jerusalem that corresponds to the "free" woman, whose son was born through the divine promise of eschatological life implicitly in this Jerusalem (4:23). "For it is written" with its focus on the "free" woman (4:22) progresses to "for it is written" with a focus on the "free" Jerusalem, who is the mother of believers. The scripture (Isa 54:1) exhorts her, and implicitly the believing children she corporately represents and personifies, including the Galatians, to engage in an act of exuberant and jubilant laudatory worship of God for the eschatological life promised to believers (3:11), as they are to "rejoice!" (4:27a).

The Jerusalem who is free and the mother of believers (4:26) is addressed as the barren one "who does not give birth" (4:27b). This contrasts with the present Jerusalem, who "gave birth" to slavery (4:24b) and is the mother who corresponds to the Hagar Sinai Mount in slavery with her children (4:25). People become children of the mother who is the Jerusalem above not by being born, but by believing. She, together with the children she represents and personifies, is to intensify her rejoicing (4:27a) by breaking out and shouting (4:27c) in joyful praise to God as an act of laudatory worship. This act of worship by believers for eschatological life in the heavenly Jerusalem resonates with and complements not only the laudatory worship of God as Father (4:6), but the doxological worship of God (1:5) for raising Jesus Christ from the dead to eschatological life in heaven (1:1).

Addressing the Galatians again as "brothers" (cf. 4:28), his fellow believers, Paul asserts that we believers are not children of the slave woman, but of the free woman (4:31). Believers are "children" of the free woman in contrast to the son of the slave woman, who will not inherit with the son of the free woman (4:30), Isaac. Like Isaac, believers are "children" of the promise (4:28), and thus those who will inherit eschatological life as heirs according to the promise (3:29) for it (3:11). By emphasizing that we believers are children of the "free" woman, Paul reinforces the scriptural exhortation for the Galatians, along with their mother, the Jerusalem who is "free" (4:26), to engage in the laudatory worship of rejoicing in God (4:27) for the eschatological life they will inherit as children of the heavenly Jerusalem. This complements the laudatory worship they can offer God as their Father (4:6), since they are no longer a slave but a son, and thus an heir, as a descendant of Abraham (3:29), with Christ (3:16), of eschatological life through God (4:7).

12

Galatians 5:1-13

THE TRUTH OF FREEDOM FROM CIRCUMCISION TO SERVE ONE ANOTHER

Through love be slaves to one another

A ¹For *freedom* Christ set us *free*; stand firm then and do not again to the yoke of *slavery* be subjected. ²Look! I, Paul, am saying to you that if you have yourselves circumcised, Christ will benefit you *nothing*. ³And I testify again to every human being who has himself circumcised that he is obligated to do the *whole* law. ⁴*You have been removed* from Christ, you who are trying to be justified by the law; you have fallen away from grace!

    B ⁵For we by the Spirit, from *faith*, the hope of justification we await.

        C ⁶ᵃFor in Christ Jesus *neither* circumcision

            D ⁶ᵇcounts for anything

        C' ⁶ᶜ*nor* uncircumcision,

    B' ⁶ᵈbut *faith* working through love.

A' ⁷You were running commendably; who hindered you from being persuaded by the truth?

⁸This persuasion is not from the one who calls you! ⁹A little leaven leavens the *whole* batch of dough! ¹⁰I have been persuaded regarding you in

the Lord that you will think *nothing* otherwise, but the one troubling you will bear the condemnation, whoever he may be. ¹¹But as for me, brothers, if I am still proclaiming circumcision, why am I still being persecuted? In that case the stumbling block of the cross *has been removed*. ¹²Would that those disturbing you might also castrate themselves! ¹³For you were called to *freedom*, brothers; only do not use the *freedom* as an opportunity for the flesh, but through love *be slaves* to one another.[1]

5:1–4 (A): For freedom Christ set us free

The A element (5:1–4) of this chiastic unit forms a chiastic pattern in itself:

a) ¹For freedom *Christ* set us free; stand firm then and do not again to the yoke of slavery be subjected.

   b) ²ᵃLook! I, Paul, am saying to you that if you have yourselves *circumcised*,

      c) ²ᵇChrist will benefit you nothing.

   b') ³And I testify again to every human being who has himself *circumcised* that he is obligated to do the whole law.

a') ⁴You have been removed from *Christ*, you who are trying to be justified by the law; you have fallen away from grace!

The statement that "Christ will benefit you nothing" in 5:2b serves as the unparalleled central and pivotal element of this chiastic subunit. Chiastic parallels progress from "circumcised" in 5:2a to "circumcised" in 5:3 and from "Christ" in 5:1 to "Christ" in 5:4.

That for "freedom" Christ "freed" us believers (5:1a) recalls how in Jerusalem the false brothers spied on the "freedom" that we believers have in Christ Jesus, that they might "enslave" us (2:4) by requiring gentile believers, like Titus, to be circumcised (2:3), and thus observe the law that is not able to give life (3:21). Christ "freed" (ἠλευθέρωσεν) us when he gave himself in self-sacrificial death for our sins, that he might "rescue" or "free" (ἐξέληται) us from the mortality of the present evil age (1:4) for an eschatological life made possible when God raised him from the dead (1:1). And, by his death on a tree, Christ "redeemed" (ἐξηγόρασεν) us (3:13; cf. 4:5) from the curse of doing all the things written in the law (3:10) to live

---

1. For the establishment of Gal 5:1–13 as a chiasm, see chapter 1 of this book.

by them (3:12).² We believers have been freed then to live an eschatological life as those who have been justified before God by faith (3:11).

Freed by Christ for freedom from the law (5:1a), the Galatian believers are to stand firm and not be subjected again to the yoke of "slavery" (5:1b), and thus become among those who were given birth for "slavery" under the law that came from Mount Sinai (4:24).³ They are not "again" to be subjected to the yoke of slavery under the law, since that would mean turning back "again" to the weak and destitute elemental powers associated with the law and being slaves of them all over "again" (4:9).⁴ Indeed, when they did not know God, before they became believers, the Galatians were slaves of things that by nature are not gods (4:8), unable to serve the true God in and through their worship. But now, freed by Christ, as those who have been crucified with Christ and so have died to the law, the Galatian believers are now able to live to and for the true God (2:19), and thus worship God by faith in this present life, in view of an eternal life with the Christ God raised from the dead (1:1).

The earnest interjection of "look," followed by the emphatic pronoun "I" before "Paul" (5:2a), recalls that "Paul" has his authority as an apostle through Jesus Christ and God the Father, who raised him from the dead (1:1). Paul is telling the Galatians that if they have themselves "circumcised," the Christ who freed gentiles from the requirement to be "circumcised" (2:3) will benefit them nothing (5:2b). Indeed, Paul testifies again to every human being who has himself circumcised that, rather than one whom Christ "will benefit" (ὠφελήσει), he will become one "obligated" (ὀφειλέτης) "to do" the whole law (5:3).⁵ Paul thus reiterates the scriptural

---

2. "The language of redemption in 3:13 and 4:5 is conceptually similar to freedom; in both these texts, redemption is from a situation having to do with the law: 'the curse of the law' in 3:13, and 'those under the law' in 4:5. And now in 5:1, Paul goes on to warn about a yoke of slavery, language that almost certainly refers to the law" (Moo, *Galatians*, 320). "This is the climax of the slavery/freedom theme that has been running vigorously since 3:22 (following its introduction in 2:4–5 and its link to the cross in the redemption language of 3:13)" (Oakes, *Galatians*, 159).

3. "For the Galatians to submit to circumcision and adopt the OT law is to return to the Sinai covenant, which is one of slavery" (Schreiner, *Galatians*, 307).

4. "The 'again' reflects the way that Paul has described the Galatian Gentiles' previous subjection to 'the elements of the world' (4:3, 9) and associated that with subjection to the law" (Moo, *Galatians*, 320–21).

5. "The verb ὠφελήσει, value, 'profit,' or 'benefit' is from the same cognate family as the noun ὀφειλέτης, obligated, in Gal 5:3. The obligations imposed upon Gentiles by circumcision would make Christ of no benefit to them" (Lyons, *Galatians*, 302).

testimony that everyone who does not remain in all the things written in the book of the law is cursed "to do" them (3:10).[6]

Paul warns the Galatians that if they are trying to be "justified" by the law, then they have been separated from Christ (5:4a), since a human being is not "justified" from works of the law, but through faith in Jesus Christ (2:16; cf. 3:24).[7] And then they will have fallen from "grace" (5:4b), which recalls that Paul, on the other hand, does not reject the "grace" of God; for if justification is through the law, then Christ died to no purpose (2:21). Also, it recalls Paul's amazement that the Galatians are so quickly turning away from the God who called them in the "grace" of Christ for a different gospel (1:6). In trying to be justified by the law, the Galatians would fall from the "grace" given to them as believers by the Lord Jesus Christ (1:3), who, as part of this grace, "gave" himself for our sins, that he might free us from the mortality of the present evil age (1:4). And they would fall from the "grace" given to them as believers by God our Father (1:3), who raised Jesus Christ from the dead, which gives us, as part of this grace, the promise of an eschatological life.[8]

5:5 (B): The hope of justification we believers await

With an emphatic "we" (ἡμεῖς), Paul invites the Galatians to join him in confessing that we believers, by the "Spirit" and from our "faith," and thus

---

6. "The word 'again' (πάλιν) here [in 5:3] does not clearly refer to 5:2 . . . It makes more sense to think that Paul reverts to the crucial argument in 3:10, where he insisted that one must keep the entire law to avoid the curse of the law" (Schreiner, *Galatians*, 314).

7. On the translation "trying to be justified" for δικαιοῦσθε in 5:4, Moo notes: "As most interpreters recognize, the present tense verb δικαιοῦσθε has a conative force, justifying the translation 'seeking to be justified' (or equivalent renderings) . . . Only this interpretation of the verb makes sense of Paul's unqualified claim elsewhere that the law cannot justify" (*Galatians*, 325).

8. "To want to predicate justification on circumcision and law observance now that Christ (faith) has come into the world (3:23-25) is to nullify God's grace (2:21a), thus to fall out of the realm of this grace and to become separated from Christ" (De Boer, *Galatians*, 315). Galatians 5:4 "describes separation from Christ. This is the opposite process from the participation in Christ, the union with Christ that is central to salvation in Galatians. Similarly, falling 'away from grace' (5:4) reverses the process of salvation. In Galatians, grace has been associated with God's calling the gentile Galatians (1:6). In turning to the law for righteousness, the Galatians abandon the terms on which they were called" (Oakes, *Galatians*, 161).

not from the law (5:4), await the hope of "justification" (5:5).⁹ This means that we believers await the eternal eschatological life that is the object of the hope promised by our being justified from faith.¹⁰ This resonates with the promise of eschatological life, which is to be brought about by the "Spirit," that we believers might receive through our "faith" (3:14), which accords with the promise that the "just one" from "faith" will live (3:11).¹¹ There is no hope of an eschatological life for those who are trying to be justified by doing the law (5:3–4), since the law is unable to give life; otherwise, "justification" would indeed be from the law (3:21). But the scripture confined all things under the power of sin, that the promise of an eschatological life from "faith" in Jesus Christ might be given to those who believe (3:22).

5:6abc (C-D-C'): In Christ neither circumcision nor uncircumcision count for anything

For believers who are "in Christ Jesus," that is, are in union with the Jesus Christ whom God raised from the dead (1:1), so that he now lives within every believer (2:20), whether one is circumcised or uncircumcised does not count for anything (5:6abc).¹² This resonates with Paul's assertion that "in Christ Jesus" all the Galatians are sons of God through faith (3:26), so that there is neither Jew nor Greek, slave nor free, male nor female, for all

---

9. The verb "we await" (ἀπεκδεχόμεθα), in a final emphatic position in the Greek sentence, "signifies eager, intense, and confident expectation" (De Boer, *Galatians*, 316). It "is always used to denote eschatological realities in Paul" (Schreiner, *Galatians*, 316).

10. The "hope" or "hoped for things" of justification "probably refer to what is summed up in the terms 'life,' 'salvation,' and 'glory'—each of which, at least in its characteristic Pauline usage, is related to justification as something to which it points forward" (Fung, *Epistle to the Galatians*, 227).

11. "We have begun by the Spirit (3:3), and by the Spirit we have entered into our present realization of the promise of 'sonship' (3:14; 4:6); moreover, by the Spirit we live in eager anticipation of final realization of the promise—life with Christ forever" (Fee, *God's Empowering Presence*, 419). "In Galatians, the Spirit of God is the agent of life-giving in believers (Gal 5:25); furthermore, it is from Spirit that believers will reap the eschatological blessing of life (Gal 6:8) and hope for it before the end (5:5). The Spirit is the source of life now and in the final age" (Boakye, *Death and Life*, 194).

12. "Christ Jesus is the sphere or realm in which the believer dwells" (Matera, *Galatians*, 182). Boakye interprets the seven uses in Galatians of the term "in Christ/in Christ Jesus" (1:22; 2:4, 17; 3:14, 26, 28; 5:6) as "in the realm/sphere of the risen Christ" (*Death and Life*, 116).

believers are one "in Christ Jesus" (3:28).¹³ This means that believers are a descendant of Abraham, heirs of eschatological life according to the promise (3:29) for it (3:11). It was "in Christ Jesus" that the blessing of Abraham (justification) came to the gentiles, so that we believers might receive, through faith, the promise of the eschatological life to be realized by the Spirit (3:14). And it is "in Christ Jesus" that we believers have the freedom to not be enslaved by the law (2:4). Indeed, through his self-sacrificial death for our sins, the Lord Jesus Christ freed us from the mortality of the present evil age (1:4) so that we believers might live an eschatological life.

5:6d (B'): Faith working through love

The "faith" from which we believers are justified before God for the hope of a future eschatological life (5:5) is a "faith" working through love (5:6d).¹⁴ That this faith is working through "love" (ἀγάπης) means that it is made operative as that faith in the Son of God who "loved" (ἀγαπήσαντός), by giving himself up in a self-sacrificial death, Paul and every believer (2:20b; cf. 1:4). As that Son of God, Christ, now lives in every believer (2:20a), the faith that works through love implies that every believer is to love God and his fellow believers in a self-sacrificial way. Every believer has been crucified with the Christ, who loved in a self-sacrificial way, so that every believer might live to and for God (2:19) in and through an ethical worship that includes a Christ-like self-sacrificial love.¹⁵

---

13. "To be *in Christ Jesus* was to belong to him, to be his people, to be members of the community of Christ-believers. Christians were to regard the distinction between Jews and Gentiles inconsequential, like all distinctions of the old order (see 3:28)" (Lyons, *Galatians*, 308-9; emphasis original). "So to Paul (representative of all believers here) the old world is no more, and with it, the merit once attached to ethno-racial classification; *both* circumcision *and* uncircumcision are inert as identity markers or indices of value (5:6; 6:15)" (Boakye, *Death and Life*, 202; emphases original).

14. "The phrase ['faith working through love'] is almost a single concept, faith-through-love, love-energized-faith . . . faith coming to expression in and through love" (Dunn, *Epistle to the Galatians*, 272).

15. "Those who are 'in Christ' by faith need to live by faith, a faith that produces works of love pleasing to God through the Spirit" (Moo, *Galatians*, 331). "Paul sees Jesus' vicarious crucifixion as the definitive example of the loving one's neighbour, and, therefore as the template for love within the community, as Gal 5:13-14 captures. Believers must imitate the sacrificial love of Christ for mankind, demonstrated through his crucifixion, in their love for one another" (Boakye, *Death and Life*, 201).

Galatians

5:7–13 (A'): Through love be slaves to one another

The A' element (5:7–13) of this chiastic unit forms a chiastic pattern in itself:

- a) ⁷You were running commendably; who hindered you from being *persuaded* by the truth? ⁸This *persuasion* is not from the one who *calls* you!

    - b) ⁹ᵃA little *leaven*

    - b') ⁹ᵇ*leavens* the whole batch of dough!

- a') ¹⁰I have been *persuaded* regarding you in the Lord that you will think nothing otherwise, but the one troubling you will bear the condemnation, whoever he may be. ¹¹But as for me, brothers, if I am still proclaiming circumcision, why am I still being persecuted? In that case the stumbling block of the cross has been removed. ¹²Would that those disturbing you might also castrate themselves! ¹³For you were *called* to freedom, brothers; only do not use the freedom as an opportunity for the flesh, but through love be slaves to one another.

At the center of this chiastic subunit is a pivot of parallels from "leaven" in 5:9a to "leavens" in 5:9b. Chiastic parallels progress from "persuaded" in 5:7 and "persuasion" in 5:8 to "persuaded" in 5:10, and from "calls" in 5:8 to "called" in 5:13.

And the a' element (5:10–13) of this chiastic subunit forms a chiastic pattern in itself:

- [a] ¹⁰I have been persuaded regarding you in the Lord that you will think nothing otherwise, but the one troubling you will bear the condemnation, whoever he may be. ¹¹ᵃBut as for me, *brothers*,

    - [b] ¹¹ᵇif I am *still* proclaiming circumcision,

    - [b'] ¹¹ᶜwhy am I *still* being persecuted?

- [a'] ¹¹ᵈIn that case the stumbling block of the cross has been removed. ¹²Would that those disturbing you might also castrate themselves! ¹³For you were called to freedom, *brothers*; only do not use the freedom as an opportunity for the flesh, but through love be slaves to one another.

At the center of this chiastic subunit is a pivot of parallels from "still" in 5:11b to "still" in 5:11c. Chiastic parallels progress from "brothers" in 5:11a to "brothers" in 5:13.

The Galatians were "running commendably" (5:7a), that is, behaving and conducting their lives in accord with the gospel proclaimed among the gentiles by Paul, who was similarly assured by the leaders in Jerusalem that he was not "running" for no purpose (2:2). In contrast to those who are zealous, but not "commendably [καλῶς]" (4:17), for the Galatians to be circumcised, the Galatians were running "commendably" (καλῶς). Paul then asks rhetorically "who" (τίς) has hindered them from being persuaded by the truth (5:7b).[16] This resonates with "who" (τίς) has bewitched them, as before their eyes Jesus Christ was publicly proclaimed as crucified (3:1), and with Paul's warning that if "anyone" (τις) is preaching to them a gospel other than the one they received, such a person is to be accursed (1:9).[17] They are being hindered from being persuaded by the "truth," that is, the "truth" Paul has been telling them (4:16), the "truth" of the gospel that uncircumcised gentiles need not live like circumcised Jews (2:14), the "truth" of the gospel that gentiles have the freedom not to be circumcised and observe the law (2:5).[18]

This persuasion away from the truth of the gospel to a requirement for gentiles to be circumcised is not from the God who calls the Galatians (5:8). The God who "calls" them is the God who, through his grace, "called" Paul (1:15) to preach the gospel about the risen Son of God among the gentiles (1:16). That this persuasion away from the gospel is not from the God who "calls" them resonates with Paul's amazement that the Galatians are so quickly turning away from the God who "called" them in the grace of Christ for a different gospel (1:6).[19] Comparing this persuasion to leaven,

16. "Paul uses indefinite and allusive language to force the Galatians themselves to identify the people who might be 'cutting in' on their successful spiritual run" (Moo, *Galatians*, 333). "Paul framed his question so as to avoid giving the Agitators free publicity. He doomed them to anonymity while negatively characterizing what they had done as an unfortunate diversion" (Lyons, *Galatians*, 312).

17. "It is difficult to know whether Paul is speaking generically in these verses or has a particular person (the leader of the group?) in view. Probably the former, since he reverts back to the plural in v. 12 (cf. 1:7; 4:17; 6:12–13)" (De Boer, *Galatians*, 320).

18. "The subtle allusion to circumcision is evident in the verb 'hindered,' ἐνέκοψεν, literally, 'cut in on,' a cognate of the verb κόπτω, 'to cut.' In v. 12, Paul will use the verb ἀποκόπτω, 'to cut away,' in connection with the caricature of circumcision as a form of castration" (De Boer, *Galatians*, 320).

19. "As often in Paul, 'call' has the sense of God's effectual call, his powerful reaching out to bring people into relationship with himself" (Moo, *Galatians*, 334). "God (through Paul's letter) is now calling them again (cf. 4:19)" (De Boer, *Galatians*, 321). "The God who has powerfully called the Galatians to faith is not, Paul affirms, speaking through the opponents" (Schreiner, *Galatians*, 324).

with a proverbial aphorism Paul warns that "a little yeast leavens the whole batch of dough" (5:9). In other words, even a slight persuasion from only a single individual (a little leaven) can lead the whole Galatian audience away from the truth of the gospel.[20] Paul's warning that a little yeast leavens the "whole" (ὅλον) batch of dough reaffirms, by way of a subtle irony, his warning that every human being who has himself circumcised is obligated to do the "whole" (ὅλον) law (5:3).

In contrast to the Galatians, who are being "persuaded" away from the truth (5:7), a "persuasion" not from the God who calls them (5:8), Paul (referring to himself with an emphatic "I") is "persuaded" regarding them, as they are now living within the realm established by the risen Lord, that they will think "nothing" otherwise (5:10a).[21] In other words, they should not think of having themselves circumcised; otherwise, Christ will benefit them "nothing" (5:2). The one "troubling" the Galatians, one among those "troubling" them by wanting to distort the gospel of Christ (1:7), will bear the condemnation (5:10b), which recalls that anyone who preaches to them a different gospel is to be accursed (1:8–9).[22] "Whoever" (ὅστις) this one troubling them may be (5:10c), he is responsible for persuading the Galatians, "who" (οἵτινες) are trying to be justified by the law (5:4) rather than from the faith by which we believers await the eschatological life that is the hope of justification (5:5).

After referring to himself again with the emphatic pronoun—"but as for *me*" (5:11a), Paul directly addresses the Galatians as "brothers," his fellow believers, as he begins to underline his contrast to the one who is troubling the Galatians (5:10) by persuading them to be circumcised. If Paul is "still" (ἔτι) "proclaiming" circumcision (5:11b), and thus "still" (ἔτι) pleasing human beings rather than God (1:10), why is he still being persecuted

---

20. "In this case the 'leaven' may be the doctrine taught by the false teachers, but considering the personal focus of this paragraph, it more likely refers to the false teachers themselves" (Moo, *Galatians*, 334).

21. "Paul's robust confidence over the final outcome finds its ultimate basis 'in the Lord,' in Christ, not in the situation in Galatia at the present moment" (De Boer, *Galatians*, 321). "Paul's expression of confidence is undoubtedly sincerely meant. Yet rhetorically this expression functions also to motivate the Galatians to live up to the confidence that Paul has in them" (Moo, *Galatians*, 335).

22. "There was surely more than one troublemaker, despite the generic singular in 5:10 . . . Paul's vague references to the Agitators were probably rhetorically motivated. Both he and the Galatians knew who they were. By refusing to name them, he added insult to his condemnation of their actions" (Lyons, *Galatians*, 317).

(5:11c)?²³ But Paul already clarified that the gospel he "proclaims" among the gentiles (2:2) does not include a requirement for gentiles to be circumcised (2:3). That Paul is still being "persecuted" recalls and reaffirms that, just as the one born according to the flesh (Ishmael) "persecuted" the one according to the Spirit (Isaac) then, so also now (4:29). The Paul who once "persecuted" the church of God (1:13, 23) is now being persecuted for proclaiming the gospel that does not require gentiles to be circumcised to be members of the church of God.

If Paul is still proclaiming the need for believers to be circumcised, then the stumbling block or offense of the cross—namely, that one is not justified from works of the law, which include circumcision, but through faith in the Jesus Christ (2:16) who was publicly proclaimed before the eyes of the Galatians as crucified (3:1)—has been "removed" (5:11d).²⁴ This reinforces for the Galatians that, if they are trying to be justified by the law, they have been "removed" from Christ (5:4). Then, in a rather stunning and sarcastic outburst, Paul exclaims his wish that those disturbing the Galatians by persuading them to be circumcised might also go so far as to castrate themselves (5:12). Since those disturbing the Galatians are those who "hindered" or, literally, "cut in on" (ἐνέκοψεν) the Galatians by persuading them away from the truth (5:7) that they need not have their foreskins cut off by circumcision, they should rather "castrate" or, literally, "cut off" (ἀποκόψονται) themselves.²⁵

With an emphatic "you," Paul again addresses his brother Galatians and reminds them that they were "called," by the God who "calls" them (5:8) to the truth (5:7), to "freedom," but they are not to use this "freedom"

---

23. "Circumcision may once have played a significant role in his life and thought, but it does so no longer, despite what the new preachers are saying" (De Boer, *Galatians*, 323). See also Hardin, "If I Still Proclaim Circumcision," 145–63. "Paul presupposed a twofold contrast between himself and the Agitators. He did not require circumcision as a condition for salvation; they did. He was being persecuted; they were not (see 6:12)" (Lyons, *Galatians*, 318).

24. "In Paul's view, the cross, or Christ crucified, is an offense not in some general sense but specifically to Jews, including Christian Jews such as the new preachers in Galatia, because it has (in Paul's understanding of the gospel) effected the destruction of the law as the reliable basis for justification and life" (De Boer, *Galatians*, 323–24).

25. "The verb ἀποκόπτω means simply 'cut off' or 'cut away,' but it is sometimes used absolutely with 'private parts' implied . . . Paul might also be wishing that the agitators would separate themselves from the Christian community" (Moo, *Galatians*, 337–38). "Those who are so taken with circumcision as a means to enter the people of God are actually cutting themselves off from God's people" (Schreiner, *Galatians*, 327).

as an opportunity for the flesh (5:13a).[26] This reaffirms that for "freedom" Christ set us believers free, so that the Galatians are to stand firm and not be subjected again to the yoke of slavery (5:1) by having themselves circumcised (5:2).[27] That they are not to use their freedom as an opportunity for the "flesh" carries literal and metaphorical connotations. They are not to use their freedom to cut off the literal flesh of their foreskins by having themselves circumcised.[28] If they do so, they who have begun to live within the realm of the Spirit would be ending by returning to the realm of the "flesh" (3:3; 4:29) as a metaphor for the present evil age, from which Christ freed us (1:4) for an eschatological life in the new and final age begun by the death and resurrection of Jesus Christ (1:1). Indeed, the risen Christ lives in every believer, who, while living in "flesh," lives an eschatological life in faith already (2:20a).

Rather, through "love," the "love" through which faith works (5:6d), the Galatians are to be slaves to one another (5:13b). The faith by which they as believers live an eschatological life is faith in the Son of God, who "loved" and gave himself up in a self-sacrificial death for Paul and every believer (2:20b).[29] If the Galatians subject themselves again to the yoke of "slavery [δουλείας]" (5:1) by being circumcised (5:2), it would mean wanting "to be slaves" (δουλεύειν) again of the weak and destitute elemental powers (4:9), the false gods which they once worshiped when "you were slaves" (ἐδουλεύσατε) to them (4:8).[30] Instead, the Galatians are "to be slaves" (δουλεύετε) to one another through the kind of self-sacrificial love

26. "The pronoun ὑμεῖς ('you') is emphatic and serves to distinguish the Galatians from those who are disturbing them (v. 12); while the agitators urge circumcision, the Galatians were called to freedom" (Matera, *Galatians*, 192).

27. "There is a warning in Gal 5:13 that the freedom afforded by rectification not be used as an 'opportunity for the flesh.' The wider context of Galatians, the call to freedom in 5:1 and the association in 5:2–4 of circumcision with legal observance suggest that flesh here denotes the decision to be circumcised and embrace Torah" (Boakye, *Death and Life*, 162).

28. "For the Galatians to yield to the Agitators' demands to be circumcised would be to give *the flesh* an opportunity. Paul insisted that no mark in human flesh justified boastful self-confidence that one was a member of the covenant community" (Lyons, *Galatians*, 326–27; emphasis original).

29. "The term 'love' in 5:6 functions as it does in 2:20, where Paul lives by faith in the son of God who *loved him. It is within the context of Jesus' loving act of self-giving that believers' faith 'works'* (Boakye, *Death and Life*, 200; emphases original).

30. "In the context of this letter, freedom means liberation from the powers of the old age: sin, the 'elements of the world,' false gods, and especially the law" (Moo, *Galatians*, 343).

they received from Christ.[31] Then, by not pleasing the human beings who are persuading them to be circumcised, they would, like Paul, be a "slave" (δοῦλος) of Christ and please God (1:10), and thus live to and for God (2:19), engaging in an ethical worship for eschatological life by becoming slaves to one another through a Christ-like self-sacrificial love.[32]

SUMMARY ON GALATIANS 5:1-13

With his authority as an apostle (5:2a), Paul tells the Galatians that if they have themselves "circumcised," the Christ who freed them as gentiles (5:1) from the requirement to be "circumcised" (2:3) will benefit them nothing (5:2b). Indeed, Paul testifies again to every human being who has himself circumcised that, rather than one whom Christ "will benefit," he will become one "obligated" "to do" the whole law (5:3). Paul thus reiterates the scriptural testimony that everyone who does not remain in all the things written in the book of the law is cursed "to do" them (3:10).

Paul warns the Galatians that if they are trying to be "justified" by the law, then they have been separated from Christ (5:4a), since a human being is not "justified" from works of the law but through faith in Jesus Christ (2:16; cf. 3:24). And then they will have fallen from "grace" (5:4b), which recalls that Paul does not reject the "grace" of God; for if justification is through the law, then Christ died to no purpose (2:21). It also recalls Paul's amazement that the Galatians are so quickly turning away from the God who called them in the "grace" of Christ for a different gospel (1:6). In trying to be justified by the law, the Galatians would fall from the "grace" given to them as believers by the Lord Jesus Christ (1:3), who, as part of this grace, "gave" himself for our sins, that he might free us from the mortality of the present evil age (1:4). And they would fall from the "grace" given to

---

31. "There can be no doubt that Paul has consciously created a paradox here, since he represents this δουλεία not as the antithesis of freedom but as its necessary outworking" (Barclay, *Obeying the Truth*, 109). "Freedom from the enslavement of Torah paradoxically means to take on a new form of 'slavery'—that of loving servanthood to one another" (Fee, *God's Empowering Presence*, 426).

32. "Believers must imitate the sacrificial love of Christ for mankind, demonstrated through his crucifixion, in their love for one another. It is this intra-community devotion that Paul describes as mutual enslavement (Gal 5:13c)" (Boakye, *Death and Life*, 201). "The life of freedom in Christ is a life of obedience and self-sacrifice... But in identifying with Christ's cross and resurrection, the Christian dies and rises to a life that is reoriented toward God" (Oakes, *Galatians*, 170).

them as believers by God our Father (1:3), who raised Jesus Christ from the dead, which gives us, as part of this grace, the promise of an eschatological life.

With an emphatic "we," Paul invites the Galatians to join him in confessing that we believers by the "Spirit" and from our "faith," and thus not from the law (5:4), await the hope of "justification" (5:5). This means that we believers await the eternal eschatological life that is the object of the hope promised by our being justified from faith. This resonates with the promise of eschatological life, which is to be brought about by the "Spirit," that we believers might receive through our "faith" (3:14), which accords with the promise that the "just one" from "faith" will live (3:11). There is no hope of an eschatological life for those who are trying to be justified by doing the law (5:3-4), since the law is unable to give life, otherwise "justification" would indeed be from the law (3:21). But the scripture confined all things under the power of sin, that the promise of an eschatological life from "faith" in Jesus Christ might be given to those who believe (3:22).

In contrast to the Galatians, who are being "persuaded" away from the truth (5:7)—a "persuasion" not from the God who calls them (5:8)—Paul, referring to himself with an emphatic "I," is "persuaded" regarding them, as they are now living within the realm established by the risen Lord, that they will think "nothing" otherwise (5:10a). In other words, they should not think of having themselves circumcised, otherwise Christ will benefit them "nothing" (5:2). The one "troubling" the Galatians, one among those "troubling" them by wanting to distort the gospel of Christ (1:7), will bear the condemnation (5:10b), which recalls that anyone who preaches a different gospel to them is to be accursed (1:8-9). "Whoever" this one troubling them may be (5:10c), he is responsible for persuading the Galatians, "who" are trying to be justified by the law (5:4), rather than from the faith by which we believers await the eschatological life that is the hope of justification (5:5).

If Paul is still proclaiming the need for believers to be circumcised, then the stumbling block or offense of the cross—namely, that one is not justified from works of the law, which include circumcision, but through faith in the Jesus Christ (2:16), who was publicly proclaimed as crucified before the eyes of the Galatians (3:1)—has been "removed" (5:11d). This reinforces for the Galatians that, if they are trying to be justified by the law, they have been "removed" from Christ (5:4). Then, in a rather stunning and sarcastic outburst, Paul exclaims his wish that those disturbing the Galatians by persuading them to be circumcised might also go so far as to castrate themselves (5:12). Since those disturbing the Galatians are those who "hindered" or, literally, "cut in on" the Galatians by persuading them away from the truth (5:7) that they need not have their foreskins cut off by circumcision, they should rather "castrate" or, literally, "cut off" themselves.

With an emphatic "you," Paul again addresses his brother Galatians and reminds them that they were "called," by the God who "calls" them (5:8) to the truth (5:7), to "freedom," but they are not to use this "freedom" as an opportunity for the flesh (5:13a). This reaffirms that it is for "freedom" that Christ set us believers free, so that the Galatians are to stand firm and not be subjected to the yoke of slavery again (5:1) by having themselves circumcised (5:2). That they are not to use their freedom as an opportunity for the "flesh" carries literal and metaphorical connotations. They are not to use their freedom to cut off the literal flesh of their foreskins by having themselves circumcised. If they do so, they who have begun to live within the realm of the Spirit would be ending by returning to the realm of the "flesh" (3:3; 4:29) as a metaphor for the present evil age, from which Christ freed us (1:4), for an eschatological life in the new and final age begun by the death and resurrection of Jesus Christ (1:1). Indeed, the risen Christ lives in every believer who, while living in "flesh," already lives an eschatological life in faith (2:20a).

Through "love," the "love" through which faith works (5:6d), the Galatians are to be slaves to one another (5:13b). The faith by which they as believers live an eschatological life is faith in the Son of God who "loved" and gave himself up in a self-sacrificial death for Paul and every believer (2:20b). If the Galatians subject themselves again to the yoke of "slavery" (5:1) by being circumcised (5:2), it would mean wanting "to be slaves" again of the weak and destitute elemental powers (4:9), the false gods which they once worshiped when "you were slaves" to them (4:8). Instead, the Galatians are "to be slaves" to one another through the kind of self-sacrificial love they received from Christ. Then, by not pleasing the human beings who are persuading them to be circumcised, they would, like Paul, be a "slave" of Christ and please God (1:10), and thus live to and for God (2:19), engaging in an ethical worship for eschatological life by becoming slaves to one another through a Christ-like self-sacrificial love.

13

Galatians 5:14–26

THE FLESH IS OPPOSED TO THE SPIRIT WHOSE FRUIT INCLUDES FAITH

If we live by the Spirit, the Spirit let us also follow

A ¹⁴For all the law is fulfilled in one statement, namely, "You shall love your neighbor as yourself" [Lev 19:18]. ¹⁵But if you go on biting and devouring *one another*, beware that you are not consumed by *one another*. ¹⁶But I say, walk by the Spirit and you will not bring to an end the *desire* of the flesh. ¹⁷For the flesh *desires* against the Spirit, and the Spirit against the flesh, for these are opposed to *one another*, so that you may not do the things you want. ¹⁸But if you are led by the Spirit, you are not under the law.

    B ¹⁹The works of the flesh *are* evident, whatever *is* sexual immorality, impurity, licentiousness, ²⁰idolatry, sorcery, hostilities, enmities, strife, jealousy, rages, rivalries, dissensions, factions, ²¹ᵃenvies, drunkenness, orgies, and similar things,

        C ²¹ᵇwhich things *I warn* you,

        C' ²¹ᶜas *I warned* before,

    B' ²¹ᵈthat those who practice such things will not inherit the kingdom of God! ²²But the fruit of the Spirit *is* love, joy, peace, patience, kindness, generosity, faith, ²³humility, self-control; such things the law *is* not against.

A' ²⁴Those who belong to Christ Jesus have crucified the flesh with its passions and *desires*. ²⁵If we live by the Spirit, the Spirit let us also follow. ²⁶Let us not become conceited, provoking *one another*, envying *one another*.¹

5:14–18 (A): *If you are led by the Spirit, you are not under the law*

The A element (5:14–18) of this chiastic unit forms a chiastic pattern in itself:

a) ¹⁴For all the *law* is fulfilled in one statement, namely, "You shall love your neighbor as yourself" [Lev 19:18]. ¹⁵But if you go on biting and devouring *one another*, beware that you are not consumed by *one another*.

  b) ¹⁶But I say, walk by the Spirit and you will not bring to an end the *desire* of the *flesh*.

  b') ¹⁷ᵃFor the *flesh desires* against the Spirit, and the Spirit against the *flesh*,

a') ¹⁷ᵇfor these are opposed to *one another*, so that you may not do the things you want. ¹⁸But if you are led by the Spirit, you are not under the *law*.

At the center of this chiastic subunit is a pivot of parallels from "desire" in 5:16 to "desires" in 5:17a and from "flesh" in 5:16 to "flesh" (twice) in 5:17a. Chiastic parallels progress from "law" in 5:14 to "law" in 5:18 and from "one another" (twice) in 5:15 to "one another" in 5:17b.

Whereas everyone who is circumcised is obligated to do the "whole" (ὅλον) law (5:3), "all" (πᾶσιν) the things written in it (3:10), "all" (πᾶς) the law is fulfilled in the one statement, the command that "you shall love your neighbor as yourself" (5:14; cf. Lev 19:18).² All the law is not merely done or observed, but "is fulfilled" eschatologically by the self-sacrificial love of the crucified Christ (2:19–20).³ This scriptural command reinforces Paul's

---

1. For the establishment of Gal 5:14–26 as a chiasm, see chapter 1 of this book.

2. "The text [Lev 19:18] does not suggest that human beings need to learn to love themselves before they can love others. Instead, it *assumes* that we love ourselves, in that we invariably seek our own interests. Love, then, seeks out the interests of others and pursues their best" (Schreiner, *Galatians*, 335; emphasis original).

3. The significance of the verb "is fulfilled" (πεπλήρωται) in the NT "suggests that it is not referring simply to obedience to the law, but to an eschatological completion

exhortation for the Galatians to be slaves to one another through "love" (5:13), the "love" through which faith works (5:6), the self-sacrificial love exemplified by the Son of God who "loved" Paul, and every believer in being crucified for us (2:20). But if the Galatians go on metaphorically biting and devouring "one another" like animals, presumably over the contentious and divisive issue of whether they need to be circumcised and observe the law, they should beware that they are not consumed by "one another" (5:15), rather than being slaves to "one another" through self-sacrificial love (5:13).[4]

Paul is telling the Galatians to "walk" (that is, to conduct their lives) by the Spirit, and they will not bring the desire of the flesh to an end (5:16). If they live now by the "Spirit," they will begin to live the future eschatological life that is the promise of the "Spirit" (3:14), and that by the "Spirit" they await as the hope of justification from faith (5:5), the faith working through their love (5:6). Living by the Spirit promises that "you will never bring to an end [τελέσητε]" or fulfill the desire of the "flesh."[5] It means a negative answer to Paul's previous question, whether, having begun with the "Spirit," now "are you ending" (ἐπιτελεῖσθε) with the "flesh"? (3:3). And it reinforces Paul's exhortation for them not to use their freedom as an opportunity for the "flesh" by being circumcised and becoming slaves under the law, but rather through self-sacrificial love to be slaves to one another (5:13). They will then be able to join Paul in declaring that the risen Christ lives in them, and insofar as they live in "flesh," they live an eschatological life in faith

---

of the law . . . the implied agent of the passive verb is Jesus Christ, who 'fulfills' the whole law . . . by going to the cross as the ultimate embodiment and pattern of sacrificial love . . . The Galatians are to serve one another 'in love' precisely because love is the true meaning and 'fulfillment' of the law in this new era" (Moo, *Galatians*, 347-48). "Love does duty instead of many of the specific commands, which the Galatians need not keep. The gentile Christians should love and need not circumcise, nor observe calendrical festivals, and so on" (Oakes, *Galatians*, 171).

4. "The division within the Galatian communities on circumcision and the Law had created a factious situation" (Lyons, *Galatians*, 331). "The world without love, Paul implies, is a dog-eat-dog world. Paul assumes that the Galatians will not want to be part of that world" (De Boer, *Galatians*, 351).

5. "The emphatic subjunctive clause ('you will never fulfill,' [οὐ μὴ τελέσητε]) should not be construed as an imperative here but as a promise" (Schreiner, *Galatians*, 343). "This way of putting things emphasizes that living life in the Spirit does not prevent one from having fleshly desires, but it does give one the power to avoid acting on these desires and so bringing them to completion" (Witherington, *Grace in Galatia*, 393).

in the Son of God who loved them and gave himself up in death for them (2:20).[6]

Since the realms of the flesh and of the Spirit are diametrically opposed to "one another," the Galatians may not do the things "you want [θέλητε]" (5:17).[7] If they give opportunity to the flesh regarding the issue of circumcision, they may not be able to be slaves to "one another" through love (5:13), but rather may be biting and devouring "one another," so that they are consumed by "one another" (5:15). If they conduct their lives by the Spirit, they may not be "under the law," as they are "wanting [θέλοντες]" (4:21).[8] Indeed, if they are led by the Spirit, they are not "under the law" (5:18).[9] This reminds them that the Son of God, born "under the law" (4:4), redeemed those "under the law," that they might receive sonship (4:5) and thus become heirs of eschatological life according to the promise for it (3:11, 29). If they are led by the Spirit, who brings to fulfillment the promise of eschatological life for those justified by faith (3:11, 14; 5:5), they are no longer held in custody "under the law" (3:23), the law that is not able to give eschatological life (3:21).[10]

5:19-23 (B-C-C'-B'): The flesh is destructive, but the Spirit gives life

By referring to the behavior that results from the desire of the flesh (5:17-18) as "the works of the flesh" (5:19), Paul closely associates, without

6. The terms "'flesh' and 'Spirit' are first of all eschatological realities, denoting the essential characteristic of the two ages, before and after Christ . . . Hence the ultimate contrasts in Paul are eschatological: life 'according to the flesh,' lived according to the present age that has been condemned through the cross and is passing away, or life 'according to the Spirit,' lived in keeping with the values and norms of the coming age inaugurated by Christ through his death and resurrection and empowered by the eschatological Spirit" (Fee, *God's Empowering Presence*, 430-31).

7. "Even though Christians enjoy the life of the age to come through the Holy Spirit, a battle with the flesh remains" (Schreiner, *Galatians*, 343-44).

8. That the verb "want" (θέλω) occurs successively in Gal 4:21 and 5:17 enhances this connection.

9. "Paul's point is that Christians, precisely because they are under the influence of the Spirit, are members of the new-covenant era in which the law of Moses no longer has binding authority" (Moo, *Galatians*, 357).

10. For Paul, "the Spirit is the principal evidence of this new eschatological existence that 'eagerly awaits' its consummation (Gal 5:5)" (Fee, *God's Empowering Presence*, 438). "In 5:18 Paul wishes to convey that the Spirit-led ones are not led by the external Torah. It is precisely because the Spirit gives the risen life to those who are of Christ that the Spirit should steer our conduct" (Boakye, *Death and Life*, 165).

equating, them with "the works of the law" (2:16; 3:2, 5, 10), the law that is not able to give life (3:21).[11] Some of the works of the flesh (sexual immorality, impurity, licentiousness, idolatry, sorcery, drunkenness, orgies in 5:19-21a) remind the audience of their idolatrous past (4:8-9), whereas the others (hostilities, enmities, strife, jealousy, rages, rivalries, dissensions, factions, envies in 5:20-21a) resonate with their present self-destructive behavior (5:15).[12] Paul repeats and thus reinforces his previous warning as he now warns the Galatians again that those who practice such things will not "inherit" (κληρονομήσουσιν) the kingdom of God (5:21). This means that they will not be "heirs" (κληρονόμοι) of eternal life, the eschatological life of the new age that is synonymous with the kingdom of God inaugurated when God raised Jesus Christ from the dead (1:1, 4), according to the promise (3:29) for it (3:11).[13]

In contrast to the flesh whose desires result in destructive, deadly works (5:19-21), the Spirit produces life-giving fruit, first and preeminently love, along with various specifications or aspects of love—joy, peace, patience, kindness, generosity, faith, humility, and self-control (5:22-23a).[14] This is

---

11. "This is not to suggest that Paul saw similarity between these two kinds of 'works.' Rather, by means of word association, he is reminding the Galatians that *both categories of 'work'* (religious observance and sins of the flesh) *belong to the past* for those who are in Christ and now walk by the Spirit" (Fee, *God's Empowering Presence*, 441; emphases original). "Through his choice of words Paul, here as elsewhere in Galatians, intimates an unholy alliance between the Flesh and the law. The 'works of the law,' instead of being the solution to 'the works of the Flesh,' are (inadvertently) part of the problem" (De Boer, *Galatians*, 357).

12. "I am suggesting then that we have a list that has an A, B, A pattern and the A has to do with sins associated with the audience's pagan past. The B list, however, found in vss. 20-21, has to do with the sins against the community of faith ... While the A list focuses on the sins of the past, the B list focuses on sins of the present or potentially the future if the agitators' agendas are followed. Paul wishes his community of converts to be like neither the community centered on the pagan temple nor the community centered upon the Mosaic Law. Rather they are to be a community centered on Christ and in the Spirit" (Witherington, *Grace in Galatia*, 399-400). For a detailed description of each of the various works listed, see Lyons, *Galatians*, 341-45.

13. "Paul regards 'the kingdom of God' as the alternative for 'corruption'; in Gal 6:8, he so regards 'eternal life.' The kingdom of God is thus the realm of 'eternal life.' The works of the Flesh have no place there, and those who 'practice' them will not inherit it" (De Boer, *Galatians*, 361). "To inherit the kingdom of God meant to participate in the future resurrection ... The Spirit assures us that we will inherit the 'new creation' and the eternal life (see Gal 6:8, 15; see 2 Cor 5:17) of the resurrection body in the future" (Lyons, *Galatians*, 346-47).

14. "Love, as loving action, is the singular fruit of the Spirit, with the remaining

the kind of love that serves as an antidote to the self-destructive behavior of the Galatians (5:15) caused by the controversy over circumcision, which involves the flesh.[15] It is the love through which the Galatians are to be slaves to one another (5:13), the love through which "faith" (πίστις) works (5:6), the "faith" (πίστις) that accompanies love as the fruit of the Spirit (5:22), the Spirit they received from the hearing of "faith [πίστεως]" (3:2, 5).[16] And it is the love by which "you shall love your neighbor as yourself" (5:14), the command of the law that Christ brought to its eschatological fulfillment when he loved Paul and every believer by giving himself up in a self-sacrificial death, so that every believer may now begin to live the eschatological life of the risen Christ (2:20) by imitating Christ's self-sacrificial love (5:6, 13).

In contrast to "such things [τοιαῦτα]" (5:21d) as the works of the flesh (5:19-21a), "such things" (τοιούτων) as the fruit of the Spirit the "law" (νόμος) is not "against [κατά]" (5:23b). This recalls that, although the "law" (νόμος) is not "against" (κατά) the promises, preeminent of which is the promise of eschatological life (3:11), the law is not able to give eschatological life (3:21).[17] Similarly, although the law is not against such things as the fruit of the Spirit, it is not able to produce the fruit that the Spirit produces in actualizing the promise of eschatological life (3:14).[18] Whereas those

---

'virtues' describing the socially discernible and relevant circumstances, dispositions, and character traits that accompany love . . . the Spirit creates the condition (freedom from the law, from Sin, from the elements of the world) in which truly responsible loving action can in fact take place. Such responsible loving action can thus be understood as the fruit of the Spirit" (De Boer, *Galatians*, 364).

15. "The headline placement of 'love' in the list of the Spirit's fruit is due both to the centrality of love within the new-covenant ethics and because it is the most important bulwark against the factional infighting that seems to be racking the Galatian churches (see v. 15)" (Moo, *Galatians*, 364).

16. Paul includes "faith" in the list "in order to reinforce the central and immediate link (for him) between the Spirit and faith. Just as it was through (hearing with) faith that they received the Spirit, so his readers should recognize that the fruit of the Spirit is not something other than that same faith. What the Spirit produces is . . . the continued expression of that same faith which they as Gentiles had first experienced and exercised when they responded to the gospel Paul had preached" (Dunn, *Epistle to the Galatians*, 311).

17. "The fruit of the Spirit is not a matter of legal prescription. Paul's peculiar use of the preposition 'against' (κατά + genitive) sharpens the point, especially if Paul intends an allusion back to 3:21, where he has emphatically claimed that the law is *not* 'against [κατά + genitive] the promises of God'" (De Boer, *Galatians*, 366; emphasis original).

18. "Paul could mean that no law prohibits the fruit of the Spirit, and hence no one

who practice "such things" as the works of the flesh will not inherit the eschatological life of the kingdom of God (5:21d), if the Galatians and all believers walk by the Spirit (5:16) and are led by the Spirit (5:18) to practice "such things" as the fruit of the Spirit, they will inherit the eschatological life of the kingdom of God. Indeed, by practicing such things as the fruit of the Spirit, preeminent of which is self-sacrificial love, believers already begin to experience and live the eschatological life that is the promise of the Spirit (3:14).

5:24-26 (A'): We live by the Spirit we are to follow

As those who are of Christ Jesus, who are heirs of eschatological life according to the promise (3:29) for it (3:11), the Galatians have crucified the flesh with its passions and desires (5:24). As those who, like Paul, have been "crucified with" Christ (2:19), so that the risen Christ lives in them (2:20), the Galatians have "crucified" the flesh. They have thus put to death, in accord with the death of the crucified Christ, the flesh with its "desires," the "desires" that are against the Spirit (5:16-17).[19] If we believers "live" by the Spirit, as those who begin to fulfill the promise that the just one from faith "will live" (3:11) ethically and eschatologically, then let us follow the lead of the Spirit (5:25).[20] The Spirit leads (5:18) those who walk by it (5:16)

---

can find fault with such virtues. Or, perhaps the point is that the law can never produce these godly qualities, but such is the result of the Spirit's work . . . The Spirit, then, produces fruit that the law cannot create" (Schreiner, *Galatians*, 350).

19. "The use of the verb 'crucify' is here decisive. It clearly points to Christ's rectifying death on the cross on their behalf. In being crucified with Christ (cf. 2:19; 6:14), the Galatian believers can be said to have crucified the Flesh, precisely as faithful participants in Christ's faithful death" (De Boer, *Galatians*, 367). "The active voice of the verb *crucified* emphasizes that believers assume personal responsibility to put an end to the rule of Flesh over their conduct" (Lyons, *Galatians*, 357; emphasis original). "The passions and desires of the flesh are not absent, but they no longer rule and reign. Those who walk by the Spirit and who are led by the Spirit find themselves, even though imperfectly and partially, triumphing over the passions of the flesh that formerly dominated them" (Schreiner, *Galatians*, 351).

20. "The verb 'to live' in v. 25a is being used ethically, as a synonym of the verb 'to walk' (cf. v. 16), and denotes a manner of conduct or existence (cf. 2:14, 19-20; 3:11-12). Because it concerns life by (and thus also in) the Spirit, that manner of conduct or existence has an eschatological dimension; it entails new life, the life of the age inaugurated by Christ. Its defining characteristic is 'being slaves of one another in love' (v. 13; cf. vv. 14, 22)" (De Boer, *Galatians*, 370). "The word 'live' (ζῶμεν) refers to eschatological life that now belongs to believers" (Schreiner, *Galatians*, 356). "This Spirit-initiated life is the

to practice the self-sacrificial love that is the preeminent fruit of the Spirit (5:22) as the ethical worship by which every believer might "live" to and for God (2:19). Along with Paul, every believer who follows the Spirit may now "live" the eschatological life of the risen Christ by faith in the Son of God who loved and gave himself up for Paul and all of us (2:20).[21]

Paul exhorts the Galatians and all believers not to become conceited, provoking "one another," or envying "one another" (5:26), as envy is one of the works of the flesh (5:21a).[22] This reinforces Paul's warning that, if they go on biting and devouring "one another," they are to beware that they are not self-destructively consumed by "one another" (5:15). It reminds them that they are not to use their freedom in Christ as an opportunity for the flesh, but to be slaves to "one another" through self-sacrificial love (5:13), and thus live a life that amounts to ethical worship pleasing to God (2:19). Thereby, as those who walk by the Spirit (5:16) and are led by the Spirit (5:18), they will follow the lead of the Spirit as those who, by the Spirit, have already begun to live the eternal, eschatological life (5:25) that we believers by the Spirit, from faith, await as the hope of justification (5:5).[23]

SUMMARY ON GALATIANS 5:14–26

Since the realms of the flesh and of the Spirit are diametrically opposed to "one another," the Galatians may not do the things "you want" (5:17). If they give opportunity to the flesh regarding the issue of circumcision, they

---

revivified eschatological life celebrated in 3:10–13; it is a new sphere and expression of existence and identity in Christ" (Boakye, *Death and Life*, 164).

21. "Galatians 5:24–25 for the second time in the letter draws together the themes of crucifixion, life and Spirit, which first arose in 2:19–3:5. Once again Spirit initiates life in those co-crucified with Jesus—in Gal 5:24, this is crucifixion of flesh. They are a new people whose identity and social praxis has a new index—Spirit" (Boakye, *Death and Life*, 184–85).

22. "The charge to resist indulging in empty glory (Gal 5:26) quite likely addresses those most impressed upon by the agitators. Perhaps, having been convinced that circumcision was significant, they believed themselves to be more authentic children of Abraham than those uncircumcised, provoking the uncircumcised and instigating a misplaced envy in them (5:26)" (Boakye, *Death and Life*, 182).

23. "The Spirit is God's effective response to the problem of the flesh, whose reign was brought to an end through Christ and whose effect in the believer is negated by the empowering of the Spirit. But what Christ and the Spirit have effected, the believer must actively participate in—by walking by, and behaving in keeping with, the Spirit" (Fee, *God's Empowering Presence*, 458).

may not be able to be slaves to "one another" through love (5:13), but rather may be biting and devouring "one another," so that they are consumed by "one another" (5:15). If they conduct their lives by the Spirit, they may not be "under the law," as they are "wanting" (4:21). Indeed, if they are led by the Spirit, they are not "under the law" (5:18). This reminds them that the Son of God, born "under the law" (4:4), redeemed those "under the law," that they might receive sonship (4:5) and thus become heirs of eschatological life according to the promise for it (3:11, 29). If they are led by the Spirit who brings to fulfillment the promise of eschatological life for those justified by faith (3:11, 14; 5:5), they are no longer held in custody "under the law" (3:23), the law that is not able to give eschatological life (3:21).

In contrast to the flesh whose desires result in destructive, deadly works (5:19–21), the Spirit produces life-giving fruit, first and preeminently love, along with various specifications or aspects of love—joy, peace, patience, kindness, generosity, faith, gentleness, and self-control (5:22–23a). This is the kind of love that serves as an antidote to the self-destructive behavior of the Galatians (5:15) caused by the controversy over circumcision, which involves the flesh. It is the love through which the Galatians are to be slaves to one another (5:13), the love through which "faith" works (5:6), the "faith" that accompanies love as the fruit of the Spirit (5:22), the Spirit they received from the hearing of "faith" (3:2, 5). And it is the love by which "you shall love your neighbor as yourself" (5:14), the command of the law that Christ brought to its eschatological fulfillment when he loved Paul and every believer by giving himself up in a self-sacrificial death, so that every believer may now begin to live the eschatological life of the risen Christ (2:20) by imitating Christ's self-sacrificial love (5:6, 13).

As those who are of Christ Jesus, who are heirs of eschatological life according to the promise (3:29) for it (3:11), the Galatians have crucified the flesh with its passions and desires (5:24). As those who, like Paul, have been "crucified with" Christ (2:19), so that the risen Christ lives in them (2:20), the Galatians have "crucified" the flesh. They have thus put to death, in accord with the death of the crucified Christ, the flesh with its "desires," the "desires" that are against the Spirit (5:16–17). If we believers "live" by the Spirit, as those who begin to fulfill the promise that the just one from faith "will live" (3:11) ethically and eschatologically, then let us follow the lead of the Spirit (5:25). The Spirit leads (5:18) those who walk by it (5:16) to practice the self-sacrificial love that is the preeminent fruit of the Spirit (5:22) as the ethical worship by which every believer might "live" to and for

God (2:19). Along with Paul, every believer who follows the Spirit may now "live" the eschatological life of the risen Christ by faith in the Son of God who loved and gave himself up for Paul and all of us (2:20).

14

Galatians 6:1–18

THE GRACE AND PEACE OF OUR LORD JESUS CHRIST TO THE BROTHERS

For neither circumcision is anything nor uncircumcision but only a new creation

A ¹*Brothers*, if indeed a person is overtaken by some wrongdoing, you who are *Spiritual* correct such a one in a *Spirit* of humility, looking to yourself, so that you also may not be tempted. ²*Bear* the burdens of one another and thus you will completely fulfill the *law* of *Christ*. ³For if anyone thinks he is something when he is nothing, he is deceiving himself. ⁴Let each one examine the work of himself, and then he will have a reason to *boast* with regard to himself *alone* and not with regard to the other. ⁵For each one *will bear* his own load. ⁶Let the one who is being instructed in the word share with the one instructing in all good things. ⁷Do not be led astray; *God* is not mocked, for a person will reap only what he sows, ⁸because the one sowing to the flesh of himself from the flesh will reap destruction, but the one who sows to the *Spirit* from the *Spirit* will reap life eternal.

    B ⁹ªLet us not lose heart in doing what is commendable, for in due *time* we will reap,

        C ⁹ᵇif we do not give up.

B' ¹⁰ So then while we have *time*, let us work the good for all, and especially for those who are members of the household of the faith.

A' ¹¹See with what large letters I am writing to you in my own hand! ¹²As many as want to make a good showing in the flesh, these are forcing you to be circumcised, *only* that for the cross of *Christ* they may not be persecuted. ¹³For those who are circumcised do not keep the *law* themselves but they want you to be circumcised, so that they may *boast* in your flesh. ¹⁴But as for me, may I never *boast* except in the cross of our Lord Jesus *Christ*, through which the world has been crucified to me and I to the world. ¹⁵For neither circumcision is anything nor uncircumcision but only a new creation! ¹⁶And as many as will follow this rule, peace and mercy upon them, that is upon the Israel of *God*. ¹⁷From now on let no one cause me troubles, for I *bear* the marks of Jesus in my body. ¹⁸The grace of our Lord Jesus *Christ* with your *spirit, brothers*. Amen![1]

6:1–8 (A): The one who sows to the Spirit from the Spirit will reap life eternal

The A element (6:1–8) of this chiastic unit forms a chiastic pattern in itself:

a) ¹Brothers, if indeed a *person* is overtaken by some wrongdoing, you who are Spiritual correct such a one in a *Spirit* of humility, looking to yourself, so that you also may not be tempted.

   b) ²*Bear* the burdens of one another and thus you will completely fulfill the law of Christ.

      c) ³For if anyone thinks he is something when he is nothing, he is deceiving *himself*.

      c') ⁴Let each one examine the work of *himself*, and then he will have a reason to boast with regard to *himself* alone and not with regard to the other.

   b') ⁵For each one *will bear* his own load.

a') ⁶Let the one who is being instructed in the word share with the one instructing in all good things. ⁷Do not be led astray; God is not mocked, for a *person* will reap only what he sows,

---

1. For the establishment of Gal 6:1–18 as a chiasm, see chapter 1 of this book.

⁸because the one sowing to the flesh of himself from the flesh will reap destruction, but the one who sows to the *Spirit* from the *Spirit* will reap life eternal.

At the center of this chiastic subunit (6:1–8) is a pivot of parallels from "himself" in 6:3 to "himself" (twice) in 6:4. Chiastic parallels progress from "bear" in 6:2 to "will bear" in 6:5, as well as from "person" in 6:1 to "person" in 6:7 and from "Spirit" in 6:1 to "Spirit" (twice) in 6:8.

Paul again addresses the Galatians as "brothers," his fellow believers, and refers to them as those who are "Spiritual" (6:1a), that is, those who live by and follow the "Spirit" (5:25). If any person among them is overtaken by some wrongdoing, presumably involving the works of the flesh (5:19–21a), they, who are "Spiritual," are to correct such a one in a "Spirit" of "humility [πραΰτητος]" (6:1a), the "humility" (πραΰτης) that is a fruit of the "Spirit" (5:23a).² They are to correct "such a one" (τοιοῦτον) so that he practices "such things [τοιούτων]" (5:23b) as the fruit of the Spirit (5:22–23a), rather than "such things" (τοιαῦτα) as the works of the flesh, by which one will not inherit the kingdom of God, eschatological life (5:21). Each individual among them is to look to "yourself" (σεαυτόν), being careful not to be tempted (6:1b) and risk being similarly overtaken by some wrongdoing rather than living by and following the Spirit. Such careful attention to oneself reminds them that, by correcting the wrongdoing of a fellow believer, they are loving their neighbor as "yourself [σεαυτόν]" (5:14).³

The Galatians are to bear the burdens, presumably including but not limited to correcting the wrongdoings (6:1), of one another, and thus they will completely fulfill the law of Christ (6:2). Rather than provoking "one another," envying "one another" (5:26), biting and devouring "one another," so that they may be consumed by "one another" (5:15), they are to bear the burdens of "one another," and thus through love be slaves to "one another" (5:13).⁴ And thereby "you will completely fulfill" (ἀναπληρώσετε) the law of Christ, the Mosaic law that was redefined by the Christ who loved us

---

2. "Πραΰτης is what is called for—humility toward oneself and considerateness regarding others—and that as the fruit of the Spirit, not some mere human disposition" (Fee, *God's Empowering Presence*, 462). Πραΰτης, "humility" or "gentleness," is "the quality of not being overly impressed by a sense of one's self-importance" (BDAG, 861).

3. "But one who truly loves others and is walking in the Spirit approaches them with firmness (since they have sinned) mingled with humility (so that they are treated gently)" (Schreiner, *Galatians*, 358).

4. "Carrying burdens was predominately if not exclusively the task of slaves in the ancient world" (De Boer, *Galatians*, 376).

by his self-sacrificial death (2:20b), when he demonstrated how "you shall love your neighbor as yourself," the one command by which all the law "is fulfilled" (πεπλήρωται) by Christ (5:14).[5] They need not do, then, all the things written in the law (3:10), in order to live eschatologically (3:12). Rather, as those justified by faith they will live (3:11), and the risen Christ will live in them (2:20a), as they repeat Christ's act of love and thus completely fulfill the law of Christ by loving one another self-sacrificially.[6]

For if anyone of the Galatians thinks he is something for correcting a fellow believer (6:1) but not looking to himself lest he be similarly tempted (6:2), so that he becomes one who is conceited (5:26), when he is nothing, he is deceiving himself (6:3).[7] Let each one examine the "work" of himself (6:4a), the result of faith "working" through love (5:6), the fruit of the Spirit (5:22).[8] Then he will have a reason to boast before God at the final judgment with regard to himself alone and not with regard to the other (6:4b), the neighbor he has loved (5:14) in bearing the burden of another (6:2).[9] He

---

5. With the statement that "you will completely fulfill the law of Christ" (6:2), "Paul is referring to fulfilling the (Mosaic) law τοῦ Χριστοῦ, and the probabilities are that this τοῦ Χριστοῦ means 'the law in its relationship to Christ,' that is, 'the law as redefined and fulfilled by Christ in love'" (Barclay, *Obeying the Truth*, 134). "Thus, 'the law of Christ' is first of all an appeal not to some new act of laws or even to some ethical standards that the gospel imposes on believers, but to Christ himself who in this letter has been deliberately described as the one 'who gave himself for our sins' (1:4) and who 'loved me and gave himself for me' (2:20). Thus, he has already served as the paradigm for the argument in 5:13-14" (Fee, *God's Empowering Presence*, 463).

6. Paul seems to have used the complex form of the verb, "you will completely fulfill" (ἀναπληρώσετε) in 6:2, rather than the simple form "is fulfilled" (πεπλήρωται) as in 5:14, "to give a hint of the motif of repetition . . . Thus, 'Bear one another's burdens, and in this way you yourselves will repeat Christ's deed, bringing to completion in your communities the Law that Christ has already brought to completion in the sentence about loving the neighbor'" (Martyn, *Galatians*, 547-48).

7. "For someone to 'think him or herself to be something [special] while being nothing [special]' is to 'become conceited' (5:26a), which means to indulge in an exaggerated sense of one's own importance" (De Boer, *Galatians*, 381).

8. "This 'work' has to do with living in line with the Spirit (5:25). The believer is to examine closely and critically one's own work for indications of deviation from the Spirit in one's dealings with others in the church . . . The 'work' to which Paul refers is then the fruit of the Spirit" (De Boer, *Galatians*, 382-83). "Those seduced by the troublemakers have engaged in *works* of the Law, but the Spirit has *worked* powerful deeds in the faithful (3:5) and faith *working* through love characterises the new community (5:6)" (Boakye, *Death and Life*, 187; emphases original).

9. "For Paul, the ground for boasting (presumably before God) is the scrutiny of one's own work" (De Boer, *Galatians*, 383). "Based on Rom. 13:8 ('the one who loves the other [ἕτερον] has fulfilled the law') and some other texts, it is possible that ἕτερον here

may not deceive "himself," but examine "himself" and boast with regard to "himself" if his love for the other/neighbor accords with the self-sacrificial love of Christ, who loved and gave "himself" up for the believer (2:20) as the one who gave "himself" for our sins (1:4). For before God, at the final judgment, each one will bear his own load (6:5).[10] He will bear the burden not just of loving the other (6:2), but of looking to (6:1) and examining himself (6:4) as to whether he has self-sacrificially loved his neighbor as himself (5:14).[11]

Each Galatian being instructed in the "word" (λόγον), generally the gospel but more specifically the one statement or "word" (λόγῳ) of the gospel in which the law is fulfilled—"You shall love your neighbor as yourself" (5:14), should share with the one instructing in all good things (6:6). By sharing with the instructor in all "good things" (ἀγαθοῖς), and thus materially supporting him, the one instructed will practice the "generosity" (ἀγαθωσύνη) which is part of the love that is a fruit of the Spirit (5:22).[12] The Galatians are not to be led astray (6:7a) from following the Spirit (5:25). God is not mocked, for a person will reap from God only what he sows to God (6:7b).[13] The one sowing to the flesh of "himself," deceiving "himself" (6:3), especially by having his flesh circumcised or not sharing

---

is equivalent to πλησίον [neighbor]" (Moo, *Galatians*, 380).

10. "[T]he future tense 'will bear' (βαστάσει) suggests that the final judgment is in view. Such an interpretation fits with 6:4 where the future tense also points to the final reward. Furthermore, 6:7–9 clearly refer to the last judgment, and Paul uses the verb 'will bear' (βαστάσει) with reference to the last judgment in 5:10" (Schreiner, *Galatians*, 362).

11. "Paul here uses another word for 'burden' (φορτίον, 'load') . . . Paul's choice of a different term indicates, however, that the (singular) 'load' of v. 5 is not simply equivalent to the (many) 'burdens' of v. 2a. The metaphorical referent is different; it refers . . . to the 'work' (ἔργον) of the believer mentioned in v. 4 . . . Each believer will carry the load of one's own 'work' before God at the last judgment" (De Boer, *Galatians*, 383–84). See also Kuck, "Each Will Bear His Own Burden," 289–97. "Obedience to 'the law of Christ' (v 2) called for the restoration of fallen brothers and sisters (v 1). There was no call for the condemnation, much less one's own self-exaltation at their expense. Those who honestly examine themselves will soon realize that they have little room for arrogance or harsh criticism of others" (Lyons, *Galatians*, 370).

12. "The exhortation of v. 6 is perhaps best understood as a specification of the exhortation to carry one another's burdens . . . Since those giving instruction carry the burden of instructing others in the gospel, the beneficiaries are to carry the burden of supporting those who instruct" (De Boer, *Galatians*, 385).

13. "Paul opts to cite a sowing-reaping metaphor here because it is ostensibly a *dying and rising* metaphor, and *Paul ultimately associates sowing to Spirit with rectification*" (Boakye, *Death and Life*, 189; emphases original).

with an instructor and thus not loving him as himself, will reap destruction (6:8a).[14] But the one who sows to God's Spirit, from the Spirit by which we live (5:25), and by which, from faith working through love (5:6), we await the life that is the hope of justification (5:5), will reap life eternal (6:8; cf. 5:16-17).[15]

6:9-10 (B-C-B'): Do not lose heart in doing what is commendable to reap life eternal

Paul exhorts the Galatians not to lose heart in doing what is commendable, for in due time we believers who sow to the Spirit will reap life eternal (6:8) if we persevere and do not give up (6:9). The Galatians will do what is "commendable" (καλόν) if they practice the love that is the fruit of the Spirit (5:22) and do not allow themselves to be circumcised by following the troublemakers, who are zealous for the Galatians but not "commendably [καλῶς]" (4:17), in contrast to Paul, whose zeal for them is "commendable" (καλόν) in a "commendable" (καλῷ) way (4:18). While we believers have the opportunity, "let us work" (ἐργαζώμεθα) the good for all from our faith "working" (ἐνεργουμένη) through love (5:6), and especially for those who are members of the household of the faith (6:10).[16] Working the good of loving fellow believers as themselves (5:14), all of the Galatian believers, as a worshiping household of the faith, will enable the risen Christ who

---

14. Paul's "use of this agricultural imagery elsewhere suggests that his appeal to it in Gal 6:7 reinforced his appeal for the Galatians to support their teachers in v 6" (Lyons, *Galatians*, 376). "The eschatological coloring of Gal 6:7-8, however, suggests that these verses have more than v. 6 in view. If the Galatians sow to their own flesh, that is, rely upon the mark of circumcision, they will reap corruption" (Matera, *Galatians*, 223). "Though what one does with one's possessions is primarily in view, it seems likely that what Paul says here reflects a wider principle as well, so that sowing to the flesh involves all actions that are evil" (Schreiner, *Galatians*, 369).

15. "The Spirit who gives life (5:25; 2 Cor 3:6) is the same Spirit by whom we await our final hope (5:5) and because of whose presence within/among us we shall also enter into the final consummation of that life ... The Spirit is both the evidence of our having entered into life in the present and the ground and guarantee of our final, full realization of that life" (Fee, *God's Empowering Presence*, 467). "'Eternal life' may here presuppose justification: divine vindication and approval (cf. 2:16d; 5:5: 'the hope of justification')" (De Boer, *Galatians*, 389).

16. "The exhortation to accomplish what is good is thus another way of underlining the importance of love, the firstfruit of the Spirit (5:22; cf. 5:13-14)" (De Boer, *Galatians*, 391).

loved them to live within them (2:20), as they live an eschatological life to and for God (2:19) through their ethical and liturgical worship.[17]

6:11–18 (A'): Neither circumcision nor uncircumcision but only a new creation

The A' element (6:11–18) of this chiastic unit forms a chiastic pattern in itself:

a) [11]See with what large letters I am writing to you in *my* own hand! [12]*As many as* want to make a good showing in the flesh, these are forcing you to be *circumcised*, only that for the *cross* of *Christ* they may not be persecuted. [13a]For those who are *circumcised* do not keep the law themselves but they want you to be *circumcised*,

    b) [13b]so that they may *boast* in your flesh.

    b') [14a]But as for me, may I never *boast*

a') [14b]except in the *cross* of our Lord Jesus *Christ*, through which the world has been crucified to me and I to the world. [15]For neither *circumcision* is anything nor uncircumcision but only a new creation! [16]And *as many as* will follow this rule, peace and mercy upon them, that is upon the Israel of God. [17]From now on let no one cause me troubles, for I bear the marks of Jesus in *my* body. [18]The grace of our Lord Jesus *Christ* with your spirit, brothers. Amen!

At the center of this chiastic subunit (6:11–18) is a pivot of parallels from "boast" in 6:13b to "boast" in 6:14a. Chiastic parallels progress from "my" in 6:11 to "my" in 6:17; from "as many as" in 6:12 to "as many as" in 6:16; from "circumcised" in 6:12 and 13a (twice) to "circumcision" in 6:15; from "cross" in 6:12 to "cross" in 6:14b; and from "Christ" in 6:12 to "Christ" in 6:14b and 18.

The "a" element (6:11–13a) of this chiastic subunit forms a chiastic pattern in itself:

---

17. "Calling the fellowship of believers a 'household' has OT roots and brings to expression one of the key NT images of the church, an extended spiritual family" (Moo, *Galatians*, 389). "Paul's resort to this description may be indebted to the fact that believers in Christ met in houses and that a household not infrequently formed the nucleus of a so-called house church. Various house churches in one city (or region such as Galatia?) might gather in a large house for worship" (De Boer, *Galatians*, 391).

[a] ¹¹See with what large letters I am writing to you in my own hand! ¹²ªAs many as *want* to make a good showing in the flesh, these are forcing you to be *circumcised*,

[b] ¹²ᵇonly that for the cross of Christ they may not be persecuted.

[a'] ¹³ªFor those who are *circumcised* do not keep the law themselves but they *want* you to be *circumcised*.

The statement that "only that for the cross of Christ they may not be persecuted" in 6:12b serves as the unparalleled central and pivotal element of this chiastic subunit. Chiastic parallels progress from "want" in 6:12a to "want" in 6:13a, and from "circumcised" in 6:12a to "circumcised" (twice) in 6:13a.

After having dictated the letter to this point, Paul now dramatically and emphatically draws special attention to its conclusion by writing it himself: "See with what large letters I am writing to you in my own hand!" (6:11).[18] The Galatians are especially to take note that as many as want to make a good showing in the "flesh," not only the literal flesh involved in circumcision but the flesh as the realm opposed to the Spirit (5:16–17; 6:8), are forcing them to be circumcised (6:12a).[19] These troublemakers (1:7) who are disturbing the Galatians (5:12) by trying to "force" them to be circumcised are thus likened to the Jews who came from James in Jerusalem (2:12) and caused Cephas, who had previously worshiped with gentiles in Antioch, now to "force" the gentiles to live and thus worship like Jews (2:14). These troublemakers are akin to the false brothers, Jewish believers in Jerusalem (2:4), who wanted to "force" the gentile Titus to be circumcised (2:3).

---

18. "Paul recapitulates one more time many of the major themes of the letter before closing. The large letters . . . signify the importance of the conclusion, provoking the readers to pay special heed to Paul's final thoughts" (Schreiner, *Galatians*, 376). "The large letters are the equivalent of boldface type or italics. Paul calls attention to them so that not only the person reading the letter aloud to the assembled Galatians but also the Galatians themselves will know that he has something important to say in closing" (De Boer, *Galatians*, 395).

19. In Gal 6:12, "σάρξ refers to the physical bodies of Paul's readers—'literally: the flesh marked by circumcision'" (Hubing, *Crucifixion and New Creation*, 210). "A deeper meaning may be that Paul accuses the new preachers of wanting to make a good showing 'in the realm of the Flesh,' with a capital F, rather than in that of the Spirit (5:13–6:10; cf. 3:3). Those 'wanting to make a good showing in the Flesh' do not know that there has been a change of regimes (3:25); they still orient their lives to the Flesh instead of to the Spirit (cf. 6:8), with all the dangers for communal life that involves (cf. 5:13–24)" (De Boer, *Galatians*, 398).

The troublemakers are forcing the Galatians to be circumcised, so that for the cross of Christ they may not be "persecuted" (6:12b).[20] They stand in contrast to Paul, who is being "persecuted" for not proclaiming circumcision, so that the stumbling block of the cross is not removed (5:11).[21] Ironically, just as at one time the one born according to the flesh (Ishmael) "persecuted" the one according to the Spirit (Isaac), so also now (4:29), the troublemakers trying to avoid persecution are persecuting the Galatians. Although everyone circumcised is obligated to do the whole law (3:10; 5:3), the circumcised troublemakers do not keep the law themselves, but they want the Galatians to be circumcised, so that they may boast to Jewish authorities about the circumcised flesh of the Galatians to avoid persecution (6:13).[22] As those who "want" to make a good showing in the flesh (6:12a), they "want" the Galatians to be circumcised (6:13a), because they "want" to exclude them from Christ (4:17), as those who "want" to distort the gospel of Christ (1:7).

In contrast to the troublemakers who want to "boast" in the circumcised flesh of the Galatians (6:13b) to avoid persecution for the "cross" of Christ (6:12b), Paul may only "boast" in the "cross" of our Lord Jesus Christ, through which the world has been "crucified" to him and he to the world (6:14). This suggests that the Galatians, as those who belong to Christ Jesus and have "crucified" (ἐσταύρωσαν) the flesh with its passions and

---

20. "The most likely reading of 6:12 is therefore that the opponents, who are Christian Jews, fear persecution from non-Christian Jews if the gentile Christians do not undergo circumcision" (Oakes, *Galatians*, 187). "The agitators have one thing in mind according to Paul: saving their skin from the threat of persecution by another entity that will be satisfied if they can compel Gentile members of Paul's churches to have some of their skin cut off" (Hubing, *Crucifixion and New Creation*, 229).

21. "'The cross of Christ' is Pauline shorthand for 'the crucifixion of Christ' and all that entails with respect to circumcision and the law. Christ's cross is an 'offense' to Jews and Christian Jews such as the new preachers in Galatia because, so Paul claims, it has brought about the end of the law as the reliable basis for righteousness and life" (De Boer, *Galatians*, 398).

22. "Paul's point would then be similar to the one that he has made in the passages earlier in the letter that touch on the same point (3:10; 5:3): accepting circumcision puts people under an obligation—to do 'the whole law'—that they are unable to fulfill. The agitators themselves exhibit this fundamental problem . . . the agitators, in taking pride in physical flesh, are also and ironically allying themselves with the power of the old age" (Moo, *Galatians*, 394–95). "Paul seems implicitly to suggest that the new preachers are counting how many new converts they have made, presumably to impress their fellow Jews, perhaps especially other Christian Jews, such as 'the false brothers' of 2:3–4, who were unable to compel Titus to become circumcised" (De Boer, *Galatians*, 400).

desires (5:24), should likewise boast in the cross of Christ rather than avoid persecution for it.[23] And it reinforces how Paul has been "crucified with" (συνεσταύρωμαι) Christ (2:19), so that now the risen Christ lives in him (2:20). That the "world" (κόσμος) has been crucified to Paul and he to the "world" (κόσμῳ) means that, through the crucifixion of Christ, he has died and been freed from slavery, to the demonic and deadly elemental powers of the "world [κόσμου]" (4:3), the present evil age (1:4), so that he may now live the eschatological life of the risen Christ.

Paul then confirms the arrival of this new eschatological life as he climactically exclaims that "neither circumcision is anything nor uncircumcision but only a new creation!" (6:15).[24] This parallels and develops his earlier statement that "in Christ Jesus neither circumcision counts for anything nor uncircumcision, but faith working through love" (5:6). It is by faith working through love, the self-sacrificial love of one's neighbor as oneself (5:14) exemplified by the self-sacrificial death of Christ (2:20), the love that is the fruit of the Spirit (5:22), that a believer already begins to live the eschatological life of the new creation. Believers can live this life of the new creation because Christ freed us from the present evil age through his death for our sins (1:4), so that the old world has been crucified to us and we to the world (6:14).[25] And it is by the Spirit, from faith, that we believers await the future eternal life that is the hope of justification (5:5), in accord with the promise that the just one from faith will live (3:11), indeed will live now and in the future to and for God (2:19) through the ethical worship of self-sacrificial love.[26]

---

23. This is the principal objective of the letter, according to Prokhorov, "Taking the Jews," 172–88.

24. "The letter has previously spoken about 'life' (2:19-20; 3:11-12, 21). The possibly closest of these to the vocabulary of creation is the comment in 3:21 about the law being unable 'to make alive'(ζῳοποιῆσαι)" (Oakes, *Galatians*, 189).

25. "This process of dying and rising is referred to then as becoming a 'new creation/creature,' over whom the world system no longer holds ultimate power, and within whom the power of God to produce life is demonstrated—even in the context of a 'present evil age' (Gal. 1.4)" (Hubing, *Crucifixion and New Creation*, 244). "The 'world' functions as the antonym to 'the new creation'" (Schreiner, *Galatians*, 379n25). "The 'life' component in Gal 6:14–15 is new creation . . . externally marked identity is mere technicality within God's new creation. For this reason, the identity of God's people effectively transcends ethnic distinction. The annihilation of this distinction marks the community of the new creation" (Boakye, *Death and Life*, 212–13).

26. "Paul's concept of new creation is an expression of his eschatologically infused soteriology which involves the individual, the community and the cosmos and which is inaugurated in the death and resurrection of Christ" (Jackson, *New Creation*, 83). "The

In contrast to "as many as" (ὅσοι) want to make a good showing in the flesh by forcing the Galatians to be circumcised (6:12a), the Galatians are to be "as many as" (ὅσοι) will follow the rule (6:16a) that neither circumcision is anything nor uncircumcision but only a new creation (6:15). The Galatians "will follow" (στοιχήσουσιν) this rule by not being circumcised, in accord with the exhortation that if we live by the Spirit, the Spirit also "let us follow [στοιχῶμεν]" (5:25). Paul prays that the "peace," the "peace" that comes from God our Father and the Lord Jesus Christ (1:3), the "peace" associated with the self-sacrificial love that is the fruit of the Spirit (5:22), as well as mercy, be upon the Galatians and all believers who follow this rule (6:16b).[27] Paul then climactically clarifies for the Galatians that they—and all believers upon whom he prays that God's peace and mercy comes—are the "Israel of God" (6:16c), not by their being circumcised, but by their being of Christ, so that they are a descendant of Abraham, heirs of eternal life according to the promise for it (3:11, 29).[28]

From now on, Paul wants no one to cause him troubles (6:17a) by continuing to trouble his converts in Galatia with a distorted gospel (1:7) that insists they be circumcised (5:10–11).[29] In accord with his statement that each one "will bear" his own load (6:5), and in contrast to the one

---

new creation is both God's newly creative act in Christ and the result of this newly creative act, a community of mutual love and service by the Spirit of Christ (cf. 5:13–24), in which the dualities of the present world (Jew/Greek, slave/free, male/female, circumcision/uncircumcision) have been abolished. Verse 15 is Paul's final brief summary of the gospel as he has repreached it to the Galatians through this letter" (De Boer, *Galatians*, 403). See also Moo, "Creation and New Creation," 39–60.

27. "Paul now adds a prayer wish for those who will walk by the rule that he has just enunciated in 6:15" (Schreiner, *Galatians*, 380).

28. "Paul's closing sentiments in Galatians revolve around a people who having been created by Spirit, order their steps by Spirit (Gal 6:14–16) . . . The rectified community was the Israel of God, a component of the new creation where the standard Jewish ethnic bifurcation of the world was erased" (Boakye, *Death and Life*, 213). "By speaking of an 'Israel *of God*' (language found only here in the NT), Paul tacitly recognizes the existence of an ethnic/national Israel, but he insists that the Israel that counts before God, the Israel that will receive the blessings of peace and mercy, is constituted on different grounds" (Moo, *Galatians*, 403; emphasis original). "In Gal 3 Paul identified Abraham's children as all believers in Christ, regardless of their ethnicity. Thus, there seems to be no reason not to take the Christian church as the Israel of God, the legitimate contemporary expression of the ancient faith of Israel" (Lyons, *Galatians*, 396). See also Filtvedt, "God's Israel," 123–40.

29. "Now that the new creation has been inaugurated, no one should trouble Paul with the requirements and regulations of the old creation by trying to impose the law on his converts" (Schreiner, *Galatians*, 383–84).

troubling the Galatians to be circumcised, who "will bear" the condemnation (5:10), Paul claims that "I bear the marks of Jesus in my body" (6:17b). In contrast to those forcing the Galatians to be circumcised so that for the cross of Christ they may not be persecuted (6:12), Paul bears the "marks" of persecution for the cross in his body.[30] This reinforces his boast in the cross of our Lord Jesus Christ, through which the world has been crucified to him and he to the world (6:14). Since masters sometimes branded slaves with a mark to indicate his ownership of them, that Paul bears the marks of Jesus on his body reinforces his claim to be a slave of Christ (1:10). Being a slave crucified with Christ (2:19c), so that the risen Christ now lives in him (2:20), enables Paul to live an eschatological life of worship to and for God (2:19b).[31]

Paul concludes the letter with an assertion that serves as an act of worship, a prayer wish: "The grace of our Lord Jesus Christ with your spirit, brothers. Amen!" (6:18). That the statement is verbless enables it to be understood as a reaffirmation of the Galatians' past reception of grace in becoming believers, as an indication of a present experience of that grace as they hear the letter, and as a prayer that they will continue to experience that grace as a result of hearing the letter. Indeed, the entire letter is placed within a framework of grace, as the closing prayer wish resonates with the one that opened the letter: "Grace to you and peace from God our Father and the Lord Jesus Christ" (1:3). This grace is the gift of eschatological life resulting from the resurrection of Jesus Christ (1:1). It is with the human "spirit" of the Galatians who have received the divine "Spirit" (3:2) from which they will reap life eternal (6:8).[32] Paul's "brothers," his fellow believers hearing the letter as a worshiping community, are invited again to add

---

30. The "marks of Jesus" thus "primarily serve to contrast the persecution willingly experienced by Paul with the persecution deliberately avoided by his 'markless' opponents" (Weima, *Neglected Endings*, 166). "The marks on Paul's body, however, belong to him because of the proclamation of the cross (5:11), and the opponents had no such marks since they avoided persecution because of their refusal to proclaim the scandal of the cross (5:11)" (Schreiner, *Galatians*, 384).

31. The word "marks" (στίγματα) "was used in the ancient world to refer to the 'brand' that masters sometimes used to mark ownership of slaves and to religious tattoos worn by some devotees of various religions... Paul probably intends these physical scars to stand in contrast to the physical mark of circumcision" (Moo, *Galatians*, 404).

32. "Paul means the 'spirit' of the Galatians as invaded and captured, thereby liberated, by 'the Spirit' of Christ" (De Boer, *Galatians*, 410).

their "amen" (cf. 1:5) to reaffirm the grace it offers them to worship for life eternal.[33]

SUMMARY ON GALATIANS 6:1–18

If anyone of the Galatians thinks he is something for correcting a fellow believer (6:1), but not looking to himself lest he be similarly tempted (6:2), so that he becomes one who is conceited (5:26), when he is nothing, he is deceiving himself (6:3). Let each one examine the "work" of himself (6:4a), the result of faith "working" through love (5:6), the fruit of the Spirit (5:22). Then he will have a reason to boast before God at the final judgment with regard to himself alone and not with regard to the other (6:4b), the neighbor he has loved (5:14) in bearing the burden of another (6:2). He may not deceive "himself" but examine "himself" and boast with regard to "himself" if his love for the other/neighbor accords with the self-sacrificial love of Christ, who loved and gave "himself" up for the believer (2:20) as the one who gave "himself" for our sins (1:4). For before God at the final judgment, each one will bear his own load (6:5). He will bear the burden not just of loving the other (6:2), but of looking to (6:1) and examining himself (6:4) as to whether he has self-sacrificially loved his neighbor as himself (5:14).

Each Galatian being instructed in the "word," generally the gospel but more specifically the one statement or "word" of the gospel in which the law is fulfilled, "You shall love your neighbor as yourself" (5:14), should share with the one instructing in all good things (6:6). By sharing with the instructor in all "good things" and thus materially supporting him, the one instructed will practice the "generosity" or "goodness" which is part of the love that is a fruit of the Spirit (5:22). The Galatians are not to be led astray (6:7a) from following the Spirit (5:25). God is not mocked, for a person will reap from God only what he sows to God (6:7b). The one sowing to the flesh of "himself," deceiving "himself" (6:3), especially by having his flesh

---

33. "With the blessings of 6:16 and 6:18 and with the final 'Amen!' Paul makes clear to the Galatians that, in listening to his letter, they have been dealing not simply with him but also and fundamentally with God" (Martyn, *Galatians*, 559). "This 'grace wish' serves, among other things, to signify just what Galatians has been all about" (Moo, *Galatians*, 405). "The 'amen' confirms and ratifies the prayer of grace" (Schreiner, *Galatians*, 385). "The final 'Amen' indicates that Paul expects his letter to the Galatians to be read aloud in the context of a gathering for worship . . . Paul invites the Galatians who will be listening to his letter to join him in a solemn affirmation of God's grace, explicitly mentioned in v. 18 and expounded in the remainder of the letter" (De Boer, *Galatians*, 410).

circumcised or not sharing with an instructor and thus not loving him as himself, will reap destruction (6:8a). But the one who sows to God's Spirit, from the Spirit by which we live (5:25), and by which, from faith working through love (5:6), we await the life that is the hope of justification (5:5), will reap life eternal (6:8; cf. 5:16–17).

Paul exhorts the Galatians not to lose heart in doing what is commendable, for in due time we believers who sow to the Spirit will reap life eternal (6:8), if we persevere and do not give up (6:9). The Galatians will do what is "commendable" if they practice the love that is the fruit of the Spirit (5:22) and do not allow themselves to be circumcised by following the troublemakers, who are zealous for the Galatians but not "commendably" (4:17), in contrast to Paul, whose zeal for them is "commendable" in a "commendable" way (4:18). While we believers have the opportunity, "let us work" the good for all from our faith "working" through love (5:6), and especially for those who are members of the household of the faith (6:10). Working the good of loving fellow believers as themselves (5:14), all of the Galatian believers, as a worshiping household of the faith, will enable the risen Christ who loved them to live within them (2:20), as they live an eschatological life to and for God (2:19) through their ethical and liturgical worship.

Paul confirms the arrival of this new eschatological life as he climactically exclaims that "neither circumcision is anything nor uncircumcision but only a new creation!" (6:15). This parallels and develops his earlier statement that "in Christ Jesus neither circumcision counts for anything nor uncircumcision, but faith working through love" (5:6). It is by faith working through love—the self-sacrificial love of one's neighbor as oneself (5:14) exemplified by the self-sacrificial death of Christ (2:20), the love that is the fruit of the Spirit (5:22)—that a believer already begins to live the eschatological life of the new creation. Believers can live this life of the new creation because Christ freed us from the present evil age through his death for our sins (1:4), so that the old world has been crucified to us and we to the world (6:14). And it is by the Spirit, from faith, that we believers await the future eternal life that is the hope of justification (5:5), in accord with the promise that the just one from faith will live (3:11), will indeed live now and in the future to and for God (2:19) through the ethical worship of self-sacrificial love.

In contrast to "as many as" want to make a good showing in the flesh by forcing the Galatians to be circumcised (6:12a), the Galatians are to be "as many as" will follow the rule (6:16a) that neither circumcision nor uncircumcision are anything, but only a new creation (6:15). The Galatians "will follow" this rule by not being circumcised, in accord with the exhortation that if we live by the Spirit, the Spirit also "let us follow" (5:25). Paul prays that the "peace," the "peace" that comes from God our Father and the Lord Jesus Christ (1:3), the "peace" associated with the self-sacrificial love that is the fruit of the Spirit (5:22), as well as mercy, be upon the Galatians and all believers who follow this rule (6:16b). Paul then climactically clarifies for the Galatians that they—and all believers upon whom he prays that God's peace and mercy comes—are the "Israel of God" (6:16c), not by their being circumcised, but by their being of Christ, so that they are a descendant of Abraham, heirs of eternal life according to the promise for it (3:11, 29).

From now on, Paul wants no one to cause him troubles (6:17a) by continuing to trouble his converts in Galatia with a distorted gospel (1:7) that insists they be circumcised (5:10–11). In accord with his statement that each one "will bear" his own load (6:5), and in contrast to the one troubling the Galatians to be circumcised, who "will bear" the condemnation (5:10), Paul claims that "I bear the marks of Jesus in my body" (6:17b). In contrast to those forcing the Galatians to be circumcised, so that for the cross of Christ they may not be persecuted (6:12), Paul bears the "marks" of persecution for the cross in his body. This reinforces his boast in the cross of our Lord Jesus Christ, through which the world has been crucified to him and he to the world (6:14). Since masters sometimes branded slaves with a mark to indicate his ownership of them, that Paul bears the marks of Jesus on his body reinforces his claim to be a slave of Christ (1:10). Being a slave crucified with Christ (2:19c), so that the risen Christ now lives in him (2:20), enables Paul to live an eschatological life of worship to and for God (2:19b).

Paul concludes the letter with an assertion that serves as an act of worship, a prayer wish: "The grace of our Lord Jesus Christ with your spirit, brothers. Amen!" (6:18). That the statement is verbless enables it to be understood as a reaffirmation of the Galatians' past reception of grace in becoming believers, as an indication of a present experience of that grace as they hear the letter, and as a prayer that they will continue to experience that grace as a result of hearing the letter. This places the entire letter within a framework of grace, as the closing prayer wish resonates with the one that opened the letter: "Grace to you and peace from God our Father and the Lord Jesus Christ" (1:3). This grace is the gift of eschatological life resulting from the resurrection of Jesus Christ (1:1). It is with the human "spirit" of the Galatians who have received the divine "Spirit" (3:2) from which they will reap life eternal (6:8). Paul's "brothers," his fellow believers hearing the letter as a worshiping community, are invited once again to add their "amen" (cf. 1:5) to reaffirm the grace it offers them to worship for life eternal.

15

Conclusion

Detailed summaries can be found at the end of each of the preceding chapters. What follows is a final brief overview recapitulating how the Galatian believers hear the chiastic structure of the letter as an exhortation to worship for eschatological life by faith in the crucified and risen Lord Jesus Christ.

That the Lord Jesus Christ gave himself for our sins (1:4a) complements the reference to his resurrection by God the Father (1:1) with a reference to his self-sacrificial and expiatory death as the source of grace and peace for the Galatian believers (1:3). And that he might free us from the present evil age (1:4b) confirms that his death and resurrection initiates a new age with a promise of life after death, a new age of freedom from the sins that prevent the proper worship of God as our Father. Paul invites his audience to join him in an initial act of doxological worship, oriented to the eschatological, eternal life that comes from God as our Father, by adding their own affirming "amen!" (1:5). This sets the tone for the whole letter and indicates that proper worship for life is a main concern and intended outcome for the letter to follow. That, together with Paul, the audience of believers are to be "slaves" who try to please Christ (1:7–10) as an object of their ethical worship, complements their doxological worship (1:5) and thus enables those who believe in the crucified and risen Lord Jesus Christ to worship for life.

Paul's preaching inspired the churches of Judea to a doxological worship of God. They were glorifying God "in me" (1:24), who was pleased to

Conclusion

reveal his Son "in me" (1:16), because Paul was now preaching the gospel about the faith that acknowledges and receives the grace and peace (1:3) that come from God's raising Jesus Christ from the dead (1:1) to life after he died for our sins to free us from the present evil age (1:4). Having led the Galatians to give glory to God for this new life (1:5), Paul implicitly invites the Galatian churches to join the Judean churches in glorifying God for Paul's gospel about this new life rather than turning away from it (1:6).

The truth of the gospel includes freedom, not only from the requirement for gentile believers to become Jewish, but from any requirement for gentile believers to observe Jewish food laws to share eucharistic meals with them (2:11–14). This reinforces Paul's implicit appeal for the Galatians to not turn away from the truth of the gospel of Christ, as preached by Paul, for a different gospel (1:6). The Galatian believers have been freed from any need to live like Jews to engage in the worship of the eucharistic Lord's Supper with any other community of believers.

Paul, and every believer he is representing, through the law to the law "died" (2:19a), so that "I might live" to and/or for God (2:19b). That "I might live for God" means to live one's present life in a way pleasing to God through cultic and ethical worship. Paul pointed out to Peter that, although he is a Jew, "you are living" like a gentile (2:14), referring to Peter's practice of sharing eucharistic meal fellowship with believing gentiles, a form of ritual worship meant to please God. For the believer to live "to God" means to live oriented to the implicit promise of future eternal life because God raised Jesus Christ from the dead (1:1) to eternal life. Living to God includes the doxological worship of glorifying God (1:5), since according to the will of God the Lord Jesus Christ gave himself for our sins, that he might free us from the mortality of the present evil age for an eternal life (1:4).

As having been and still being crucified with the Christ (2:19c) God raised from the dead (1:1) to life, Paul and every believer yet lives. But the life a believer lives is not animated and directed by oneself, but by the risen Christ "who lives in me" (2:20a). "I," Paul and every believer, still live "in flesh," that is, in the realm of the mortality of the present evil age (1:4), the realm in which not any "flesh" will be justified and thus given life from works of the law (2:16). But while "I live in flesh, in faith I live" (2:20b), that faith of accepting the grace of a new life given by the Son of God who loved "me" and "gave" himself up for "me" (2:20c). Here Paul makes personal for every believer that Christ "gave" himself for "our" sins, that he might free "us" from the mortality of the present evil age (1:4). Living by faith in the Son of God and accepting the grace of a new life from the risen Christ who "lives in me" means that "I might live to and for God" (2:19b), and thus by faith worship God in this present life in the realm of mortal flesh in view of an eternal life with the risen Christ.

Not from works of the law, but from faith, the Galatians were justified and received the life-giving divine Spirit of the crucified-but-risen Christ, which empowers them to live to and for God (2:19) as the people of God through their cultic and ethical worship (3:1–2). And they continue to experience various gifts of the Spirit for their communal worship, not from the works of the law, but from their faith in Christ (3:5). Thus, Paul reminds the Galatians that God continues to supply them, as believers, with the Spirit, enabling them to work mighty deeds as they live to and for God (2:19) in and through their worship.

That by the law no one is justified before God (cf. 2:16) is clear, for "the just one from faith will live" (3:11; cf. Hab 2:4). In the Galatian context, this scriptural quotation has a double meaning. It promises that one who is justified or just from faith (not law) will live a future divine eternal life, and it asserts that the just one will live presently a life of worship from faith (not law). That the just one from faith "will live" a life of worship presently and for the future resonates with the life "I [every believer] live" in flesh, in faith "I live," that faith in the Son of God who loved me and gave himself up for me, so that "I live," no longer I, but the risen Christ "lives" in me (2:20). It recalls and reinforces that to the law "I died," so that "I might live" for God presently and to God in view of future eternal life (2:19). And, that "will live" connotes a life of worship accords with "you are living" as a reference to Peter sharing meal fellowship and thus worshiping with gentiles (2:14). As a just one, every believer is to live a life of worship from faith (not law) now to live eternally in the future.

Christ redeemed us from the curse of the law through his crucifixion (3:13) "that to the gentiles the blessing of Abraham might come in Christ Jesus" (3:14a). The blessing of Abraham refers to the gentiles being justified by God from faith (3:8–9), that is, believing in the God who raised Christ Jesus from the dead (1:1) to new life. The Abrahamic blessing of justification came to the gentiles, so that the promise of the Spirit "we" (all believers) might "receive" through faith (3:14b). This reinforces Paul's point that the Galatians "received" the Spirit from the hearing of faith (3:2, 5). The "promise of the Spirit" refers not to the promised Spirit, but to the promise

Conclusion

of eschatological life that believers receive by being justified through faith and that the Spirit will bring to fulfillment. The promise, then, accords with the scriptural promise that the just one from faith "will live" (3:11) not only presently but eternally.

Believers who were baptized into Christ in an act of communal worship that ritualizes their faith in Christ have clothed themselves with Christ (3:27), in implicit contrast to the ritual act of circumcision, which places one under the curse of doing all the works of the law (3:10). That all baptized believers have metaphorically and sacramentally "clothed" themselves with Christ corresponds to every individual believer having died to the law and been crucified with Christ, so that the risen Christ now lives in each believer (2:19–20). Just as clothing identifies and unites with its wearer, so the risen Christ identifies and unites with all believers baptized into Christ so that they have clothed themselves with the risen Christ who lives in them. The sacrament of baptism, then, plays an essential role in the worship for life by faith in the crucified and risen Lord Jesus Christ.

The Spirit that God sent into our hearts enables us believers to address God in an act of filial worship as "Abba, Father" (4:6), implicitly praising and thanking God as the "Father" (4:2) who sent his Son to redeem us (4:4–5). This act of joyous laudatory worship thus complements the doxological worship of "our God and Father, to whom be glory for the ages of the ages. Amen!" (1:4–5). It praises and thanks God for the grace and peace that come from God our "Father" (1:3), the "Father" who raised Jesus Christ from the dead (1:1) to eternal life. That every believer, as a son, is an "heir" (4:7) reaffirms that believers are "heirs" of eschatological life according to the promise for it (3:29; cf. 3:11, 14). They are heirs through "God" (4:7), the "God" who sent not only his Son to redeem those under the law (4:4–5a), but also the Spirit of his Son, enabling believers who have received sonship (4:5b), so that they are now heirs, to worship God as their "Father" (4:6) for the eschatological life God as their "Father" has entitled them to inherit (4:2).

That, as believers, the Galatians are now recognizing God (4:9a), resonates with their worship, as sons, of the true and living God as their Father (4:6). But they can so worship God only because they were first recognized by God (4:9b) when God sent the Spirit of his Son into their hearts, so that they are no longer slaves but sons, and thus heirs (4:6–7), of eschatological life. If, by having themselves circumcised, they were to place themselves under the curse of the law (3:10), they would again be slaves of things that are not gods (4:8), serving and worshiping the weak and destitute elemental powers (4:9c) associated with the law (4:3–5). They are already observing various times for worship that suggests they are beginning to observe the law (4:10). And so, Paul fears that, in bringing them to faith in the gospel whereby the Spirit enabled them to worship the true and living God as their Father, he may have labored for them "in vain" (4:11).

Addressing the Galatians again as "brothers" (cf. 4:28), his fellow believers, Paul asserts that we believers are not children of the slave woman, but of the free woman (4:31). Believers are "children" of the free woman, in contrast to the son of the slave woman, who will not inherit with the son of the free woman (4:30), Isaac. Like Isaac, believers are "children" of the promise (4:28), and thus those who will inherit eschatological life as heirs according to the promise (3:29) for it (3:11). By emphasizing that we believers are children of the "free" woman, Paul reinforces the scriptural exhortation for the Galatians, along with their mother, the Jerusalem who is "free" (4:26), to engage in the laudatory worship of rejoicing in God (4:27) for the eschatological life they will inherit as children of the heavenly Jerusalem. This complements the laudatory worship they can offer God as their Father (4:6), since they are no longer a slave but a son, and thus an heir, as a descendant of Abraham (3:29) with Christ (3:16), of eschatological life through God (4:7).

Through "love," the "love" through which faith works (5:6d), the Galatians are to be slaves to one another (5:13b). The faith by which they as believers live an eschatological life is faith in the Son of God who "loved" and gave himself up in a self-sacrificial death for Paul and every believer (2:20b). If the Galatians subject themselves again to the yoke of "slavery" (5:1) by being circumcised (5:2), it would mean wanting "to be slaves" again of the weak and destitute elemental powers (4:9), the false gods which they once worshiped when "you were slaves" to them (4:8). Instead, the Galatians are "to be slaves" to one another through the kind of self-sacrificial love they received from Christ. Then, by not pleasing the human beings who are persuading them to be circumcised, they would, like Paul, be a "slave" of Christ and please God (1:10), and thus live to and for God (2:19), engaging in an ethical worship for eschatological life by becoming slaves to one another through a Christ-like self-sacrificial love.

As those who are of Christ Jesus, who are heirs of eschatological life according to the promise (3:29) for it (3:11), the Galatians have crucified the flesh with its passions and desires (5:24). As those who, like Paul, have

Conclusion

been "crucified with" Christ (2:19), so that the risen Christ lives in them (2:20), the Galatians have "crucified" the flesh. They have thus put to death, in accord with the death of the crucified Christ, the flesh with its "desires," the "desires" that are against the Spirit (5:16–17). If we believers "live" by the Spirit, as those who begin to fulfill the promise that the just one from faith "will live" (3:11) ethically and eschatologically, then let us follow the lead of the Spirit (5:25). The Spirit leads (5:18) those who walk by it (5:16) to practice the self-sacrificial love that is the preeminent fruit of the Spirit (5:22) as the ethical worship by which every believer might "live" to and for God (2:19). Along with Paul, every believer who follows the Spirit may now "live" the eschatological life of the risen Christ by faith in the Son of God who loved and gave himself up for Paul and all of us (2:20).

Paul confirms the arrival of this new eschatological life as he climactically exclaims that "neither circumcision is anything nor uncircumcision but only a new creation!" (6:15). This parallels and develops his earlier statement that "in Christ Jesus neither circumcision counts for anything nor uncircumcision, but faith working through love" (5:6). It is by faith working through love, the self-sacrificial love of one's neighbor as oneself (5:14) exemplified by the self-sacrificial death of Christ (2:20), the love that is the fruit of the Spirit (5:22), that a believer already begins to live the eschatological life of the new creation. Believers can live this life of the new creation because Christ freed us from the present evil age through his death for our sins (1:4), so that the old world has been crucified to us and we to the world (6:14). And it is by the Spirit, from faith, that we believers await the future eternal life that is the hope of justification (5:5), in accord with the promise that the just one from faith will live (3:11), and indeed will live now and in the future to and for God (2:19) through the ethical worship of self-sacrificial love.

Paul concludes the letter with an assertion that serves as an act of worship, a prayer wish: "The grace of our Lord Jesus Christ with your spirit, brothers. Amen!" (6:18). That the statement is verbless enables it to be understood as a reaffirmation of the Galatians' past reception of grace in becoming believers, as an indication of a present experience of that grace as they hear the letter, and as a prayer that they will continue to experience that grace as a result of hearing the letter. This places the entire letter within a framework of grace, as the closing prayer wish resonates with the one that opened the letter: "Grace to you and peace from God our Father and the Lord Jesus Christ" (1:3). This grace is the gift of eschatological life resulting from the resurrection of Jesus Christ (1:1). It is with the human "spirit" of the Galatians who have received the divine "Spirit" (3:2) from which they will reap life eternal (6:8). Paul's "brothers," his fellow believers hearing the letter as a worshiping community, are invited once again to add their "amen" (cf. 1:5) to reaffirm the grace it offers them to worship for life eternal.

Bibliography

Adewuya, Ayodeji J. *Holiness in the Letters of Paul: The Necessary Response to the Gospel.* Eugene, OR: Cascade, 2016.
Arnold, Clinton E. "Returning to the Domain of the Powers: *Stoicheia* as Evil Spirits in Galatians 4:3, 9." *NovT* 38 (1996) 55–76.
Barclay, John M. G. *Obeying the Truth: Paul's Ethics in Galatians.* Edinburgh: T. & T. Clark, 1988.
Barth, Gerhard. "πίστις." *EDNT* 3.91–97.
Bedford, Nancy Elizabeth. *Galatians.* BELIEF: A Theological Commentary on the Bible. Louisville: Westminster John Knox, 2016.
Berger, Klaus. "χάρις." *EDNT* 3.457–60.
Beutler, Johannes. "ἀδελφός." *EDNT* 1.28–30.
Boakye, Andrew K. *Death and Life: Resurrection, Restoration, and Rectification in Paul's Letter to the Galatians.* Eugene, OR: Pickwick, 2017.
Borchert, Gerald L. *Worship in the New Testament.* St. Louis: Chalice, 2008.
Bruce, Frederick Fyvie. *The Epistle to the Galatians: A Commentary on the Greek Text.* NIGTC. Grand Rapids: Eerdmans, 1982.
Bryant, Robert A. *The Risen Crucified Christ in Galatians.* SBLDS 185. Atlanta: Society of Biblical Literature, 2001.
Burke, Trevor J. *Adopted into God's Family: Exploring a Pauline Metaphor.* New Studies in Biblical Theology 22. Downers Grove: InterVarsity, 2006.
Burton, Ernest De Witt. *A Critical and Exegetical Commentary on the Epistle to the Galatians.* ICC. New York: Scribner's, 1920.
Capes, David B. *The Divine Christ: Paul, the Lord Jesus, and the Scriptures of Israel.* Acadia Studies in Bible and Theology. Grand Rapids: Baker Academic, 2018.
Chester, Stephen J. "Paul and the Galatians Believers." In *The Blackwell Companion to Paul,* edited by Stephen Westerholm, 63–78. Malden: Wiley-Blackwell, 2011.
Costa, Tony. *Worship and the Risen Jesus in the Pauline Letters.* StBibLit 157. New York: Lang, 2013.
De Boer, Martinus C. *Galatians: A Commentary.* NTL. Louisville: Westminster John Knox, 2011.
Di Mattei, Steven. "Paul's Allegory of the Two Covenants (Gal 4.21–31) in Light of First-Century Hellenistic Rhetoric and Jewish Hermeneutics." *NTS* 52 (2006) 102–22.
Dunn, James D. G. *The Epistle to the Galatians.* BNTC. Grand Rapids: Baker Academic, 1993.
———. "Faith, Faithfulness." *NIDB* 2.407–23.

Bibliography

———. *The Theology of Paul the Apostle*. Grand Rapids: Eerdmans, 1998.

Eastman, Susan G. "'Cast Out the Slave Woman and her Son': The Dynamics of Exclusion and Inclusion in Galatians 4.30." *JSNT* 28 (2006) 309–36.

———. *Recovering Paul's Mother Tongue: Language and Theology in Galatians*. Grand Rapids: Eerdmans, 2007.

Elliott, Susan M. *Cutting Too Close for Comfort: Paul's Letter to the Galatians in Its Anatolian Cultic Context*. LNTS 248. London: T. & T. Clark, 2003.

Elmer, Ian J. *Paul, Jerusalem and the Judaisers*. WUNT 2.258. Tübingen: Mohr Siebeck, 2009.

Fee, Gordon D. *God's Empowering Presence: The Holy Spirit in the Letters of Paul*. Peabody: Hendrickson, 1994.

———. *Jesus the Lord according to Paul the Apostle: A Concise Introduction*. Grand Rapids: Baker Academic, 2018.

———. *Pauline Christology: An Exegetical-Theological Study*. Peabody: Hendrickson, 2007.

Filtvedt, Ole J. "'God's Israel' in Galatians 6.16: An Overview and Assessment of the Key Arguments." *CurBR* 15 (2016) 123–40.

Fredriksen, Paula. "The Question of Worship: Gods, Pagans, and the Redemption of Israel." In *Paul within Judaism: Restoring the First-Century Context to the Apostle*, edited by Mark D. Nanos and Magnus Zetterholm, 175–201. Minneapolis: Fortress, 2015.

Fung, Ronald Y. K. *The Epistle to the Galatians*. NICNT. Grand Rapids: Eerdmans, 1988.

Gaventa, Beverly Roberts. *Our Mother Saint Paul*. Louisville: Westminster John Knox, 2007.

Hardin, Justin K. *Galatians and the Imperial Cult: A Critical Analysis of the First-Century Social Context of Paul's Letter*. WUNT 237. Tübingen: Mohr Siebeck, 2008.

———. "'If I Still Proclaim Circumcision' (Galatians 5:11a): Paul, the Law, and Gentile Circumcision." *Journal for the Study of Paul and His Letters* 2 (2013) 145–63.

Heil, John Paul. *1 Peter, 2 Peter, and Jude: Worship Matters*. Eugene, OR: Cascade, 2013.

———. *1–3 John: Worship by Loving God and One Another to Live Eternally*. Eugene, OR: Cascade, 2015.

———. *The Book of Revelation: Worship for Life in the Spirit of Prophecy*. Eugene, OR: Cascade, 2014.

———. "The Chiastic Structure and Meaning of Paul's Letter to Philemon." *Bib* 82 (2001) 178–206.

———. *Colossians: Encouragement to Walk in All Wisdom as Holy Ones in Christ*. ECL 4. Atlanta: Society of Biblical Literature, 2010.

———. *Ephesians: Empowerment to Walk in Love for the Unity of All in Christ*. Studies in Biblical Literature 13. Atlanta: Society of Biblical Literature, 2007.

———. *Hebrews: Chiastic Structures and Audience Response*. CBQMS 46. Washington, DC: Catholic Biblical Association of America, 2010.

———. *The Letter of James: Worship to Live By*. Eugene, OR: Cascade, 2012.

———. *The Letters of Paul as Rituals of Worship*. Eugene, OR: Cascade, 2011.

———. *Philippians: Let Us Rejoice in Being Conformed to Christ*. ECL 3. Atlanta: Society of Biblical Literature, 2010.

Hubing, Jeff. *Crucifixion and New Creation: The Strategic Purpose of Galatians 6.11–17*. LNTS 508. London: Bloomsbury, 2015.

Bibliography

Hunn, Debbie. "Πίστις in Galatians 5.5–6: Neglected Evidence for 'Faith in Christ.'" *NTS* 62 (2016) 477–83.
Hurtado, Larry W. "Worship, NT Christian." *NIDB* 5.910–23.
Jackson, T. Ryan. *New Creation in Paul's Letters: A Study of the Historical and Social Setting of a Pauline Concept.* WUNT 2.272. Tübingen: Mohr Siebeck, 2010.
Jeon, Paul S. *1 Timothy: A Charge to God's Missional Household: Vol. 1.* Eugene, OR: Pickwick, 2017.
———. *1 Timothy: A Charge to God's Missional Household: Vol. 2.* Eugene, OR: Pickwick, 2017.
———. *1 Timothy: A Charge to God's Missional Household: Vol. 3.* Eugene, OR: Pickwick, 2017.
———. *To Exhort and Reprove: Audience Response to the Chiastic Structures of Paul's Letter to Titus.* Eugene, OR: Pickwick, 2012.
John, Felix. *Der Galaterbrief im Kontext historischer Lebenswelten im antiken Kleinasien.* FRLANT 264. Göttingen: Vandenhoeck & Ruprecht, 2016.
Kahl, Brigitte. *Galatians Re-Imagined: Reading with the Eyes of the Vanquished.* Minneapolis: Fortress, 2010.
Kellermann, Ulrich. "ἀφωρίζω." In *EDNT* 1.183–84.
Kim, Jung Hoon. *The Significance of Clothing Imagery in the Pauline Corpus.* LNTS 268. London: T. & T. Clark, 2004.
Kuck, David W. "Each Will Bear His Own Burden: Paul's Creative Use of An Apocalyptic Motif." *NTS* 40 (1994) 289–97.
Lee, Chee-Chiew. *The Blessing of Abraham, the Spirit, & Justification in Galatians: Their Relationship and Significance for Understanding Paul's Theology.* Eugene, OR: Pickwick, 2013.
Lincoln, Andrew T. *Paradise Now and Not Yet: Studies in the Role of the Heavenly Dimension in Paul's Thought with Special Reference to His Eschatology.* NTSMS 43. Cambridge: Cambridge University Press, 1981.
Longenecker, Richard N. *Galatians.* WBC 41. Grand Rapids: Zondervan, 1990.
Lyons, George. *Galatians: A Commentary in the Wesleyan Tradition.* NBBC. Kansas City, MO: Beacon Hill, 2012.
Martyn, J. Louis. *Galatians: A New Translation with Introduction and Commentary.* AB 33A. New York: Doubleday, 1997.
Matera, Frank J. *Galatians.* SP 9. Collegeville, MN: Liturgical, 1992.
Matthews, Victor H. "Clothe Oneself, To." In *NIDB* 1.696.
McGowan, Andrew B. *Ancient Christian Worship: Early Church Practices in Social, Historical, and Theological Perspective.* Grand Rapids: Baker Academic, 2014.
Milinovich, Timothy. *Beyond What Is Written: The Performative Structure of 1 Corinthians.* Eugene, OR: Pickwick, 2013.
Moo, Douglas, J. "Creation and New Creation." *BBR* 20 (2010) 39–60.
———. *Galatians.* BECNT. Grand Rapids: Baker Academic, 2013.
Nanos, Mark D. *The Irony of Galatians: Paul's Letter in First-Century Context.* Minneapolis: Fortress, 2002.
Neutel, Karin B. *A Cosmopolitan Ideal: Paul's Declaration 'Neither Jew Nor Greek, Neither Slave Nor Free, Nor Male and Female' in the Context of First-Century Thought.* LNTS 513. London: Bloomsbury, 2015.
Oakes, Peter. *Galatians.* Paideia Commentaries on the New Testament. Grand Rapids: Baker Academic, 2015.

Bibliography

Peterson, David. *Engaging with God: A Biblical Theology of Worship*. Downers Grove: InterVarsity, 1992.

Prokhorov, A. V. "Taking the Jews out of the Equation: Galatians 6.12–17 as a Summons to Cease Evading Persecution." *JSNT* 36 (2013) 172–88.

Schreiner, Thomas R. *Galatians*. ZECNT. Grand Rapids: Zondervan, 2010.

Silva, Moisés. "Galatians." In *Commentary on the New Testament Use of the Old Testament*, edited by G. K. Beale and D. A. Carson, 785–812. Grand Rapids: Baker, 2007.

Taylor, Joan E. "Baptism." In *NIDB* 1.390–95.

Thiessen, Matthew. *Paul and the Gentile Problem*. New York: Oxford University Press, 2016.

Trick, Bradley R. *Abrahamic Descent, Testamentary Adoption, and the Law in Galatians: Differentiating Abraham's Sons, Seed, and Children of Promise*. NovTSup 169. Leiden: Brill, 2016.

Weima, Jeffrey A. D. *Neglected Endings: The Significance of the Pauline Letter Closings*. JSNTSup 101. Sheffield: JSOT, 1994.

Wendt, Heidi. "Galatians 3:1 as an Allusion to Textual Prophecy." *JBL* 135 (2016) 369–89.

Witherington, Ben. *Grace in Galatia: A Commentary on Paul's Letter to the Galatians*. Grand Rapids: Eerdmans, 1998.

Wright, Brian J. *Communal Reading in the Time of Jesus: A Window into Early Christian Reading Practices*. Minneapolis: Fortress, 2017.

Scripture Index

OLD TESTAMENT

Genesis

12:3	9, 66, 67, 72
12:7	9, 67, 71, 77n4
13:15	9, 67, 71
15:3–4	77n4
15:6	66, 67
16:1	100
16:15	100
17:8	9, 67, 71
18:18	9, 66, 67, 72
21:3	100
21:10	14, 99, 105
22:17	9, 67, 71
24:7	9, 67, 71

Leviticus

18:5	9, 66, 69
19:18	16, 122, 123

Deuteronomy

21:23	9, 66, 70, 73
27:26	9, 66, 68, 69, 72

Psalms

143:2	49, 50, 52, 52n8

Habakkuk

2:4	9, 66, 68, 73, 150

Isaiah

49:1	34n3
49:6	34n6
54:1	13, 98, 102, 103, 104, 106

Jeremiah

1:5	34n3

NEW TESTAMENT

Mark

14:36	86n8

Scripture Index

Acts

1:15	35
2:14	35
2:37–38	35
9:1–22	35
12:17	36
13–14	26
15:13	36
21:18	36
22:5–16	35
26:12–20	35

Romans

8:15	86n8
10:16–17	62

Galatians

1:1–10	3–4, 5, 19, 21, 24–31
1:1–2	3, 25–26
1:1	3, 22, 24, 25, 26, 28, 29, 30, 31, 34, 36, 37, 38, 42, 51, 55, 56, 57, 58, 68, 71, 72, 73, 74, 77, 78, 81, 85, 86, 86n10, 87, 88, 103, 106, 109, 110, 112, 118, 121, 126, 143, 146, 148, 149, 150, 151, 154
1:2	3, 19, 22, 23, 24, 25, 26, 27, 30, 33, 34
1:3–5	23
1:3–4	4, 26–27, 86n10
1:3	3, 4, 19, 22, 24, 26, 28, 31, 36, 37, 38, 57, 86, 88, 111, 119, 120, 142, 143, 146, 148, 149, 151, 153
1:4–5	86, 88, 151
1:4	3, 22, 24, 26, 27, 28, 29, 30, 31, 33, 34, 36, 37, 38, 42, 51, 52, 55, 56, 57, 58, 59, 62, 65, 70, 78, 85, 87, 91, 109, 111, 113, 118, 119, 121, 126, 136, 141, 144, 145, 148, 149, 150, 153
1:5	3, 4, 22, 23, 24, 27, 28, 30, 31, 37, 38, 55, 58, 103, 106, 144, 147, 148, 149, 154
1:6–7	56, 57, 59, 95
1:6	3, 4, 19, 24, 28, 29, 31, 34, 37, 38, 47, 48, 51, 57, 61, 93, 111, 115, 119, 149
1:7–10	3, 3n5, 28–30, 31, 148
1:7	3, 24, 28, 29, 30, 33, 51, 61, 68, 72, 93, 94, 104, 116, 120, 139, 140, 142, 146
1:8–9	31, 116, 120
1:8	3, 24, 28, 29, 94
1:9	3, 24, 28, 29, 61, 115
1:10	3, 5, 24–25, 28, 29, 30, 34, 36, 91, 116, 119, 121, 143, 146, 152
1:11–24	4–5, 6, 19–20, 21, 32–38
1:11–16	5, 33–35
1:11–12	33
1:11	4, 5, 32, 33, 42, 48, 72, 96, 104
1:12	4, 5, 32, 33, 34, 37, 38, 41
1:13	4, 5, 32, 33, 34, 36, 37, 117
1:14	4, 32, 33, 34, 35
1:15–16	33, 36, 41
1:15	4, 32, 33, 34, 37, 45, 57, 115
1:16	4, 5, 20, 32, 33, 34, 35, 37, 38, 57, 59, 78, 79, 115, 149
1:16b–19	5
1:17–19	35–36
1:17	4, 32, 35, 36, 38, 101
1:18–19	35, 36, 38, 41
1:18	4, 5, 32, 35
1:19	4, 32, 35, 36
1:20	4, 5, 33, 36
1:21	4, 5, 33, 36, 38
1:22–24	5, 37
1:22	4, 5, 33, 37
1:23	4, 5, 6, 20, 33, 37, 94, 117
1:24	4, 5, 33, 37, 38, 148
2:1–14	5–6, 7, 20, 21, 39–48
2:1–5	6, 40–42
2:1–3	41

Scripture Index

2:1	5, 6, 39, 40, 41	3:1–5	8, 9, 20, 21, 60–65
2:2	5, 6, 39, 40, 41, 115, 117	3:1–3	8, 60–63
2:3–5	47, 94	3:1–2	65, 150
2:3	5, 39, 40, 41, 47, 109, 110, 117, 119, 139	3:1	8, 60, 61, 62, 65, 94, 94n12, 115, 117, 120
2:4	5, 20, 39, 40, 42, 109, 113, 139	3:2	8, 22, 60, 61, 62, 64, 65, 68, 71, 73, 126, 127, 130, 143, 147, 150, 154
2:5	5, 6, 20, 39, 40, 42, 48, 115		
2:6	5, 6, 39, 42–43, 44, 45, 48	3:3	8, 60, 61, 62, 63, 65, 118, 121, 124
2:7–14	6, 43–47		
2:7–9	44	3:4	8, 20, 60, 63, 65, 91
2:7	6, 20, 39, 43, 44, 45	3:5	8, 22, 60, 64, 65, 68, 71, 73, 126, 127, 130, 150
2:8	6, 20, 39–40, 43, 44, 45		
2:9	6, 20, 40, 43, 44, 45, 57	3:6–16	8–9, 10, 20, 21, 66–74
2:10	6, 40, 43, 44, 45		
2:11–14	45–46, 48, 149	3:6–9	9, 67–68
2:11	6, 40, 43, 44, 45, 46	3:6–8	77
2:12	6, 20, 40, 43, 44, 45, 46, 105, 139	3:6–7	72
		3:6	8, 9, 66, 67, 72, 74
2:13	6, 40, 44, 45, 46	3:7	8, 9, 66, 67, 79
2:14	6, 7, 20, 40, 44, 46, 47, 55, 58, 69, 73, 94, 115, 139, 149, 150	3:8–9	68, 71, 73, 79, 150
		3:8	8, 9, 66, 67, 68, 72, 74
		3:9	9, 66, 67, 68, 72
2:15–21	7, 20, 21, 49–59	3:10	9, 66, 68, 69, 70, 72, 73, 77, 79, 79n10, 81, 84, 85, 87, 91, 96, 109, 111, 119, 123, 126, 140, 151
2:15–17	7, 50–53, 58		
2:15	7, 49, 50, 52		
2:16	7, 49, 50, 51, 52, 54, 55, 58, 59, 62, 67, 68, 73, 111, 117, 119, 120, 126, 149, 150	3:11	9, 66, 68–69, 72, 73, 74, 78, 79, 81, 82, 87, 88, 101, 102, 104, 105, 106, 110, 112, 113, 120, 125, 126, 127, 128, 130, 135, 141, 142, 145, 146, 150, 151, 152, 153
2:17	7, 49, 50, 52		
2:18	7, 49, 53, 54, 58		
2:19–21	7, 53–57		
2:19–20	80, 82, 92n8, 123, 151		
2:19	7, 49, 53–54, 55, 56, 57, 58, 59, 61, 62, 63, 64, 65, 69, 70, 73, 85, 87, 92, 95, 96, 97, 110, 113, 119, 121, 128, 129, 130, 131, 138, 141, 143, 145, 146, 149, 150, 152, 153	3:12	9, 66, 69–70, 73, 110, 135
		3:13	9, 20, 66, 70, 71, 73, 85, 85n6, 87, 109, 150
		3:14–16	9, 71–72
		3:14	9, 22, 67, 71, 72, 73, 74, 77, 79, 79n9, 86, 87, 88, 104, 112, 113, 120, 124, 125, 127, 128, 130, 150, 151
2:20	7, 20, 49, 54, 56, 57, 58, 59, 61, 62, 69, 70, 73, 79, 85, 87, 92, 95, 96, 97, 112, 113, 118, 121, 124, 125, 127, 128, 129, 130, 131, 135, 136, 138, 141, 143, 144, 145, 146, 149, 150, 152, 153		
		3:15–16	76
		3:15	9, 67, 71, 72, 96, 104
		3:16	9, 10, 67, 71, 72, 74, 77, 79, 81, 84, 87, 101, 105, 107, 152
2:21	7, 8, 49, 54, 57, 59, 63, 65, 67, 77, 111, 119	3:17–29	10–11, 20–21, 23, 75–82
		3:17–22	11, 76–78

Scripture Index

3:17	10, 11, 75, 76	4:6	11, 22, 83, 85, 86, 86n10, 87, 88, 91, 94, 96, 103, 105, 106, 151, 152
3:18	10, 11, 75, 76, 77, 78, 79, 81, 82, 100		
3:19	10, 11, 75, 76, 77, 78, 79, 81, 84, 84n2, 87	4:7	11, 12, 83, 85, 86, 88, 90, 94, 95, 97, 100, 105, 107, 151, 152
3:20	10, 75, 76, 77, 81		
3:21–22	78, 81	4:8–20	12, 13, 14, 20, 21, 89–97
3:21	10, 11, 75, 76, 77, 78, 92, 96, 109, 112, 120, 125, 126, 127, 130	4:8–11	13, 90–91
		4:8–9	126
3:22	10, 11, 75, 76, 77, 78, 84, 87, 112, 120	4:8	12, 13, 89, 90, 90n3, 91, 96, 101, 110, 118, 121, 152
3:23–25	78, 87	4:9	12, 13, 89, 90, 91, 94, 95, 96, 100, 101, 110, 118, 121, 151, 152
3:23–24	11		
3:23	10, 75, 78, 84, 100, 125, 130		
3:24	10, 11, 75, 78, 81, 111, 119	4:10	12, 89, 90, 91, 96, 152
3:25	10, 11, 75, 78, 81, 84	4:11	12, 20, 89, 90, 91, 96, 152
3:26–29	10, 79–81	4:12c–20	13, 92–95
3:26	10, 76, 79, 79n9, 80, 81, 82, 86, 92, 94, 96, 112	4:12	12, 13, 89, 91–92, 92n8, 93, 94, 95, 96, 97, 104
3:27	10, 21, 76, 79, 79n10, 80, 81, 82, 151	4:13	12, 89, 92, 93
		4:14	12, 89, 92, 93, 94
3:28–29	92n8	4:15	12, 89, 92, 94, 94n12
3:28	10, 76, 79, 80, 81, 82, 92, 94, 96, 113	4:16	12, 89, 92, 94, 115
		4:17	12, 12n6, 13, 89, 92–93, 94, 95, 105, 115, 137, 140, 145
3:29	10, 11, 76. 79, 81, 82, 84, 87, 88, 92, 96, 101, 104, 105, 106, 107, 113, 125, 126, 128, 130, 142, 146, 151, 152	4:18	12, 13, 89, 93, 95, 96, 137, 145
		4:18b–20	93
4:1–7	11, 12, 20, 21, 83–88	4:19	12, 13, 90, 93, 95, 95n15, 96, 101, 103, 103n14
4:1–4a	11, 83–84		
4:1–2	87	4:20	12, 13, 14, 90, 93, 95, 96
4:1	11, 83, 84, 86	4:21–31	13–14, 16, 20, 21, 98–107
4:2	11, 83, 84, 84n2, 86, 86n10, 87, 88, 91, 151	4:21–27a	14, 99–102
		4:21–24a	99–100
4:3–5	91, 96, 152	4:21	13, 14, 98, 99, 100, 105, 125, 125n8, 130
4:3	11, 83, 84, 85, 86, 87, 90, 141		
		4:22	13, 14, 20, 98, 99, 100, 102, 106
4:4–5	86, 87, 88, 151		
4:4	11, 12, 83, 84, 85, 87, 100, 125, 130	4:23	13, 14, 98, 99, 100, 101, 102, 104, 106
4:4b–5a	85	4:24	13, 14, 98, 99, 100, 101, 102, 106, 110
4:5b–7	11, 85–86		
4:5	11, 12, 20, 83, 85, 85n6, 86, 87, 88, 100, 109, 125, 130, 151	4:25	13, 13n7, 14, 98, 99, 101, 102, 104, 106
		4:26	13, 14, 98, 99, 102, 104, 105, 106, 152
4:6–7	91, 96, 151	4:27e–31	14, 103–5

162

Scripture Index

4:27	13, 14, 98, 99, 102–3, 103n14, 104, 105, 106, 152	5:14	16, 17, 122, 123, 127, 130, 134, 135, 135n6, 136, 137, 141, 144, 145, 153
4:28	13, 14, 98, 103, 104, 105, 106, 152	5:15	16, 17, 122, 123, 124, 125, 126, 127, 129, 130, 134
4:29	13, 14, 98, 103, 104, 117, 118, 121, 140	5:16–17	128, 130, 137, 139, 145, 153
4:30	13–14, 20, 98–99, 103, 105, 106, 152	5:16	16, 17, 20, 122, 123, 124, 128, 129, 130, 153
4:31	14, 15, 99, 103, 104, 105, 106, 152	5:17–18	125
5:1–13	15, 16, 17, 20, 21, 108–21	5:17	16, 17, 20, 122, 123, 125, 125n8, 129
5:1–4	16, 109–11	5:18	16, 122, 123, 125, 128, 129, 130, 153
5:1	15, 16, 20, 108, 109, 110, 118, 119, 121, 152	5:19–23	125–28
		5:19–21	126, 130
5:2	15, 16, 108, 109, 110, 116, 118, 119, 120, 121, 152	5:19–21a	17, 126, 127, 134
		5:19	16, 17, 20, 122, 125
5:3–4	112, 120	5:20–21a	126
5:3	15, 16, 108, 109, 110, 116, 119, 123, 140	5:20	16, 122
		5:21d-23	17
5:4	15, 16, 108, 109, 111, 111n7, 112, 116, 117, 119, 120	5:21	16–17, 122, 126, 127, 128, 129, 134
		5:22–23a	126, 130, 134
5:5	15, 16, 108, 111–12, 113, 116, 120, 124, 125, 129, 130, 137, 141, 145, 153	5:22	17, 20, 122–23, 127, 129, 130, 135, 136, 137, 141, 142, 144, 145, 146, 153
5:6	15, 16, 20, 108, 112–13, 118, 121, 124, 127, 130, 135, 137, 141, 144, 145, 152, 153	5:23	17, 123, 127, 134
		5:24–26	17, 128–29
		5:24	17, 20, 123, 128, 130, 141, 152
5:7–13	16, 114–19	5:25	17, 18, 123, 128, 129, 130, 134, 136, 137, 142, 144, 145, 146, 153
5:7	15, 20, 108, 114, 115, 116, 117, 120, 121		
5:8	15, 108, 114, 115, 116, 117, 120, 121	5:26	17, 123, 129, 134, 135, 144
5:9	15, 16, 108, 114, 116	6:1–18	17–18, 19, 21, 132–47
5:10–13	114		
5:10–11	142, 146	6:1–8	19, 133–37
5:10	15, 16, 108–9, 114, 116, 120, 143, 146	6:1	17–18, 19, 132, 133, 134, 135, 136, 144
5:11	15, 16, 20, 109, 114, 116, 117, 120, 140	6:2	18, 19, 132, 133, 134, 135, 135n6, 136, 144
5:12	15, 109, 114, 117, 121, 139	6:3	18, 132, 133, 134, 135, 136, 144
5:13	15, 16, 17, 20, 109, 114, 118, 121, 124, 125, 127, 129, 130, 134, 152	6:4	18, 19, 132, 133, 134, 135, 136, 144
		6:5	18, 19, 132, 133, 134, 136, 142, 144, 146
5:14–26	16–17, 18, 19–20, 21, 122–31		
5:14–18	17, 123–25	6:6	18, 132, 133, 136, 144

Scripture Index

6:7	18, 19, 132, 133, 134, 136, 144	6:13	18, 19, 133, 138, 139, 140
6:8	18, 19, 23, 132, 134, 137, 139, 143, 145, 147, 154	6:14	18, 19, 133, 138, 140, 141, 143, 145, 146, 153
6:9–10	137–38	6:15	18, 133, 138, 141, 142, 145, 146, 153
6:9	18, 19, 132, 137, 145	6:16	18, 19, 133, 138, 142, 146
6:10	18, 19, 133, 137, 145	6:17	18, 19, 133, 138, 142, 143, 146
6:11–18	19, 138–44	6:18	18, 19, 22, 23, 133, 138, 143, 146, 153
6:11–13a	138–39		
6:11	18, 133, 138, 139		
6:12	18, 19, 133, 138, 139, 139n19, 140, 142, 143, 145, 146		

Author Index

Adewuya, Ayodeji J., 54n14
Arnold, Clinton E., 84n3

Barclay, John M. G., 119n31, 135n5
Barth, Gerhard., 51n7
Bedford, Nancy Elizabeth., 1n2
Berger, Klaus., 52n7
Beutler, Johannes., 25n4
Boakye, Andrew K., 25n2, 34n4, 50n2, 51n4, 51n6, 55n18, 56n22, 72n15, 101n6, 104n15, 104n16, 112n11, 112n12, 113n13, 113n15, 118n27, 118n29, 119n32, 125n10, 128n20, 129n21, 129n22, 135n8, 136n13, 141n25, 142n28
Borchert, Gerald L., 23n10
Bruce, Frederick Fyvie., 35n7, 36n9, 64n16, 69n7, 77n5, 78n7
Bryant, Robert A., 27n9, 61n5
Burke, Trevor J., 86n7
Burton, Ernest De Witt., 61n2

Capes, David B., 26n7
Chester, Stephen J., 26n5
Costa, Tony., 23n10

De Boer, Martinus C., 26n6, 34n4, 36n9, 37n11, 41n2, 45n9, 45n10, 53n13, 56n20, 56n24, 61n4, 62n10, 63n14, 68n5, 69n8, 70n11, 77n5. 78n6, 78n8, 90n2, 92n9, 94n11, 94n14, 100n3, 100n5, 101n7, 102n11, 104n16, 105n18, 105n19, 111n8, 112n9, 115n17, 115n18, 115n19, 116n21, 117n23, 117n24, 124n4, 126n11, 126n13, 126n14, 127n17, 128n19, 128n20, 134n4, 135n7, 135n8, 135n9, 136n11, 136n12, 137n15, 137n16, 138n17, 139n18, 139n19, 140n21, 140n22, 141n26, 143n32, 144n33
Di Mattei, Steven., 101n7
Dunn, James D. G., 51n6, 53n12, 113n14, 127n16

Eastman, Susan G., 103n14, 105n18
Elliott, Susan M., 26n5
Elmer, Ian J., 26n5

Fee, Gordon D., 34n4, 55n19, 62n7, 63n13, 64n15, 71n13, 85n5, 86n8, 112n11, 119n31, 125n6, 125n10, 126n11, 129n23, 134n2, 135n5, 137n15
Filtvedt, Ole J., 142n28
Fredriksen, Paula., 23n10
Fung, Ronald Y. K., 77n5, 112n10

Gaventa, Beverly Roberts., 95n15, 95n17

Hardin, Justin K., 26n5, 117n23
Heil, John Paul., 1n3, 23n10
Hubing, Jeff., 139n19, 140n20, 141n25
Hunn, Debbie., 51n6
Hurtado, Larry W., 46n12

Jackson, T. Ryan., 141n26
Jeon Paul S., 1n3
John, Felix., 26n5

Author Index

Kahl, Brigitte., 26n5
Kellermann, Ulrich., 46n13
Kim, Jung Hoon., 80n13
Kuck, David W., 136n11

Lee, Chee-Chiew., 71n13
Lincoln, Andrew T., 102n11
Longenecker, Richard N., 94n12
Lyons, George., 27n9, 27n11, 35n5, 42n4, 42n5, 45n11, 54n14, 55n18, 62n6, 63n14, 70n10, 78n7, 80n14, 86n8, 90n3, 102n12, 105n20, 110n5, 113n13, 115n16, 116n22, 117n23, 118n28, 124n4, 126n12, 126n13, 128n19, 136n11, 137n14, 142n28

Martyn, J. Louis., 22n9, 26n6, 29n12, 30n13, 34n2, 35n6, 41n3, 46n13, 135n6, 144n33
Matera, Frank J., 30n13, 118n26, 137n14
Matthews, Victor H., 80n12
Milinovich Timothy., 1n3
Moo, Douglas, J., 13n7, 25n3, 26n8, 34n4, 36n10, 42n6, 43n7, 45n8, 47n15, 50n3, 51n6, 53n11, 54n14, 54n16, 55n17, 56n20, 57n25, 61n3, 62n9, 63n12, 67n2, 68n3, 68n6, 70n9, 77n3, 77n5, 86n11, 94n13, 95n16, 100n2, 100n3, 101n8, 101n9, 102n10, 103n13, 103n14, 104n15, 105n17, 105n18, 110n2, 110n4, 111n7, 113n15, 115n16, 115n19, 116n20, 116n21, 117n25, 118n30, 123n3, 125n9, 127n15, 135n9, 138n17, 140n22, 142n26, 142n28, 143n31, 144n33
Nanos, Mark D., 26n5
Neutel, Karin B., 80n15

Oakes, Peter., 56n21, 57n26, 67n2, 72n14, 80n14, 80n15, 92n7, 93n10, 101n8, 110n2, 111n8, 119n32, 124n3, 140n20, 141n24

Prokhorov, A. V., 141n23

Schreiner, Thomas R., 35n8, 36n10, 41n2, 42n6, 45n8, 47n14, 51n5, 51n6, 52n9, 52n10, 54n15, 62n8, 63n11, 68n4, 69n7, 76n2, 77n3, 80n15, 81n16, 84n3, 84n4, 90n3, 93n10, 95n17, 102n12, 103n13, 104n16, 110n3, 111n6, 112n9, 115n19, 117n25, 123n2, 124n5, 125n7, 127n18, 128n19, 128n20, 134n3, 136n10, 137n14, 139n18, 141n25, 142n27, 142n29, 143n30, 144n33
Silva, Moisés., 51n6, 52n8

Taylor, Joan E., 80n11
Thiessen, Matthew., 71n13
Trick, Bradley R., 67n2

Weima, Jeffrey A. D., 143n30
Wendt, Heidi., 61n3
Witherington, Ben., 27n10, 36n10, 47n14, 55n17, 70n12, 86n9, 124n5, 126n12
Wright, Brian J., 100n2

www.ingramcontent.com/pod-product-compliance
Lightning Source LLC
Chambersburg PA
CBHW031434150426
43191CB00006B/504